# LANFORD WILSON
## *21 SHORT PLAYS*

"*Since the first evening I sat spellbound
in the theatre listening to the writings
of Lanford Wilson – the honesty of his ideas
and emotions, the beauty of his language –
I was desperate to be included in his world of
the theatre. He is the greatest writer I have
ever had the privilege of knowing and
working with.*" Patricia Wettig

A Smith and Kraus Book
Published by Smith and Kraus, Inc.
Copyright © 1993 by Lanford Wilson
All rights reserved

COVER AND TEXT DESIGN BY JULIA HILL
Manufactured in the United States of America

First Edition: October 1993
10 9 8 7 6 5 4 3 2 1

Wilson, Lanford, 1937–
      [Plays. Selections]
      Lanford Wilson : 21 short plays. —1st ed.
          p. cm. —(Plays for actors)
      ISBN 1-880399-31-8 : $14.95 paper $23.95 cloth
          I. Title. II. Title: 21 short plays. II. Series.
      PS3573.I458A6   1993
      812'.54--dc20
                                        93-34434
                                          CIP
                                          AC

# LANFORD WILSON
## *21 SHORT PLAYS*

*Contemporary Playwrights Series*

## SK
A Smith and Kraus Book

# LANFORD WILSON

Lanford Wilson received the 1980 Pulitzer Prize for Drama and the New York Drama Critic's Circle award for *Talley's Folly*. He is a founding member of Circle Repertory Company and one of twenty-one resident playwrights for the company.

His work at Circle Rep includes: *The Family Continues* (1972), *The Hot L Baltimore* (1973), *The Mound Builders* (1975), *Serenading Louie* (1976), *5th Of July* (1978), *Talley's Folly* (1980), *A Tale Told* (1981), *Angels Fall* (1982), all directed by Marshall Mason, and the one-act plays *Brontosaurus* (1977) and *Thymus Vulgaris* (1982).

His other plays include: *Balm In Gilead* (1965), *The Gingham Dog* (1966), *The Rimers Of Eldritch* (1967), *Lemon Sky* (1969) and some twenty-five produced one-acts. He has also written the libretto for Lee Hoiby's opera of Tennessee Williams' *Summer And Smoke*, and two television plays, *Taxi:* and *The Migrants* based on a short story by Tennessee Williams.

Other awards include the New York Drama Critics' Circle Award, the Outer Critics' Circle Award and an Obie for *The Hot L Baltimore*, an Obie for *The Mound Builders*, a Drama-Logue Award for *5th Of July* and *Talley's Folly*, the Vernon Rice award for *The Rimers Of Eldritch*, and Tony Award nominations for *Talley's Folly, 5th Of July*, and *Angels Fall*. He is the recipient of the Brandeis University Creative Arts Award in Theatre Arts and the Institute of Arts and Letters Award.

Mr. Wilson has completed an entirely new translation of Chekhov's *Three Sisters*, which was commissioned and produced by the Hartford Stage Company. His play, *Talley and Son* (the third play in the Talley Trilogy) opened in New York City on September 24, 1985.

His play, *Burn This*, opened at the Mark Taper Forum in Los Angeles in January 1987 starring John Malkovich and Joan Allen and opened on Broadway in October 1987 with the same cast. He is currently writing the screenplay for the film version. *Burn This* was also done in London, starring John Malkovich in 1990.

His newest play, *Redwood Curtain*, opened in Seattle in January 1992 and in Philadelphia in March, and at the Old Globe in San Diego, California in January of 1993. It opened at the Brooks Atkinson Theatre on Broadway on March 30, 1993.

He is a member of the Dramatists Guild Council and makes his home in Sag Harbor, New York.

# LANFORD WILSON *21 SHORT PLAYS*

## Contents

# INTRODUCTION

To read this anthology of Lanford Wilson's short plays is to take an exhilarating free fall through three decades of history — the history of the American theater from its absurdist heyday until now, the parallel history of America itself from the eve of the Vietnam era through its long aftermath, and the history of Wilson's own development as a quintessential American artist. All three of these histories are compelling, and all are inextricably intertwined.

The very soil of American democracy seems embedded in Wilson's work. Sometimes this is literally the case: In *This is the Rill Speaking* (1965), like the full-length play, *The Rimers of Eldritch,* it prefigures, the ground threatens to talk; the voices of the author's rural native Missouri rise like specters from the land. Once Wilson begins to absorb his adopted home of New York City, the range of voices in his plays expands demographically and emotionally to form a cacophonous oral tapestry of America singing, bitching, laughing, mourning. Is there another American playwright whose pitch extends from the heartland children and parents of the Midwest to a screaming downtown queen (*The Madness of Lady Bright*) to the dyspeptic Manhattan alumnae of Bryn Mawr and Bergdorf's (*The Great Nebula in Orion*) to the terminally knowing summer sophisticates of Long Island's tony South Fork (*Say de Kooning*)?

Of course Wilson's talent for capturing and empathizing with a diversity of characters is legendary: His epic breakthrough play, *Balm in Gilead* (1965), set more than two dozen characters to gabbing in an Upper Broadway coffee shop. A tour through his one-act works further allows the reader (and potential actor, director and designer) to appreciate that this prolific writer's wide range extends to form as well as character. Though Wilson is now best known for the lyrical naturalism of his Talley plays, especially *Fifth of July* (1978) and *Talley's Folly* (1979), his writing has evolved through the years, echoing the constant evolution of the New York theater in which he has played so consistent and conspicuous a role. In the early *Home Free!* (1964), the imaginary characters and Surprise Box echo the experiments of Edward Albee, among other writers who were reinventing American theatrical forms in the early 1960's; *Sextet(Yes)* (1969) cuts through the night air like Beckett or Pinter. As is the case with many of the early plays in this collection, the sheer brio of the writing, its liberation from dowdy conventions, summons the try-anything excitement of Caffé Cino and the accompanying Off Off Broadway movement that would remake the American stage. Beginning in the early 1970s, Wilson's artistic marriage to an acting company, the Circle Repertory Company, expanded his technical expertise and took him in other esthetic directions that can be appreciated most fully in his major plays. Yet all of his writing has been marked by an uncanny ability to merge character and performer: If the early *The Madness of Lady Bright* (1963) fuses perfectly with its original interpreter, Neil Flanagan, so the much later *A Betrothal* (1984) expresses the sensibility of two much different (if equally distinctive) actors, Herbert Berghof and Uta Hagen.

At the same time, Wilson has never been an insular writer, bound by the world of the theater. The real world always invades his work. Without being ideological, journalistic or preachy about it, Wilson's plays have given constant voice to the dispossessed — the lost or shunned American souls who have been cast out of the mainstream, sometimes by specific cataclysms (the Vietnam War) but just as often by their refusal to march in step with familial, sexual or capitalist orthodoxy. By the time you reach a later piece like the guts-spilling monologue *A Poster of the Cosmos*, which seethes with the tendernesses and horrors of the ongoing age of AIDS, you will begin to grasp the extraordinary emotional, historical and theatrical span of a writer who illuminates the deepest dramas of American life with poetry and compassion.

*Frank Rich*
*September, 1993*

**LANFORD WILSON** *21 SHORT PLAYS*

# HOME FREE!  (March 1963)

## AUTHOR'S NOTE

Lawrence and Joanna were inspired by two couples, one brother and sister, the other lovers, and a few of the second couple's friends, who lived, I'm afraid, very much like HOME FREE! Surprise box, imaginary characters and all. This was the first play I wrote after moving to New York, also the first play based loosely on people I knew; it takes a while to be convinced you're supposed to write about something you know.

Two of the first people I met in New York were Bill Hoffman, the playwright/poet and the composer John Corigliano. (25 years later they collaborated on GHOSTS OF VERSAILLES, the best American opera yet written.) They went to great lengths to get a copy of HOME FREE! to Gian Carlo Menotti for his Spoleto Festival. It was past the deadline but Menotti could get it in, they said, but it couldn't be done anywhere else as the plays at the festival that year were all to be world premiers. I waited six months to hear from him, long past the festival. It turned out he liked the play very much but had left the script on the plane.

When it was finally done at the Caffé Cino, on January 16, 1964, beautifully directed by Neil Flanagan, we were surprised at the stir it caused. Working in the world of the play we became so involved with the spirit of the characters' imagination, we forgot completely that they were living in an incestuous relationship.

The play was rewritten and produced again a few months later. It was at that production, directed by William Archibald, that I first met Marshall W. Mason, who now directs almost everything I write. If you find something that works, stick with it. Marshall was a big star at the Cino, as he had gone on to direct real live professional Off-Broadway plays, for money. On being introduced to him, I said, "Don't you love the rewrite?" The first thing Marshall ever said to me was, "No, I think you're ruined it." Later, since he directed very successful productions of the play both here and in London, I believed he changed his mind.

This version of HOME FREE! was first presented by Joseph Cino at the Caffé Cino, New York City on August 23, 1964. It was directed by William Archibald with the following cast:

LAWRENCE: Michael Warren Powell
JOANNA: Maya Kenin
Sets and lighting by Mr. Archibald; assistant to the director was Charles A. Golden.

A subsequent production was staged by Theater 1965 at the Cherry Lane Theatre, New York City, on February 2, 1965, as part of their New Playwrights Series. It was directed by Marshall W. Mason with the following cast:

LAWRENCE: Michael Warren Powell
JOANNA: Joanna Miles


**CHARACTERS**

LAWRENCE BROWN
JOANNA BROWN

Both are dark, attractive, about twenty-five or twenty-six.


**SCENE**

A small, cluttered room, where they eat and sleep. There may be a door to the kitchen, and there should be a front door. The room is several flights up. Important furnishings include a bed with a brightly colored quilt, a desk littered with paper, notebooks, etc. A candelabra, a music box, perhaps a dresser for Joanna. There is a Ferris wheel that Lawrence has made; a large, colorful, highly–decorated wheel that turns and has (perhaps ten or twelve) seats that swing as the wheel turns, all but two seats are on the wheel. A colorful box with a decorated lid, the Surprise Box, where gifts are placed. Perhaps a blackboard somewhere, and stools or chairs for Edna and Claypone, two imaginary characters who share the room. Joanna is about six months pregnant.

# HOME FREE!

*At rise we see Lawrence in the room alone. He is tapping the wall with the end of a coat hanger to get the attention of his "audience": Claypone and Edna, his students for the moment.*

**LAWRENCE**  Now, if you'll only pay attention! The Pleiades are called the Seven Sisters because they're grouped closely together and with the unaided eye you can only see seven of them. Actually there're about thirty stars in the whole cluster. Now you know that the universe is expanding; we discussed that—Billy, sit down and don't chew your eraser—we discussed that last time. I know your name isn't Billy, Claypone, but you're pre*tend*ing to be Billy: can't you just sit still like a good student? You're in Astronomy 101. If Edna can sit quietly, so can you. Now. As the universe is expanding and all of our galaxy is rotating, within the galaxy the stars are moving at incredible speeds in various directions. It's part of the expansion—Edna!—theory that all stars are moving farther and farther from each other. But the Seven Sisters, although they seem to be perfectly stationary to us, it has been proved that they are shooting away from the center—moving apart, at an incredible speed—every one getting farther from the others, so in a million years we won't be able to tell that they ever were a part of the same cluster. They're shooting out this way! (*Drawing, as with chalk, on the wall.*) And over here, and zoom—at about a hundred light-years a minute! Up and down and out and across— (*Getting uncontrollably excited, he starts tracing their path around the room as if following an exploded skyrocket.*)—and bang! And pow! And, if we were there, Whizz! Burn! Zing! Sssssstt Sssssstt! Zooommmm! Kachowwie! Whamm! (*He has knocked some papers off the desk. He turns to Claypone, calming down.*) Hey, did I scare you? Did I? Where's Edna? (*His eyes focus under the desk across the room. Panting.*) You—come on back here, now. Come on. Sit down. You too, Claypone. It's part of the lesson. I'm busy now. You do something. I don't care; do anything. Don't bother me. (*He walks to the Ferris wheel, sitting, looking at it; turning it gently. To himself.*) No, no, if it went faster you wouldn't need the seats, because the gravity would throw you against the bars; either that or it would throw you off altogether. Well, that way is all right, too; it's just that it's a different ride altogether. You'll have to experiment and see which principle applies to this particular size model. Well it might mean the death of a hundred thirty-seven human guinea pigs, but if it's for the advancement of entertainment, what's a sacrifice? I am an engineer, a scientist, I can only make the models; you can either use them or disregard my advancements. (*To Claypone and Edna.*) No, she went to the grocery—she'll be back in a minute. No, you can't go out and look for her. They'd grab you and lock you in jail in a minute. Because you don't watch for street lights. You do not—every time— (*He is getting nervous, frightened.*) —you go out, you get almost hit with some car or truck and it just drives me crazy trying to keep track of you. And besides you hate it out there. You know how you are! You make me so ashamed—stuttering! And not talking to a person and wilting into some corner like a shade plant. No. She'll be back! She went to the grocery to get a few things! (*Almost uncontrolled.*) And she said she'll be back and she will. You must stay here. No, you stay too. You're not going to leave me here alone; you'd wilt into some corner and they'd come and take you off. (*He forces himself down between the desk and bed, on the floor.*) She'll be right back. She promised. And we'll look in the Surprise Box. She promised. You promised. She just went out for a minute; and she'll be back like always and tell us about the adventure, now. (*Pause. Music. Sweetly now.*) You just sit now, like you were at a social tea with ice cream and cake and peppermint frosting and little sugar cookies with butter and almond flavoring. And little sugar crystals on top that are red and blue and yellow and white. . . . (*There is a soft but very urgent knock at the door.*) Shhhhhhh! (*Violently whispered to Claypone and Edna.*) Be quiet! (*The knock is repeated a little louder.*) Shhh!

JOANNA    (*From outside in a very urgent whisper.*) Quick, Lawrence. It's me. Quick; hurry. They're coming.

LAWRENCE    (*Hurries to the door, looks toward Claypone and Edna.*) It's okay, it's her. Sit down now and act like you've just been waiting nicely. Don't disappoint her. You just sit there. I'm coming.

JOANNA    Hurry.

LAWRENCE    (*To Claypone and Edna.*) You be good. (*He unlocks the door. Joanna slips in and shuts it quickly. She stands just inside the door, her back to the wall. She locks the door quietly.*)

JOANNA    Shhh! She saw me! (*Still whispering.*) She saw me coming in. She was right behind me. She's right outside. Shh! Listen!

LAWRENCE    (*As soon as she comes in he begins to whine. Over above.*) Where have you been? They were just awful, they got so upset I hardly could control them.

JOANNA    Shhh! (*Now Lawrence listens at the door too.*)

LAWRENCE    (*Quickly to Claypone and Edna.*) Don't say anything.

JOANNA    She was right behind me. I think she's outside the door. Listen.

**LAWRENCE**  Did she see you?

**JOANNA**  I don't think so. (*Stops a moment; listens. In a normal voice, very casual.*) No, it's okay, now.

**LAWRENCE**  (*Still at the door*). Shhh! Listen!

**JOANNA**  (*A little winded.*) No, it's okay now. Let me tell you!

**LAWRENCE**  I thought I heard something.

**JOANNA**  No, she's gone now. Sit down and I'll tell you about the adventure. (*Still not able to catch her breath, she lays her hand against her pregnant belly.*) Oh, poor old Tiberius and Coriolanus. They must wonder what I'm doing running upstairs. I'm sorry, Tiberius. I'm sorry, Coriolanus. My heart is just beating away.

**LAWRENCE**  Shhh! You aren't listening.

**JOANNA**  No. It's okay now. My heart is just pounding like crazy.

**LAWRENCE**  (*Over, to Claypone and Edna*). You two!

**JOANNA**  Am I turning blue?

**LAWRENCE**  (*Still whispering*). That isn't fair!

**JOANNA**  Feel how it's pounding. I shouldn't have run up those stairs but Pruneface was after me.

**LAWRENCE**  I'll feel the baby.

**JOANNA**  (*Disgusted.*) No. Claypone, sit down.

**LAWRENCE**  They were just awful while you were out. They were just terrible. I told Edna I was just gonna spank her good! If she didn't sit down and behave.

**JOANNA**  (*Taking off her head scarf.*) Well, she's young yet.

**LAWRENCE**  I said when my sister gets back here she's just gonna spank you good and proper.

**JOANNA**  Oh! (*Big announcement.*) He knows! Mr. Fishface knows. He asked about you. I've decided he knows the whole thing.

**LAWRENCE**  He asked after me?

**JOANNA**  Oh, he's getting so smarty, I'd like to just pinch him good. He said, "Where's your brother, Miss Brown?" And I said, "He isn't my brother, he's my husband; we're going to have a baby."

**LAWRENCE**  He said that?

**JOANNA**  Naturally I lied. He'll believe anything: I said, "He's my husband and he's in Bermuda just now and when he comes back he'll have a lovely dark tan." So you have to get a tan.

**LAWRENCE**  No.

**JOANNA**  Well, I'll think of something. Now. Sit down so I can tell you about the adventure.

**LAWRENCE**  Okay, Claypone sit there, she's going to tell us about the adventure. Edna, you stand there. And keep quiet!

**JOANNA**  Edna has to leave the room.

**LAWRENCE**  Edna, you must leave the room. Yes, you must! Through the kitchen and *into* the scullery and shut the door. And not a whimper out of you—

**JOANNA**  (*In exactly the same voi*ce.) —young miss! Go on this minute. (*She looks at Edna a moment.*) Well, I—!

**LAWRENCE**  What?

**JOANNA**  No, I wouldn't have said that. You can't say things that I wouldn't have said when I was a little girl. (*She has started out reprovingly but softens now.*) You might grow up to be different from me. You must wear tall black stockings and a long gray skirt and a wine-colored apron and your hair will be combed straight back and pulled into a bun and clipped with— (*She makes a sudden, violent attack.*) *Yes, it will, I did!* (*Instantly sweet again.*) And clipped with a tortoise-shell bow. And you will sit with both your hands on your knees or folded in your lap and you will not think about what's between little boys' legs and you will speak when you're spoken to. (*She watches her go to the kitchen.*)

**LAWRENCE**  She's left.

**JOANNA**  She's listening. She has her ear against the door, she always does. (*Abruptly.*) Snoop! (*Listens.*) She's gone now. You know where she gets that—from that busybody landlady, Pruneface. (*She surveys Claypone and Lawrence and finds the situation satisfactory.*) Now. Actually, I only asked her to leave because I have an announcement to make. I will stand to— (*As she starts to rise she catches her heart—lightly. Her voice now is surprised, serious.*) Oh, golly! (*Sits.*)

**LAWRENCE**  (*Over a bit*). No, no, no announcements. You have to tell us about the adventure.

**JOANNA**  No, wait, golly—I shouldn't run. Well. This is.

**LAWRENCE**  (*To Claypone*). She's going to tell us about the adventure.

**JOANNA**  I will deliver my announcement from a seated position. Claypone, I want you to pay particular attention because you're involved.

**LAWRENCE**  I don't want to hear any old—

**JOANNA**  On my way outside to the grocery, this afternoon, Miss Pruneface was in the hallway and she made me stop—

**LAWRENCE**  (*Over.*) What a silly thing to say—I don't know anybody by that name at all.

**JOANNA**  (*Without pause.*) And she said, "Mrs. Brown, I have told you before, you will have to move. You make too much noise as it is and—"

**LAWRENCE**  (*Over.*) She didn't say any such thing.

**JOANNA**  "And I'm afraid it will be impossible for you to live here after your baby is born."

**LAWRENCE**  (*Over a little*). She did not. (*Both speak at once.*)

**JOANNA**  "And I'm afraid it will be impossible for you to live here with an infant. You know I told you that when you moved in here." And I told you—and I told her we would—I did—you were not either—I was there. I told her we would be out next week!

**LAWRENCE**  She didn't even say one word to you. She didn't say anything. I went out. I was there. I went out after you did and she said we could stay here like we have been and we could stay on, she said as long as we wanted to!

**JOANNA**  (*Wins.*) So there!

**LAWRENCE**  No.

**JOANNA**  She looks at me in the hall and shakes her finger at me.

**LAWRENCE**  You told her a hundred times that we were moving and she never says anything more. You say that every week.

**JOANNA**  No. She looks at me and she says I can't have the baby here—because they don't want the noise, Lawrence.

**LAWRENCE**  It doesn't matter what they want. (*There is a fast exchange between them.*)

**JOANNA**  They don't want the mess.

**LAWRENCE**  We just won't talk to her, then.

**JOANNA**  No, she'll throw us out in the street—!

**LAWRENCE**  We won't answer the door—Claypone, shut up!

**JOANNA**  (*Almost panicked.*) They're afraid of the baby, don't you know that?

**LAWRENCE**  Claypone's making noise!

**JOANNA**  They don't want the pain!

**LAWRENCE**  We won't go! We're not going. If you're not going to tell me about the adventure, I'm going to call Edna back into the room—Claypone go get Edna.

**JOANNA**  You sit right back down.

**LAWRENCE**  Well, then, we're going to look in the Surprise Box—it's wonderful.

**JOANNA**  No. No, you can't until two o'clock today.

**LAWRENCE**  No, come on— It's especially lovely, I bet, today.

**JOANNA**  Not until after I tell you about the adventure. I have not told you.

**LAWRENCE**  Very well—first she's going to tell us about the adventure.

**JOANNA**  To begin—there was a shadow across the door downstairs.

**LAWRENCE**  The sun is shining.

**JOANNA**  (*She notices the interruption but goes on.*) It was all crooked because of the panels in the door, as usual; exactly the same number of squares in the sidewalk from here to the corner.

**LAWRENCE**  (*Quickly.*) Eighteen.

**JOANNA**  And—(*Pause. Sharply.*) I guess you just don't want to hear about it, do you?

**LAWRENCE**  (*Meaning* "What did I do?") What?

**JOANNA**  (*Continuing to look sharply at him.*) The same number of parking meters from here to the corner. (*Lawrence starts to speak up automatically; her look intensifies; he stops without really knowing why. When she is satisfied he is not going to interrupt she continues.*) Out of which eight were expired this morning. If you must know, I was thinking about the Ferris wheel most of the time I was out.

**LAWRENCE**  Do you want to look in the Surprise Box?

**JOANNA**  I don't think so; not till it's time. Unless you want to. It wasn't much of an adventure except for Mr. Fishface at the market. The Skinner was watching me so I couldn't slip anything. I think he's catching on. Old Fishface, though, he said: "*Oh,* how's your brother, Miss Brown?" I said, "It's Mrs. Brown, and he's not my brother as you are mistakenly referring to the gentleman whose company you've seen me in. That's Mr. Brown, and he's away in the Canary Islands trapping finches but we're expecting him shortly, Mr. Fishface. I'll give him your best."

**LAWRENCE**  Lie.

**JOANNA**  I said that. I did.

**LAWRENCE**  You didn't say, "Mr. Fishface."

**JOANNA**  I most certainly did.

**LAWRENCE**  Claypone, she didn't. (*They are beginning to laugh.*)

**JOANNA**  I did. And I said, "How's Mrs. Fishface?"

**LAWRENCE**  (*Laughing.*) You did not.

**JOANNA**  (*Laughing.*) And all the little tadpoles that must be swimming around at home. And all—

**LAWRENCE**  —And the pollywogs! And—(*They degenerate into a giggling mess, falling all over each other and slapping at each other. They fall onto the bed, giggling.*)

**JOANNA**  And the little baby perch.

**LAWRENCE**  And the whole Fishface family. (*They try to stop laughing. Joanna tries to sit up on the bed.*)

**JOANNA**  Come on. Be serious.

**LAWRENCE**  (*Pulling her back down.*) No.

**JOANNA**  (*Sitting up again.*) Yes—Go away, Claypone—sit down. (*To Lawrence.*) I don't know why we keep him around, he's so stupid. (*As he tries to pull her back down.*) Oh, don't—I get dizzy today. You know I can't play much at a time.

**LAWRENCE**  Oh, you're always dizzy. Now let's look in the Surprise Box.

**JOANNA**  No, wait! I forgot the most important part! A cat! (*This is used to draw his attention away from the Surprise Box as she slips a foun-*

*tain pen into it a bit later.*) A yellow and gray and white and brown and—

**LAWRENCE**   Not brown. Lie!

**JOANNA**   Brown! With black ears—all spots—ran across from the market and under a parked car. I called to her but she wouldn't come. She only looked out from behind a tire and wouldn't come.

**LAWRENCE**   How did you know it was a she-cat?

**JOANNA**   Because she was fat and pregnant like me! No tomcat is going to have kittens.

**LAWRENCE**   Maybe you'll have kittens though! Spotted kittens!

**JOANNA**   Oh! Wouldn't that be *rare?* Why how rare! But I know I won't. I just couldn't. Nothing ever happens like that. Seldom ever.

**LAWRENCE**   Or pups! You never know what can happen. (*Joanna slips the pen into the box.*) Now let's look in the Surprise Box. (*The lid bumps softly.*) Did you peek? You peeked!

**JOANNA**   Lie! I never did. (*To Claypone.*) Tell him! Now see?

**LAWRENCE**   Okay. Let's look now. (*They walk to either side of the box.*)

**JOANNA**   Okay. (*They both close their eyes.*)

**LAWRENCE**   Open it. (*She does.*)

**JOANNA**   It's open. (*They open their eyes.*)

**LAWRENCE**   A pen! Where did you find it?

**JOANNA**   I have no idea where it came from. Maybe you can use it to write your book. (*Looking into the box with wonder.*) Ohh! I'll bet *someone* has sure been busy. Another seat for the Ferris wheel. (*She slips it out gently.*) Oh, it's lovely. It's so lovely. This is the best one so far—it's so fragile!

**LAWRENCE**   It's not too fragile, though, I don't think.

**JOANNA**   Oh, no. It just looks—

**LAWRENCE**   Where do you suppose it came from?

**JOANNA**   I'll bet I know. I'll bet Lawrence Brown made it while I was out.

**LAWRENCE**   Do you suppose . . .

**JOANNA**   I certainly do suppose. Can I put it on? You can come over, Claypone, and watch.

**LAWRENCE**   (*Nods.*) Carefully.

**JOANNA**   Well, I won't break it. It's my surprise, after all. (*She sets it gently on the Ferris wheel.*) There. Is that all? Count them, Claypone.

**LAWRENCE**   One more to go yet.

**JOANNA**   Then it'll be totally finished.

**LAWRENCE**   I'll bet no one has anything at all like this Ferris wheel.

**JOANNA**   After you get just one more seat done—

**LAWRENCE**   And then we can get in it and ride like mad. (*Joanna turn-*

*ing it very slowly.*) Easy! (*Said softly to Joanna but as she starts to frown at him he adds quickly.*) Claypone, easy! (*Joanna automatically switches her frown to Claypone and they both frown briefly at him.*)

**JOANNA**  Clutz. (*To Lawrence.*) Why we have to harbor a forty-three-year-old imbecile!

**LAWRENCE**  (*As the Ferris wheel turns.*) Up we go.

**JOANNA**  I don't think it's for us to ride. I think it's for the baby.

**LAWRENCE**  Well, maybe all three—or you two and I'll turn.

**JOANNA**  It's lovely. The last seat is the best, I think anyway. Technically.

**LAWRENCE**  I can make this pen work. It's 14 carat gold.

**JOANNA**  Where?

**LAWRENCE**  There. And Parker. There.

**JOANNA**  You can use it to write your book with.

**LAWRENCE**  Hey, wonderful.

**JOANNA**  What do you think we should call it, Lawrence?

**LAWRENCE**  We? I get to name my book by my—

**JOANNA**  No. no. no. Not your old book. You're so stupid.

**LAWRENCE**  Lie!

**JOANNA**  Claypone, isn't he stupid?

**LAWRENCE**  Lie!

**JOANNA**  Lie! Lawrence, you're stupid. My *baby*. What will we name it?

**LAWRENCE**  *Our* baby.

**JOANNA**  Our baby. What will we call it?

**LAWRENCE**  I thought we settled on something yesterday. Boy or girl?

**JOANNA**  I think girl.

**LAWRENCE**  We'll name her—Miss Brown.

**JOANNA**  (*Starting to say no*). Well, why not? Perfect!

**LAWRENCE**  The name will be perfect but I don't suppose we can expect the baby to be. I don't see how Miss Brown can help being deformed a little.

**JOANNA**  Mmmm. Maybe no arms.

**LAWRENCE**  Very well: no arms. At least she won't go around breaking things. You should concentrate on no voice box too.

**JOANNA**  I don't think that's nice. You hate children. What kind of father is that? You have no business being a father at all if you hate children.

**LAWRENCE**  I don't hate them. I hate the noise they make.

**JOANNA**  Claypone, what can you do with a father who hates children?

**LAWRENCE**  Well, what's so unusual about that? Besides, I don't hate them all. I think I begin to like them as soon as they're about fifteen years old.

**JOANNA**  What do I do with her till then?

**LAWRENCE**  I don't know. Send her to camp!

**JOANNA**  (*Delighted at the idea.*) Of course. Send her to camp Lackawalla Nursery, then Lackabellabella Camp and Miss Lackamannamanna's Home for Young Ladies.

**LAWRENCE**  And we'll be home riding the Ferris wheel. She's going to be no problem. (*Puts his head to Joanna's stomach.*) Are you going to be a problem, Miss Brown? What was that? You're all muffled. She says no.

**JOANNA**  Well, she's *diff*erent.

**LAWRENCE**  That's right, I'd forgotten.

**JOANNA**  (*Calling.*) You can come back now, Edna. Here, quick; kiss me. (*They kiss; she looks up as Edna enters.*) Oh, you weren't supposed to see that.

**LAWRENCE**  We were discussing things you're not old enough to understand, young lady. When you grow up maybe we'll tell you.

**JOANNA**  And maybe we won't.

**LAWRENCE**  Now let's go. I want to go off to bed. Come on.

**JOANNA**  No. Not now.

**LAWRENCE**  What kind of wife are you? It's part of the common law— you have to come when I tell you to.

**JOANNA**  I'm not your wife, I'm your sister.

**LAWRENCE**  Well, what kind of sister are you?

**JOANNA**  Only if I'm in agreement, and I don't fancy it. I want to at two o'clock. And nothing will—

**LAWRENCE**  Shhhh! Listen! I thought I heard something. That's twenty minutes. We can start now.

**JOANNA**  No, we won't start now. That *isn't* fair. There's no point in having a schedule if you don't stick to it religiously.

**LAWRENCE**  That's absurd.

**JOANNA**  Not at all. I have a very simple timetable here I've worked out. I'm quite mathematical, you know.

**LAWRENCE**  You are not mathematical at all. But I'll wait till two o'clock. And we can take Colonel Polarfuz with us. No, Edna, you slept with him last night. Wipe your nose!

**JOANNA**  Colonel Polarfuz was with us when I got pregnant. Everytime you take the teddy bear I get pregnant.

**LAWRENCE**  That isn't true. He's been with us a hundred times and you haven't got pregnant but once.

**JOANNA**  Well, I will again. On top of Miss Brown. Or maybe Miss Brown will get pregnant. I'll have one and in three months I'll have another and the first thing you know I'll be turning them out like Volkswagens. Besides, when I have Miss Brown we have to move away.

**LAWRENCE**   No, Joanna. You can't have it if we have to move away.

**JOANNA**   Yes. Are we going to be good parents?

**LAWRENCE**   No.

**JOANNA**   Yes, we are.

**LAWRENCE**   Okay. The perfect parents. We can even get married.

**JOANNA**   But we have to move. The city isn't any place to prepare a child anyway. She can't grow up in the city—

**LAWRENCE**   —Ha! Prepare—

**JOANNA**   What's funny? What's funny, Edna?

**LAWRENCE**   You said "prepare." (*To Edna.*) She said "prepare." The city is no place to prepare a child—

**JOANNA**   Well, it isn't.

**LAWRENCE**   (*Pretending to be a chef.*) To prepare one City Child, stew softly in mother's milk for two hours or until tender—

**JOANNA**   (*Joining in.*) Turning frequently. City Children are poached in milk.

**LAWRENCE**   And in the country—

**JOANNA**   The Country Child is simmered in butter—

**LAWRENCE**   And onions! (*Takes up a paper and pencil.*)

**JOANNA**   Chop twelve large red onions very fine—

**LAWRENCE**   That's too fast, let me write it down.

**JOANNA**   Chop twelve large Bermuda onions—we'll send it to *Good Housekeeping.* "Dear Cooking Editor. This recipe has been in our family for nine centuries—"

**LAWRENCE**   Generations. For nine generations.

**JOANNA**   —Grease lightly one Dutch oven.

**LAWRENCE**   And there has to be vegetables—

**JOANNA**   (*Quitting the game abruptly.*) We have to move anyway. Lady Pruneface looks at me every time I pass her in the hall or on the stairs. She looks at my bulging middle.

**LAWRENCE**   Well, if you'd learn to hold your stomach in like I told you.

**JOANNA**   She's thinking when Miss Brown comes out—we go out.

**LAWRENCE**   Maybe it won't be Miss Brown—maybe it'll be kittens. With kittens she'd look the other way.

**JOANNA**   I saw a cat!

**LAWRENCE**   You told us. Honestly, sometimes you don't have all your marbles.

**JOANNA**   I didn't tell you, Edna. Besides I saw another one: a dead one.

**LAWRENCE**   Why didn't you get it? You should have brought it home free.

**JOANNA**   It was too dead.

**LAWRENCE**   What color?

**JOANNA** I couldn't tell.

**LAWRENCE** Gray then. Maybe it won't be kittens. Maybe it'll be pups. Pups she'd look the other way.

**JOANNA** Not a chance. It's too rare. It seldom ever happens any more. You know that.

**LAWRENCE** It's almost two o'clock. I can't wait.

**JOANNA** You've got to. Sit down and wait. I don't mind going back on my word in front of Claypone, but not Edna. We should be an example to her. Why don't you work on your book?

**LAWRENCE** I decided to illustrate it myself.

**JOANNA** I didn't realize you were talented.

**LAWRENCE** I'm not, silly—but it's going to be very, very modern. (*To Edna.*) No, you can't! In color. (*He gets pencil and paper at his desk and sits.*) It'll be about Miss Brown and getting lost in the woods.

**JOANNA** And you must describe the woods in every possible detail. Every leaf and every bird.

**LAWRENCE** Very well. Don't bother me then, I'm going to write until two o'clock and then we'll go to bed. Now sit down. You too, Edna. And Claypone. Sit there. Now! And don't say a word. (*Pause while he thinks. Joanna sits.*)

**JOANNA** Don't chew your pencil.

**LAWRENCE** Shhhh!

**JOANNA** Well, I'm not sitting here and watching you devour a perfectly good pencil. Chew a cigar or something if you want to chew.

**LAWRENCE** Shhhhh!

**JOANNA** (*Pause. Helpfully.*) Would you care for a stick of gum?

**LAWRENCE** No thank you, Joanna. Just sit there and be still. (*Without looking up.*) Edna, stop fidgeting. (*Pause. He thinks and writes a few words. Joanna becomes restless. Gets up and wanders to the Surprise Box. She winds the music box, he reacts. She stops. Then opens music box for one note. He snorts. She closes it, turns around, and studies him.*)

**JOANNA** A boy looked at me on the subway last night. (*Pause. No reaction.*) He said "hello"!

**LAWRENCE** When? (*Pause. No reaction.*) When?

**JOANNA** I didn't say anything, I looked the other way. Last night.

**LAWRENCE** What'd he say?

**JOANNA** He said hello and I turned my hand so he could see I was married and I looked the other way.

**LAWRENCE** Lie. You went away with him.

**JOANNA** Lie, I looked the other way. (*To Edna.*) I did too, young lady, you just shut your mouth or I'll wash it out with soap! (*To Lawrence.*) I looked the other way and he got off the train. Now go on writing.

**LAWRENCE** What'd he look like?

**JOANNA** I didn't notice.

**LAWRENCE** What'd he *look* like?

**JOANNA** I didn't notice, now go on writing. (*Beat.*) He had blond curly hair and a very square jaw and a sweater with a big red "R" on it. (*Quickly to Edna.*) I did not, young lady, you shut up!

**LAWRENCE** Some college boy, they'll flirt with married women, it makes them feel big.

**JOANNA** Well, I looked the other way and he got off the train. Aren't you going to write?

**LAWRENCE** I can't do anything if you're going to talk all the time. You're just jealous because you don't have anything to do. I'll do something else.

**JOANNA** Lie! I certainly am not.

**LAWRENCE** Well, I'll do something else anyway. Let's go to bed.

**JOANNA** Shhhh! (*Listens.*) Not now.

**LAWRENCE** What? I'll move the clock up.

**JOANNA** That isn't fair. You're a cheat.

**LAWRENCE** You are. Edna, leave the room!

**JOANNA** I said I wouldn't. (*To Edna.*) You sit right back down, young miss. You just do what I do. (*To Lawrence.*) Edna and Claypone may read. (*To them.*) You may read. I don't care—anything. (*To Lawrence.*) And you and I will talk about moving.

**LAWRENCE** I won't talk about any such thing!

**JOANNA** We have to talk about it. We have to. She's right behind the door and besides Miss Brown will probably be blue!

**LAWRENCE** Not blue. Shut up about blue.

**JOANNA** If I was a blue baby she'll be a blue baby. It's simple heredity.

**LAWRENCE** You were not a blue baby. You just make it up so you'll sound exceptional.

**JOANNA** Mother said I was a blue baby and they sewed me back up and I am too exceptional.

**LAWRENCE** What does she know about it?

**JOANNA** ... Besides I can feel the catgut.

**LAWRENCE** I don't want to hear about your pains and catgut. Honestly, sometimes you can really be nauseating ... (*Mumbling.*) Catgut.

**JOANNA** I had another one.

**LAWRENCE** I don't want to hear about it.

**JOANNA** (*Holding her shoulder.*) I felt it here. Feel.

**LAWRENCE** That shows what you know about it. Heart pains are felt in the bottom of the stomach.

**JOANNA** Well, mine hurts me here. You know it does. You were scared once.

**LAWRENCE**   When was I? I was not. You were faking and I knew it.

**JOANNA**   Lawrence Brown, you were so.

**LAWRENCE**   Joanna Brown, I was not. I wasn't. You made it up; you did.

**JOANNA**   I didn't.

**LAWRENCE**   I wasn't. You never had one of your pains!

**JOANNA**   I feel it all the time.

**LAWRENCE**   I won't listen to you. I have to write.

**JOANNA**   (*Louder.*) I feel it in my shoulder like someone pinching me!

**LAWRENCE**   (*Louder.*) I won't listen to you. I'll sing!

**JOANNA**   (*Louder.*) I DO! I can feel it right now!

**LAWRENCE**   (*Singing loudly.*) My country tis of thee—sweet land of liberty! Of thee I sing! Land where!—

**JOANNA**   Okay!! They are trying to read. You can at least be civil. I know it's difficult for you, but if you will only try.

**LAWRENCE**   You started it by faking.

**JOANNA**   Well, I feel it!

**LAWRENCE**   (*Sings two notes very loudly*). Land where!

**JOANNA**   But I won't talk about it. Shhh! Listen.

**LAWRENCE**   What?

**JOANNA**   Shhh! She's gone. You won't learn, will you?

**LAWRENCE**   Well, you started it by faking . . . you think you're so very exceptional.

**JOANNA**   Well, I *am exceptional!*

**LAWRENCE**   You are not! You're blue and that's not exceptional.

**JOANNA**   *You* shut up!

**LAWRENCE**   Turn blue for me. Just once!

**JOANNA**   I. Will. Not!

**LAWRENCE**   You can't.

**JOANNA**   I could if I wanted to. I wouldn't be inclined to for you.

**LAWRENCE**   (*Pause.*) Are we really going to be turned out? Did she honestly say no children?

**JOANNA**   She only told us a dozen times.

**LAWRENCE**   Well, what does she expect a young married couple to do?

**JOANNA**   We're not married.

**LAWRENCE**   Well we told her we were. We'll get a lawyer.

**JOANNA**   We can't. He'd guess. You know how lawyers are. They'd even take away Miss Brown. (*To Edna.*) They can *have* you!

**LAWRENCE**   He'd guess from your eyes.

**JOANNA**   Certainly not! You'd tell him. You'd stammer and stutter and he'd know. You always stutter when you talk to anyone but me!

**LAWRENCE**   I do not!

**JOANNA**   You stutter and stammer and just wilt into a corner like some shade plant.

**LAWRENCE**  Stop.

**JOANNA**  You just can't—(*Whining.*)—cross the street—Oh, I can't *talk* to anyone. Oh, that truck is going to hit me!

**LAWRENCE**  Don't.

**JOANNA**  (*Calmer.*)  You always embarrass me when you talk to the landlady.

**LAWRENCE**  Well, I can't talk to Pruneface. She's wrinkled. She has white hair, that's the reason. (*Joanna smiles and doesn't speak.*) It is, too!

**JOANNA**  I didn't say a word. I agree with you. I really do. (*Pause.*) Mr. Fishface doesn't have white hair and you stutter to him!

**LAWRENCE**  He's got a fish—

**JOANNA**  I didn't hear you.

**LAWRENCE**  He's got—

**JOANNA**  I didn't say a word.

**LAWRENCE**  I have to write. Why don't we go to bed and play?

**JOANNA**  I'm not in the mood. You'd stutter.

**LAWRENCE**  Lie! That *was* a lie! Tell her, Claypone.

**JOANNA**  You're just a mess.

**LAWRENCE**  You are! You live in common law!

**JOANNA**  So do you.

**LAWRENCE**  So do you!

**JOANNA**  It's different with me. I'm a girl. (*To Edna.*) We girls are very exceptional.

**LAWRENCE**  You live in common law.

**JOANNA**  I was a blue baby! And besides, I have a pain.

**LAWRENCE**  I'll give you a pain. You always have a pain when you're in the wrong. I'll kiss it and make it well.

**JOANNA**  Go away. It feels like pinching. Really.

**LAWRENCE**  You're faking. You want attention because you're pregnant.

**JOANNA**  That's a perfectly acceptable reason. Ask any woman—until the child is born any woman is a very, very special and wonderous thing. (*Regally.*) As a matter of fact, I'm royalty. I'm a queen! (*Simply.*) I have blue blood.

**LAWRENCE**  A queen! (*Music for two or three bars, very faint.*) A queen! I should have recognized it. Queens are always pregnant with somebody or other. Prince Claypone! Fetch her the crown. Lady Edna, Lady Edna—into the kitchen and supervise those wenches. Into the kitchen with you!

**JOANNA**  (*Assuming the air of a gruff queen.*) Bring me a pickled flamingo, Lady Edna!

**LAWRENCE** (*Bringing a chair.*) Sit here on this throne. Up with your feet on the ottoman.

**JOANNA** (*Kicking aside the chair.*) Down with the Ottomans! Behead every one of them. Barbarians! I won't have them in the kingdom! Where's my filet of flamingo? Behead that girl!

**LAWRENCE** (*With a quilt from the bed.*) You must have a mantle. This robe, your pregnancy, was made by four hundred Hungarian virgins who went blind sewing seed pearls. (*Getting a candelabrum.*) And a scepter! Is there anything else, your pregnancy? (*He tucks in the quilt.*)

**JOANNA** (*Gruffly.*) Careful with me, you fool. I'm with child! You're *jostling* the future king!

**LAWRENCE** (*Excited. Again singing. Loud.*) For unto us a child is given. For unto us a son is born. And the government shall be upon his shoulders! And his name shall be—

**JOANNA** Silence! Silence that racket or off with your shoulders!

**LAWRENCE** Oh, no. Not that. Not that, your pregnancy. Not my shoulders! Throw me in the briar patch, but not my shoulders!

**JOANNA** (*Saintly*). I knight. Thee. (*Pause.*) Sir Stutter! Ha!

**LAWRENCE** That's not fair. You're a whore. (*Takes away quilt.*) You're not a queen. Fetch your own filet of flamingos. Edna—forget the flamingos. She's not a queen, she's a whore.

**JOANNA** Oh! I *am not!*

**LAWRENCE** I bet you are!

**JOANNA** I bet I am not!

**LAWRENCE** I bet you go around trying to stir up some look in boys' eyes.

**JOANNA** I bet I do not.

**LAWRENCE** Lie!

**JOANNA** Lie! I do not. Only you. You know it's true. I couldn't get away if I wanted to. Besides, now I'm pregnant.

**LAWRENCE** I'd hold you in. (*Moving behind her.*) I'd bite the nape of your neck and pull you back like a tomcat.

**JOANNA** (*Playfully.*) Ouch! It tickles.

**LAWRENCE** Of course it tickles. Let's take a shower.

**JOANNA** No. Oh, sometimes you're really vulgar. Sometimes you really shock us.

**LAWRENCE** Shock you. I do not.

**JOANNA** You do, too. You do.

**LAWRENCE** Let me feel the baby. (*Reaches around her. To Edna.*) Do you want to feel the baby?

**JOANNA** (*To Edna.*) No! No, you can't. You'd hit. I know you.

**LAWRENCE** I think she's asleep. (*Joanna touches her shoulder.*)

**JOANNA** Ouch, Lawrence!

**LAWRENCE**  I'm not hurting. You don't suppose she's asleep. Hey, wake up, Miss Brown. God, you don't suppose she's going to be lazy, do you? Edna, you knock over that Ferris wheel and I'll hit you good!

**JOANNA**  Of course she's not going to be lazy.

**LAWRENCE**  If there's anything I can't tolerate it's laziness. Why doesn't she kick or something?

**JOANNA**  I like it when she takes these little cat naps—

**LAWRENCE**  Do you suppose she'll really be a whole litter of kittens?

**JOANNA**  —Lord knows she kicks me enough when she's awake. (*To Edna.*) She's going to take after you, you little sadist. (*Touches her shoulder.*) Oh, golly.

**LAWRENCE**  What's wrong?

**JOANNA**  I had a little pain is all.

**LAWRENCE**  Miss Brown kicked you!

**JOANNA**  In the shoulder. You don't seem to realize that Mrs. Pruneface is just outside that door and she's going to kick us out onto the street and I have a pain.

**LAWRENCE**  Oh, that! (*To Edna.*) Don't believe her.

**JOANNA**  You never believe anything I say. None of you. Well, you'll see.

**LAWRENCE**  Hey. Come to bed with me now.

**JOANNA**  I will, I guess. If you'll only be quiet. It's nearly time.

**LAWRENCE**  (*Singing.*) It's nearly time, it's nearly time.

**JOANNA**  And if you'll promise to talk about moving away afterwards.

**LAWRENCE**  Afterwards they lay on the soft grass and talked about moving away.

**JOANNA**  (*Happy.*) I wish I wasn't pinching.

**LAWRENCE**  I'll teach you to pinch.

**JOANNA**  The whole world pinches me!

**LAWRENCE**  (*Singing.*) He's got the whole world—between his fingers and thumb.

**JOANNA**  You always sing when I say we'll go to bed!

**LAWRENCE**  It makes me happy. I like it.

**JOANNA**  That's all you know. Hop in bed. You're a funny rabbit.

**LAWRENCE**  I'm a funny rabbit. (*To Edna.*) Are you a funny rabbit?

**JOANNA**  Impossible rabbit. I love an impossible rabbit. Oh, God!

**LAWRENCE**  What?

**JOANNA**  Well, think of all the number of offspring rabbits have.

**LAWRENCE**  Wonderful.

**JOANNA**  That's all perfectly well for the buck—but I have to bear all those scratchy little monsters. Fuzzy little monsters.

**LAWRENCE**  You'll die laughing! It sounds like fun.

**JOANNA**  Everything sounds like fun to you.

**LAWRENCE** Everything is.

**JOANNA** How do you suppose a female rabbit keeps from giggling? I mean, think how furry a baby rabbit is.

**LAWRENCE** They really are, you know. (*To Edna.*) Of course they are, Edna. And long tickly ears. But giggling isn't bad.

**JOANNA** Well, maybe not—but it certainly would destroy the seriousness of the situation.

**LAWRENCE** You giggle better than any rabbit anyway.

**JOANNA** Oh, I never giggle. (*Picks up music box.*)

**LAWRENCE** Oh, you don't?

**JOANNA** What?

**LAWRENCE** You never giggle. You don't, huh? (*He starts advancing slowly toward her.*)

**JOANNA** No-o-o-a.

**LAWRENCE** You don't giggle ever, huh?

**JOANNA** Now you stay away. I can't play like that. (*She is smiling.*)

**LAWRENCE** Not even with someone playing the piano on your ribs? Get back, Claypone.

**JOANNA** (*Touching her shoulder.*) You stay away now. I don't giggle. (*They are laughing now.*)

**LAWRENCE** Edna? Did you hear what she said? She said she doesn't snicker. Not even a little. Whatta you think of that?

**JOANNA** Now that isn't true. (*They are circling the room.*) I didn't say I don't snicker. I said I don't giggle. I snicker all the time.

**LAWRENCE** You giggle too. Admit it.

**JOANNA** I snicker like a horse. It's *disgusting* the way I snicker. (*She half throws, half lays the music box on a chair.*) Move back, now Edna, don't you help him. (*There is a fullscale chase.*)

**LAWRENCE** You're going to giggle. (*He knocks the chair over.*)

**JOANNA** Stay back, I said! (*From the floor the music box plays.*)

**LAWRENCE** No. We're going to make you giggle.

**JOANNA** No, you aren't.

**LAWRENCE** I am. Claypone, head her off.

**JOANNA** Don't do it, Claypone. I'll tell Mother on you.

**LAWRENCE** Mother's in heaven and Mother can't hear you.

**JOANNA** Mother's in Hoboken and if I yell loud enough she'll *hear me*. The whole *building* will hear me!

**LAWRENCE** They'll hear you giggle when I catch you.

**JOANNA** They won't! (*She pulls out a chair and runs behind the table. Sudden stop. Scream. Joanna's expression is one of terror and great pain. Lawrence is still playing. He thinks she is joking.*)

**LAWRENCE** Everyone will hear you laugh your—

**JOANNA** Get away. (*She can't speak further.*)

**LAWRENCE**  What's wrong? (*She turns to him.*) Oh, come on! That's not fair. That isn't fair. Edna, don't believe her, she's joking. She's pretending.

**JOANNA**  (*Starting to collapse.*) It's pinching me . . .

**LAWRENCE**  I don't believe you. (*Still he takes her and starts to help her to the bed.*)

**JOANNA**  Oh, really, Lawrence, really!

**LAWRENCE**  I don't believe you. That's foolishness. I'm not going to get frightened again, if that's what you're trying.

**JOANNA**  Am I blue?

**LAWRENCE**  Really? You truly hurt? (*He is getting scared and excited.*) I'll help you, don't worry. I'll get you something. What do you want, Joanna?

**JOANNA**  A doctor. Oh, please.

**LAWRENCE**  A doctor? They know everything. I'll get you a doctor. (*But he stays by the bed.*) I will.

**JOANNA**  Lawrence, go. Go on, hurry.

**LAWRENCE**  I will. I'll get you anything, Joanna. (*Panicked.*) Tell me what you want, rabbit.

**JOANNA**  Downstairs and on the corner—get me a doctor.

**LAWRENCE**  No, now I can't go out there, Joanna, you know I don't go out there, you said I—

**JOANNA**  Please, Lawrence—

**LAWRENCE**  —never had to go out there—now, I can't do something—

**JOANNA**  (*Scream, but the wind cuts away from her voice.*) No. Go on, Lawrence. Look, it's okay. It's okay. There's nothing out there that will hurt you, it's—

**LAWRENCE**  (*Lawrence has gone to the door.*) No, she's out there— she's right on the other side of the door. I can't go out there.

**JOANNA**  Lawrence, it's never been like this. Go on!

**LAWRENCE**  (*Crumpling at the door.*) No, I can't. I can't. Don't make me. Don't make me. Please don't make me. I can't go out. They'll take me off. I can't go, don't make me, Joanna, please don't.

**JOANNA**  (*Over the above, coaxingly*). Lawrence, look, baby, it's okay, baby, there's nobody out there who can hurt you, baby, Lawrence, for me. Please. Please. (*Her strength fails.*)

**LAWRENCE**  Joanna? Say things to me, Joanna. (*She looks at him.*) Joanna?

**JOANNA**  Please. (*She takes a jar and knocks it violently against the wall, calling.*) Miss Williams! Miss Williams!

**LAWRENCE**  NO! Don't call old Pruneface! I'll get you a doctor, I really will, Joanna. It's okay. Quick, quick, EDNA! Put on your coat, child, this is an emergency. (*He runs and opens the door just enough* *for Edna to squeeze through.*) As fast as you can or she'll die. There's a doctor's sign over the drugstore on the corner.

**JOANNA**  No, Lawrence! You go. You go. YOU GO!

**LAWRENCE**  (*Turning to her.*) It's all right. She went for him. You have to be patient. Can I get you something? You'd feel better if you sat up and talked, I'll bet. (*She has tried to sit up. She falls back.*) Here, I'll sit by you and hold your hand. (*He takes her hand; it falls lifeless and unnoticed from his.*) Now, don't go to sleep, she'll be right back in no time. I told her to hurry. It's after two o'clock already. I wish you'd sit up and—I know what—I want to show you something. (*He gets a seat for the Ferris wheel from the table where he'd hidden it.*) If there's something in the Surprise Box. (*He puts it in but is too excited to leave it there.*) Joanna, I bet there's something in the Surprise Box. (*He opens it.*) I wonder . . . Look. (*He brings it over to her.*) See? I made two of them and this one is . . . If I put it on the Ferris wheel, will you sit up? If—I tell you—you can put the last one on . . . If I—what if I— look. (*He sets it on the wheel.*) Joanna? Look at that! It's all finished, Joanna. Are you going to sleep? It's all finished—you're supposed to be the very first one to turn it . . . Look, if I let you . . . If I turned it for you then you—would you—then would you? Huh? Look, what . . . if I see? (*He turns it slowly around.*) See? Well, If I If I If I If I took—If I went—let you take—if I got, then, would . . . If I then would—you . . . would . . . you . . .

**CURTAIN**

# THE MADNESS OF LADY BRIGHT  (December 1963)
*for Neil Flanagan*

## AUTHOR'S NOTE

I saw THE FUNNYHOUSE OF THE NEGRO, the wonderful play by Adrienne Kennedy, and didn't understand it or like it at all. It's about a young African American girl quietly going mad in her apartment.

Hanging around the Cino, bitching the play, I said, "Who cares? I'd as soon see a play about a screaming queen going stark raving –" and stopped dead. I suddenly understood Adrienne's play and loved it completely. The subject and form of LADY BRIGHT owes everything to FUNNYHOUSE. In other words I ripped Adrienne off totally. The play was written on the typewriter at the Americana Hotel (now a Sheraton) where I was working the night shift, down in the basement, quite alone, manning the reservation phones. I believe the idea for the play shocked me. I called Neil Flanagan and said,"What can we do at the Cino? I mean can we just do anything? Could we, for instance, do a play about a screaming queen?" (To my knowledge LADY BRIGHT was the first on stage. Robert Patrick's THE HAUNTED HOST had been written but wasn't produced for another 6 months. And the host is very funny, and very gay, but really not a queen.) Neil said, "Write it and we'll see." I took him the script a few days later. HOME FREE! was running at the Cino; I watched the performance while Neil and his wife, Jackie, read LADY BRIGHT in the dressing room. When the show was over he came to my table and said, "You're going to have to get a very good director for this." I was crestfallen. I told him I was hoping he would direct it. "No," he said, "I'm going to play it." I said he was nothing like what I had imagined in the part. "That's why you're going to have to get a very good director." We did. Neil got his first Obie for his really stunning performance. Historical note: Jerry Tallmer reviewed the play (favorably, thank God, or thank Tallmer) in *The New York Post*, the first review of an Off-Off Broadway play in a major New York daily.

THE MADNESS OF LADY BRIGHT was first presented by Joseph Cino at the Caffé Cino on May 19, 1964. It was directed by Denis Deegan with sets by Joseph Davies, lighting by John Torrey, and had the following cast:

LESLIE BRIGHT: Neil Flanagan
GIRL: Carolina Lobravico
BOY: Eddie Kenmore

The production was revised with new casts and a redirection by William Archibald to run a total of 168 performances at the Cino.

## CHARACTERS

LESLIE BRIGHT  A man of about forty; he is a screaming, preening queen, rapidly losing a long-kept "beauty."

BOY AND GIRL  Both are very attractive, perhaps twenty-five, dressed in dark, simple, casual clothes.

## SCENE

The stage within a stage is set as Leslie Bright's one-room apartment. The walls are light and covered over with hundreds of signatures, or autographs, mostly only names, in every conceivable size and writing medium. The name "Adam" is prominent on one wall; on another is "Michael Delaney." There is a dresser with nail polish, hair brush, lipstick, various clutter across the top. A desk, chair, papers, telephone. A portable phonograph that works passably well, and records. The room seems tucked like a pressing book with mementos, post cards, letters, photographs, pictures of men from body-building magazines. A bed with pink and white silk sheets is against one wall. A window looks out to the back of buildings across the back yard below, a scene like the seventies between Amsterdam and Columbus avenues in upper Manhattan. The room is very sunny. A hot, still summer afternoon.

# THE MADNESS OF LADY BRIGHT

*The characters of the Boy and Girl are used to move the action—
to Leslie's memories, moods. They express, as actors, various people, voices, lovers. Sometimes they should be involved, sometimes
almost bored, impatient, sometimes openly hostile, as the people
he has known.*

*At curtain the three walk on and assume their positions. The
Boy and Girl sit to the side, or either side; Leslie, entering, carrying a telephone, in character, sits at the desk and dials a number.
After a moment of half-listening, a doubletake, he turns to the
couple.*

**LESLIE**  (*Broadly.*) Do you know what is comforting the world on Dial-
A-Prayer this abysmally hot Saturday afternoon?

**GIRL**  (*Prefatorily, to the audience.*) Abysmally Hot Saturday Afternoon . . .

**LESLIE**  (*Cutting in, superior.*) You think lately perhaps you've been
overly preoccupied with sex; you should turn to deeper, more solemn
matters, and Dial-A-Prayer gives you: "The Lord is my Shepherd, I
shall not want. He maketh me to *lie down* in green pastures." God,
what an image. Out in a green pasture, yet. Well, Adam, if that isn't
heaven. . . . Why didn't you maketh me to lie down in green pastures,
Adam? Why didn't you just maketh me to lie down? Why didn't you
maketh me? (*He has been looking through an address book.*) Well,
who would be home? (*Dials.*) Stalwart queen, I can't believe even you
would walk the street in this heat. (*Hanging up.*) One day you're going
to melt into the sidewalk (*Looking through the book*) into this little
puddle of greasy rouge and nylons. (*Dials.*) Ring. Ring. (*Holds telephone receiver between his shoulder and ear, picks up the bottle of
nail polish and polishes one nail.*) Ring. (*Looking at the hand.*) Ten
rings, dear, that's enough for any girl. One for every finger. Cheap
damn Chinese red. Junk. No one. No one is home. (*Waving hand to
dry.*) *That's* ten, sweetheart—okay, one extra for the index finger—
eleven, that's all, sorry. (*Hangs up sloppily.*) So, no one is home.

**BOY**  You're home.

**LESLIE**  (*Cutting in.*) *I'm* home, of course. Home. (*Looks around.*) Oh,
god! Well, face it, girl; you'll drive yourself stir if you can't find someone else to drive. . . . (*He fans through the address book.*) Oh, to hell
with you. (*Tossing it aside.*) You bore me. (*Affected voice.*) You bore

me! (*Rather seriously.*) You are a pile of paper addresses and memories, paper phone numbers and memories, and you mean nothing to me. (*Trying to catch the line just said.*) You—I am surrounded—I am left with (*Rather desperately trying to catch the right phrasing of the line to write it down.*) a—with paper memories and addresses. . . . (*Finds a piece of paper at the desk. With a pencil, bent over the desk.*) I am—how?

**BOY**   I am left with a—with paper memories.

**GIRL**   With paper addresses.

**BOY**   You are a pile of addresses and remembrances.

**LESLIE**   How did it go?

**GIRL**   (*Singing.*) "Memories, memories . . ."

**LESLIE**   How did it go?

**BOY**   I am a paper.

**LESLIE**   Oh, to hell with it. I should go out. (*Looking at the polished nail.*) If nothing else in the world, I am certain that that is the wrong color for me. (*Sitting down.*) I—I— (*Totally different thought.*) I should never wear anything other than blue. Aqua. The color of the sea. (*Rising.*) I am Venus, rising from . . . and matching eye shadow. And nothing else. (*He looks in the mirror for the first time. Stops. Looks bitchily at his reflection.*) You. Are a faggot. There is no question about it any more—you are definitely a faggot. You're funny but you're a faggot. (*Pause.*) You have *been* a faggot since you were four years old. Three years old. (*Checking the mirror again.*) You're not *built* like a faggot—necessarily. You're built like a disaster. But, whatever your dreams, there is just no possibility whatever of your ever becoming, say, a lumberjack. You know? (*He has risen and is wandering aimlessly about the room.*)

**GIRL**   You know? (*Music, very softly from outside.*)

**LESLIE**   I know. I just said it. None whatever. Oh, you're spinning around in your stupid room like Loretta Young for Christsake. You should have a long circular skirt and . . . (*Long stretching motion with his arm as he turns, imitating Loretta Young's television entrance.*) "Hello. John?" (*He stops. They all hear the music now, a Mozart concerto, very faint.*) Why, how lovely.

**GIRL**   How soft, distant. Isn't that lovely?

**BOY**   It is. (*The three drift toward the window.*)

**LESLIE**   It must be coming from someone's apartment. Some faggot's apartment. (*They are at the window.*) He's turned on the Bach—no, it's Mozart. And he's preparing dinner nervously, with some simple salad and some complex beef stew. And they'll dine by candlelight and ruin their eyes. Sometimes in summer it seems the only way to remain sane is listening to the radios playing in the neighborhood. I haven't a radio myself; I discovered I was talking back to it so I kicked it out. I have only the phonograph you saw and some worn-out records. (*The boy and girl have become visitors.*)

**GIRL**  The music is lovely.

**BOY**  Where's it coming from, can you tell?

**LESLIE**  I don't know. Somewhere. It's nice at a distance like that. Sometimes in summer it seems the only way to remain sane is by listening to—of course, it's a mixed neighborhood. Oh, well. I get Spanish guitars and a good deal of Flamenco music as well. Of course I enjoy that too. At a distance like that.

**GIRL**  So soft, like that.

**BOY**  It's all right. (*They turn from the window.*)

**LESLIE**  Mozart has always been one of my favorites; I know, you'll say how ordinary, but Mozart and Bach, I believe they have—oh, I don't know. It's so immature to try to analyze music. (*The window has become the doorway to a symphony hall; they exit, moving away slowly, and Leslie lights a cigarette, as at intermission.*)

**BOY**  It isn't necessary to talk about it; you just listen to it.

**LESLIE**  Exactly. I know. But they'll intellectualize and say that *this* is like a sunset and *that*—I mean it's so phony.

**GIRL**  It is.

**LESLIE**  I get really passionately upset by that sort of thing. Music is not like a sunrise, it's like (*They are laughing at his joke before it is finished.*) music, isn't it? I mean, isn't it?

**GIRL**  That's so true.

**BOY**  That's true. (*They walk away. Leslie remains standing in the same position. The music has faded away.*)

**LESLIE**  (*Continuing.*) I go to these concerts only to listen to the music, not to see the white cliffs of wherever-it-is. I only . . . (*Listens.*) It's stopped. (*Goes to window again.*) Why do you always hear that stupid concerto, the same one? There is no one out there who would have been playing it, is there? (*To the walls.*) Is there, Autographs? (*Listens.*) What was that? (*This is bawdy—Judy Garland yelling to her doting audience.*) What was that once more? (*Big.*) We'll stay all night and sing 'em all! (*A bow. Drops his cigarette.*) God damn! Burn the place down.

**BOY**  (*Correcting; this exchange is rapid with almost sadistic inanity.*) Up.

**GIRL**  Burn the place up.

**LESLIE**  Up or down?

**GIRL**  Up or down.

**BOY**  (*Echo.*) Up or down?

**LESLIE**  Down or up? (*Leslie sits at dresser.*)

**GIRL** (*Cutting in.*) You're so damn sloppy; if you've got to smoke . . .

**LESLIE** (*Cutting in.*) I don't *have* to smoke, I *prefer* to smoke.

**GIRL** (*Cutting in.*) Got to smoke you could at least take a few elementary precautions not to burn the place down.

**BOY** Up.

**GIRL** Not to burn the place up.

**LESLIE** (*Cutting in.*) I am a very nervous person and I have to have something to do with my hands and I *prefer* to smoke, if you don't mind! If you don't *mind!*

**GIRL** Well, you can buy your own cigarettes; don't expect me to supply cigarettes for you, and don't think I don't notice when you steal mine.

**LESLIE** I wouldn't touch yours. . . .

**GIRL** You can march down to the store and buy your own—if you're not ashamed to be seen there. (*The Boy has laughed chidingly at "march."*)

**LESLIE** Why would I be . . . (*Breaks off, turns to mirror.*) Hmm. (*Hands to sides of eyes, testily.*) Oh, not good. Not good at all. All those spidery little wrinkles showing your a-g-e. Exposing yourself, aren't you? And a gray hair or two—and your whole face just collapsing. Built like a disaster. (*Turning mirror away.*) Oh, do go away. (*To the back of mirror.*) You should be preserved somewhere. You are a very rare specimen that should be saved for posterity. *Lowered* into the La Brea tar pits in a time capsule as a little piece of the twentieth century that didn't quite come off. Along with an Olivetti typewriter and a can of cream of celery soup. (*Turning mirror back again.*) Whatever you're telling me I don't want to hear it. I've heard it before from every bitchy queen alive. The old fey mare ain't what she used to be. But she's well preserved, you've got to give her that. *A line or two,* but holding together. By a thread. (*Rising.*) But she can sing like a nightingale. Well, nearly. And dance like Giselle. Giselle was a little willie—a willie is a fairy who dances in the woods. (*Almost as though telling a story to the Boy and Girl.*) And, well, they tried to make Giselle's husband dance all night and she danced all night in his place. (*Aside.*) Didn't you, Giselle? You did. You saved his life. (*To the walls.*) Now, what have I done for you? All my visitors—all the men who have visited this stupid apartment for the last ten or so years—what have I ever done for you? Well, let's face it, what did you ever do for me? Look at it that way. Precious little. (*Jumping onto the bed, tapping a finger against a crossed-out name.*) Oh, you! Quentin! I scratched your name off over a year ago; you gave me—what particular social disease was it you gave me? You with your neat little signature. Tight, like-a-spring-little signature. You can always tell a man by the way he signs his name, and a tight signature is very, very bad, Quentin.

**BOY**  How come?

**LESLIE**  (*Walking away. Only mildly scolding.*) I have studied graphology and believe me, it is very, very *bad*, Quentin. You will undoubtedly give me some dreadful social disease. And you, another meek little signature. In pencil. But you were only an edge bashful, only shy. For a meek little signature, Arnold Chrysler, you weren't really bad. You were not Adam, but there was only one. You were none of you like—anything like—Adam. Well, Michael Delaney was wonderful indeed; marvelous indeed, but he was not Adam. (*Cheek to Adam's name.*) You were everything. You are what I remember. Always the dreams are you. (*Turning away, laughing.*) Dreams? Oh, my dear. Fantasies. Oh, you are definitely cracking. (*Into mirror.*) Mirror, you are—I am sorry to report—cracking up. (*Frustrated.*) I am losing my mind. I am. I am losing my faggot mind. I'm going insane. (*The Mozart returns, but never important—very distantly, and only to a few bars.*) It's this stupid apartment and the goddamned heat and *no one ever being at home!* (*To telephone.*) Why don't you answer? (*To himself.*) You are growing old and fat and insane and senile and old. (*Goes to phone, dials. Ends the nervous note, says with the phone:*) "The Lord is my"—yes, we know all that. (*Hangs up. Dials.*) All of you are never, ever, ever at home. (*Looking about the room as the phone rings on and on.*) *You* at least never had homes. You never lived in one place more than a week. Bums and vagabonds, all of you; even Adam, admit it. Tramp around the world, hustling your box from Bermuda to Bangkok! From Burma to Birmingham. How was Birmingham, Adam? What? Oh, don't lie to me, *everyone* has hustled his box in Birmingham. (*Notices the phone is in his hand, hangs up.*) Never home. At least you can count on Dial-A-Prayer being home. (*Tosses book on the desk.*) You, you whores, tramp-the-street bitches. Dial-A-Prayer, and weather and the correct time and Pan American Airways travel information and TWA and American and Delta and Ozark—and the public library. You can count on—but an acquaintance? Don't count on it. There is no one outside. (*Laughs.*) Well! (*To the Boy and Girl.*) A little action, huh? (*They laugh, party-like.*) I hate beer, just a coke, please: Yes, I know they're both fattening, you whore, I don't have to worry about that *yet!* Beauty isn't everything! . . . But then what is? Come on.

**GIRL**  Come on. (*A rock and roll record comes up.*)

**BOY**  Come on. Let's dance.

**LESLIE**  Let's dance. (*Girl dances with Boy. Leslie dances with imaginary partner. The Boy talks both for himself and Leslie's partner. But Leslie doesn't know the dance.*) What is it? What on earth? Oh, God, I couldn't do that. Zat new? Huh? Well tell me the steps anyway.

**BOY**  Zeasy.

**LESLIE**  Walk through it once.

**BOY**  Just follow.

**LESLIE**  I'll try. Oh, God. (*Catching on, but not completely getting it.*)

**BOY**  Zit.

**LESLIE**  Is it? (*They continue to dance, very fast, very tiring, until the end of the record and it goes off. General noise.*)

**GIRL**  Swell.

**BOY**  Thanks. (*They walk away.*)

**GIRL**  Wheeh! It's so warm.

**BOY**  Yeah.

**LESLIE**  Is that all? Hell, it's over; put another quarter in. Ha! (*Comes out of it.*) Goddamn. Every time, all over sweat. You crazy loon. Stupid bitch. You should get dressed up and go down to the beach, it's so damn muggy and hot they must need a little something to liven up the beach about now. (*Makes a quick single enormous cabbage rose of the top sheet and puts it on his head as a fashionable hat—walks across the room as in a beauty contest, singing low:*) "There she is, Miss America. . . ." (*Takes rose from head, holds it to cover himself—a vision of total nudity, raises his eyes to the imaginary Judge's bench. With sunny brightness.*) Good morning, Judge! (*Pause.*) Your Honor. (*Tosses it aside, goes to dresser.*) Oh, dear. (*Pause. Boy and Girl have been ignoring him.*)

**BOY**  (*To the actress quietly, privately.*) Did you go somewhere?

**LESLIE**  (*Tossing the sheet back to the bed.*) No.

**GIRL**  When?

**BOY**  Last night. Did you go out for a while?

**GIRL**  Oh, yes. I went for cigarettes.

**BOY**  I missed you. I rolled over for a second and stretched, you know — and you weren't there—and I thought where the hell—then I must have drifted off again. Got up and got dressed?

**GIRL**  I went out for a few minutes down to the drug store.

**BOY**  I wondered.

**GIRL**  It was raining.

**BOY**  (*Faking a hurt voice.*) Well, you might consider—I looked over expecting you to be there—and there was nothing but loneliness.

**LESLIE**  (*To himself—listening in spite of himself.*) Loneliness. (*He is not looking toward them.*)

**GIRL**  You were asleep when I came back.

**BOY**  It's a terrible thing to wake up to loneliness. (*Leslie looks sharply toward him at the word repeated.*)

**GIRL**  I came right back; it was wet as hell. You know?

**LESLIE**  You know nothing about loneliness. (*Long pause.*) I should go out. (*Seeing name on the wall.*) I should go out and look for you. . . . (*Creeping up on the name.*) Mich-ael De-lan-ey— (*Grabbing the wall.*) Gotcha! (*Turning from the wall.*) Good Lord—eight years ago— you would be how old by now? Oh well, old hustlers never die, they just start buying it back! (*Turning back to the wall.*) You were very good, I remember that. And who else? (*Going over the names.*) So-so; fair; clumsy, but cute anyway; too intelligent; Larry; good, I remember, A minus, and that's very good; undersized; very nice; *over*sized, but I'm not complaining. (*Suddenly angry.*) Samuel Fitch! (*Runs to the desk for a pencil.*) Samuel Fitch! (*Scratches the name off.*) No, I thought you were gone! You bitch! You liar! You vicious faggot! You *Queer*! You were not a man, you were some worm. Some smelly worm. (*Feeling better.*) Of course, you couldn't help it. You were *born* a worm. Once a worm always a worm, I always say. (*Looking back at the erased name.*) Oh. Poor Samuel. You really couldn't help it, could you? You were queer but you couldn't help it. Domineering mother, probably. What was it—that was sweet—you said. You said my body was smooth. (*The Mozart is back, softly but getting louder.*) Hairless, that's what you liked about it. You said I moved well, too, didn't you? Well, *I do* move well. I move *exceptionally* well. (*Sits on the side of the bed. Giselle music is added to the Mozart, and in a moment the rock and roll also begins.*) And I haven't a hair on my body. I'm as hairless and smooth as a newborn babe. I shave, of course, my underarms; no woman would go around with hair under her arms. It's just not done. Lately. In America anyway. (*Stretches his legs.*) And my legs—they're smooth. They are. (*Feeling the backs of his legs.*) I have– I (*Nervously.*) I have varicose veins in my legs. I can't wear hose. I have hideous, dreadful legs. I have blue, purple, *black* veins in my legs. They give me pain—they make me limp, they ache, they're ugly. They used to be beautiful and they are bony and ugly. Old veins. (*The Boy and Girl begin to rub their legs and arms and to moan low.*) Old legs, dancing legs; *but the veins!* They get tired. And when they get (*Fast.*) old they get tired and when they get tired they get slow and when they get slow they get stiff and when they get stiff they get brittle and when they get brittle they break and the veins break and your bones snap and your skin sags. . . . The veins in my arms and legs—my veins are old and brittle and the arteries break—your temples explode your veins break like glass tubes—you can't walk you can't dance you can't speak; you stiffen with age. Age takes you over and buries you; it buries you under—under—my *veins*, my arms, my body, my heart, my old callused hands; my ugly hands; my face is collapsing. I'm losing my mind. (*The boy finally screams a long, low, "Oh." The Girl. screams nervously, "I'm going insane."*) I'm going insane. I'm going insane!

**BOY**  My veins, my arteries.

(*The Boy and Girl speak the next two lines simultaneously.*)

**GIRL**  I'm being buried.

**BOY**  I'm old; I'm growing old.

**GIRL**  (*Singing.*) "Memories, memories." (*The music has now reached its loudest point.*)

**LESLIE**  (*Speaking over Girl's singing.*) I'm losing my *mind. I'm losing my mind. Oh, God, I'm losing my mind.* (*He falls panting onto the bed. The only music left is the Mozart, very far away. After a moment he gets up. He notices his pants leg is pulled up; he slowly pulls it down.*) I. . . .

**GIRL**  (*Chattering madly.*) If you must smoke you could at least buy your own.

**BOY**  How did it go, memories and paper and addresses on the walls and . . . ?

**GIRL**  And don't tell me . . .

**LESLIE**  (*Sits on side of the bed. To himself.*) I should.

**GIRL**  And don't tell me you don't snatch mine; I've seen you. I sometimes count them, you know. Did you ever think about that?

**LESLIE**  I—I should go out. (*Rises, walks to desk, sits.*) That way insanity, Leslie. That way the funnyfarm, Lady Bright. The men in white, Mary. And watch it, because you know you look like a ghost in white. You have never, ever worn white well. (*Rising.*) You should never be seen in any color other than pink. Candy pink. Candy pink and white candy stripes. Silk.

**GIRL**  Well, of course.

**LESLIE**  (*Walking toward the window.*) Someone is playing their radio; I wonder what station plays Mozart all day long. (*The Boy has moved to beside the bed. He is buckling his belt.*) I know you don't understand it, but I do. Your pants are on the chair.

**BOY**  Yeah, I found them. You're good, I'll say that.

**LESLIE**  (*Pleased.*) Sometimes I just like to stand and listen to the music from someone's radio. I've done that a lot this summer. I live alone. (*He continues to look out the window, away from the Boy.*)

**BOY**  I said you're good.

**LESLIE**  Well, of course. You see the names. Did you notice the names on the wall?

**BOY**  (*Seeing them.*) Yeah. I mean I see them now. You do it?

**LESLIE**  Of course not! They're autographs. No one has refused me. And I'll want yours, too, of course.

**BOY**  My what?

**LESLIE**  Your name, your autograph.

**BOY**  On the wall?

**LESLIE**  Yes. Whenever you want to write it. There's an ink pen on the table if you haven't one.

**BOY**  (*finding it and going to the wall.*) Yeah. Okay, you got it.

**LESLIE**  Don't tell me where. Move away now. (*He turns.*) Now. (*Surveying the walls.*) There. Oh, so large, you egoist; it surely wasn't difficult to find it. Michael Delaney. You're Irish?

**BOY**  Yeah.

**LESLIE**  Irish. (*Distantly disappointed.*) Well, it isn't romantic, is it? It's not Russian or Sicilian or one of those, but I've got nothing against the Irish. Any more. You have raised my opinion of them, I'll admit, considerably. (*The Boy walks away, sits down.*) I thought you only drank a good deal, but I find you have a capacity for other things as well. And it's just as well to add a favorite nationality; I was guessing you as Jewish; you don't mind me saying that—the dark hair, you know—but with a name like Michael Delaney you couldn't be anything else. (*The music has faded slowly out. Leslie looks out the window again.*) They've turned the radio down so I can't hear it now. I tell you (*A quick glance at the name.*) Michael, it's no fun. It's no fun living here in this stupid apartment by myself listening to my few records and the neighbor's radio; I should like someone, I think sometimes (*Being delicate.*) living here some times. Or maybe somehow not living here but coming here to see me often. Then I'd wash the walls—wash off everyone else. Wash them off and kiss them good-by—good riddance. I've even thought I wouldn't mind, you know, just letting someone live here, scot free; I could prepare the meals—and do things. I—want to *do things* for someone who could live here. And he could sleep here, every night. It's really lovely—or would be—with the music. I'd like something like that, it (*Turning.*) gets so lonely here by . . . (*But of course, he's gone. Leslie glances at the Boy sitting. To the Girl.*) This dumb room. (*To the walls.*) Dumb! Mute! All you goddamned cobwebby corners, you stare down at me while I die of boredom; while I go insane because everyone I call is gone off somewhere. Once more. (*Goes to phone, dials, listens to the ringing.*) Once. Twice. Thrice. Quadrice. Screw. (*Limply he puts his finger on the cradle, clicking off. Raises it and dials from memory another number.*)

**GIRL**  Good afternoon, American Airlines. May we help you?

**LESLIE**  Yes. (*Pause.*) Fly me away from here. (*Clicks her off, leaving his finger on the phone. Long pause. Reflecting, bitchily.*) Oh, well, fly yourself fairy; you've got the wings. All God's chil'un got wings, Leslie. That's your disastrous body: wings and ass.

**BOY**  You've got a nice body. You know, a young body. How old are you, about nineteen? (*Leslie is surprised, almost stunned by the line.*

*The Boy repeats the cue.*) How old are you, about nineteen? (*The Boy has entered the room.*)

**LESLIE** (*Sadly; remembering.*) Twenty. (*The scene now is played with young, fresh buoyancy.*) And you're what? The same age about, aren't you?

**BOY** Twenty-one. Get drunk legally, any state.

**LESLIE** I've never—I'm almost embarrassed—I've never met anyone as—well, I'm never at a loss for words, believe me. I don't know what you have—anyone so good looking as you are. (*Boy laughs.*) What do you do? Are you a weight lifter?

**BOY** Who—me? I don't do nothing. Bum around.

**LESLIE** Bum around.

**BOY** Been in every state.

**LESLIE** Just bumming around?

**BOY** One state pays for the next, you know?

**LESLIE** You hustle, I guess. I mean—do you only hustle? I . . .

**BOY** (*Cutting in.*) That's right. Oh, well, for kicks too; sometimes. Why not? When the mood hits me.

**LESLIE** I wish to God it would hit you about now.

**BOY** Yeah. Rough night, kid. Sorry.

**LESLIE** Oh.

**BOY** (*Looking around.*) Come on, they'll be other nights. I said I like you; you're a nice kid. We'll make it. I'll promise you.

**LESLIE** You will?

**BOY** I'll promise you that.

**LESLIE** Good. Then I'll wait.

**BOY** How long you been in this pad?

**LESLIE** About a month. Everything's new. I painted the walls myself.

**BOY** You ever seen one of these?

**LESLIE** What? A grease pencil? Sure, I used to work in the china department of this stupid store; we marked dishes with them.

**BOY** Mind if I do something?

**LESLIE** What am I supposed to say? (*Earnestly.*) No. I don't mind if you do something. Anything.

**BOY** Something to remember me by. (*Goes to wall.*)

**LESLIE** What? *What?* Are you writing—your name? Hey, on my fresh wall? (*The Boy turns smilingly to him.*) What the hell, it looks good there.

**BOY** Yeah. I'll see you around.

**LESLIE** Where are you going? (*No answer. Leslie is in the present now. The Boy walks to his chair and sits.*) Where are you going? Not you. Don't leave now. Don't. Adam. You're not leaving. Come back here, don't go away; you were the one I wanted. The only one I wanted,

Adam! Don't go away! (*Wildly.*) Don't go, Adam; don't go, Adam.

**GIRL**  Unrequited love is such a bore.

**BOY**  Sad.

**GIRL**  Left him flat, didn't he?

**BOY**  The only one he wanted.

**LESLIE**  Oh, God, that way, honey, is madness for sure. Think about Adam and you've had it, honey. Into the white coat with the wrap-around sleeves.

(*The following dialogue between the Boy and Girl takes place simultaneously with Leslie's next speech.*)

**GIRL**  It's sad, really.

**BOY**  It is. It really is. The only one he wanted really was Adam.

**GIRL**  And he never had him.

**BOY**  Never saw him after that.

**GIRL**  Of course he would have gone mad either way, don't you think?

**BOY**  Oh, yes.

**GIRL**  Drove himself to it, I mean. He couldn't have possibly lived a sane life like that.

**BOY**  Some pansies live a sane life and some don't. Like anyone else, I suppose.

**GIRL**  Well, not exactly.

**BOY**  I mean some go nuts and some don't. Some just go insane.

**GIRL**  Mad.

**BOY**  Nuts.

**GIRL**  Lose their balance, you know.

**LESLIE**  (*Over the above. Moves to the record player and goes through the records, finds one.*) What I should have is some music. I'm so sick of music for companionship. But it's better than (*Looks at the telephone.*) you queens! Never-at-home sick queens! (*Puts a record on. It is Judy Garland, singing a fast, peppy number. The volume is kept very low.*) Now that's better. That's a little better. I can dance to that one. (*He dances, as with a partner, but he dances a slow, sexy number as the music continues fast.*) There. I like the way you . . . Oh, you think I follow well. I'm glad you think I follow—I have a good sense of rhythm, I've always been told that I move well. I get lonely, but I've been told I move well. I sometimes just stare at the corners of my room, would you believe that, *and pray* (*He stops dancing and stands still.*) *And pray for* . . . (*Stops, panting.*) I want—*I want* . . . (*But he can't say it.*)

**GIRL**  (*With comic remove.*) He wants to die, I believe.

**BOY**  I think that's what he's trying to say.

**GIRL**  Well, it's easy to understand; I mean you couldn't expect him to live like that.

**BOY**  He's effeminate.

**GIRL**  No one can want to live if they're like that.

**BOY**  It's all right on girls.

**LESLIE**  Why do you let me live if you know it?

**GIRL**  (*To Boy.*) What could we do?

**LESLIE**  Why?

**BOY**  No one should live who's like that.

**LESLIE**  Giselle. Giselle, you saved him. You danced all night and you danced till dawn and you saved him. You did, you saved him; you danced for him. They let you save him.

**GIRL**  He used to be an intelligent fellow.

**BOY**  He was. He was a bright kid.

**GIRL**  Quick-thinking.

**LESLIE**  Why do you let me live if you know it? Can't you see I'm going insane alone in my room, in my hot lonely room? Can't you see I'm losing my mind? I don't want to be the way I am.

**GIRL**  He doesn't like the way he is.

**BOY**  He'd like to be different.

**GIRL**  He looks different enough to me.

**BOY**  Extraordinary, I'd say.

**LESLIE**  You could have killed me as a child, you could have.

**GIRL**  Christ! How can you play those goddamned records? Do you have to blare that *music? Do you? You dance around in your room all day.* Do something worthwhile why don't you?

**LESLIE**  You could have.

**GIRL**  Do something worthwhile.

**LESLIE**  (*As before to Michael Delaney.*) I'd like to do something. (*Suddenly.*) No. We won't have this music. (*He's wild now, excited.*) We won't have this music. (*Strip music comes in over the Garland.*) We'll have a party. We'll have a show. I'll give you a show!

**BOY**  He's going to give you a show. I think.

**GIRL**  Turn that off!

**LESLIE**  (*Goes to music. He turns it by accident to full volume, gets nervous, scratches the needle all the way across the record, at full volume. It clicks off. The other music goes off too. Turning to them.*) What would you like?

**BOY**  (*To Girl.*) What would you like?

**GIRL**  (*To Leslie.*) What would you like?

**LESLIE**  (*Happy.*) Oh, me! God, I—would—like . . . We won't have a show, we'll have a royal dance; a cotillion; a nice beautiful dance,

**GIRL**  A ball! Wonderful!

**BOY**  Lady Bright requests your presence . . .

**LESLIE**  A beautiful party. (*Grabs the sheet and winds it around*

*himself.*)

**BOY**   May I have the pleasure?

**GIRL**   I hardly know what to say. (*Mozart music comes up.*)

**LESLIE**   And I shall be the queen! I dance with the most grace. I will be selected queen by popular demand. I dance like a flower on the water. (*Mozart up. They dance around in a whirl.*) I dance like a flower. I shall dance with Adam and you shall dance with whom you please. No, I have no more room on my program, I am dreadfully sorry, young man . . . (*Still dancing.*) I am dancing tonight with only one man, you know what that means.

**GIRL**   She's so lovely.

**BOY**   She's so beautiful.

**GIRL**   Did you catch her name?

**LESLIE**   My name is Giselle! I am Giselle! (*Running to mirror.*) I'm the fairest at the ball. I am the loveliest. *I am young. I am young and lovely. Yes, I am young!* (*He bends over the dressing table and returns to the mirror. He takes up lipstick and smears it across his lips, half his face.*) I am young tonight. I will never be old. I have all my faculties tonight. (*The people have continued to dance. Leslie returns and they whirl about. Other music joins the Mozart—Giselle, the rock and roll, the strip number.*) I am beautiful. I am happy! (*Leslie falls down. They continue to dance about him. The music stops. Then comes on. Stops. Returns. A pulsating effect.*) Excuse me, I must have . . . (*Music continues loudly.*) My arms are so tired. My legs. I have bad legs; I don't walk too well. The veins in my legs are getting old, I guess . . . (*This is light, chattery talk.*) I grow tired easily. *I grow brittle and I break. I'm losing my mind, you know. Everyone knows when they lose their mind. But I'm so lonely!* (*The music stops. Leslie looks up. The boy and girl exit to opposite sides. As if to a man standing over him.*) I'm sorry. I just slipped and . . . (*Turning to the other side. There is a "man" there, too.*) Oh, thank you. (*Allowing the man to help him up, still with the sheet as a gown; softly to the man, intimately.*) I'm sorry—I hate to trouble you, but I—I believe I've torn my gown. I seemed to have ripped . . . Oh, no, it can be repaired. Yes, I'm sure it can. But would you take me home now, please? (*There is a pause.*) Just take me home, please; take me home, please. Take me home now. Take me home. *Please take me home.* (*The music now comes on and builds in a few seconds to top volume. Leslie screams above it. He drops the sheet; it falls down around him.*) TAKE ME HOME, SOMEONE! TAKE ME HOME! (*The music stops. Leslie has run to the wall, to a far-off area, leaning against the wall. The Mozart is the only music remaining. Softly, whispering against the wall—to himself.*) Take me home. Take me home. Take me home. Take me home. Take

me home. Take me home. Take me home. Take me home. Take me
home. . . . (*The lights fade out slowly.*)

**CURTAIN**

# LUDLOW FAIR  (November 1964)

## AUTHOR'S NOTE

Michael Warren Powell and I arrived in New York City on July 5th, 1962. (With $7 between us, but that's another story.) One of the first acting jobs Michael got was Roderigo in OTHELLO at Hunter College. Neil Flanagan, who was everywhere in those days, was Iago. One of the student assistants was a mildly hysterical girl who had turned in her boyfriend for stealing her paycheck and found the larcenous creep was wanted in a dozen states. I've always used whatever was at hand, and when I wrote LUD-LOW FAIR, a year or so later, her story was very handy. While the play was running at the Cino I bumped into the girl from Hunter and encouraged her to drop by and see my play, completely forgetting I had used her story. Neil, who directed, must have known the origin of Rachel, but I don't remember if we discussed it. I'm sorry I missed that performance. When I came by later they told me a rather odd thing had happened. In the middle of the play some girl had jumped up screaming, "Oh, my God, that's me! That's me!"

LUDLOW FAIR was first presented by Joseph Cino at the Caffé Cino, New York City, on February 1, 1965. It was directed by Neil Flanagan with the following cast:

RACHEL: Martha Galphin
AGNES: Jennie Ventriss

Lighting by Dennis Parichy, sets by Mr. Flanagan. Stage manager Renée Mauguin.

## CHARACTERS

RACHEL  An attractive young woman in her mid-twenties.

AGNES  On the heavy side, busty, not unattractive, but no raving beauty, in her mid-twenties. She would be considered "a great deal of fun."

## SCENE

The bedroom of their apartment. Two twin beds on one wall, a vanity dresser across the room. A desk with books. The room is neat and in good taste. On the table between the beds is a phone. On the desk, is a dictionary, among other books; on the vanity is, among the usual paraphernalia, a box of large hair rollers and a bottle of nail polish. One exit is to the bathroom, another to the living room. Rachel wears a gown and robe; Agnes, pajamas and robe.

# LUDLOW FAIR

**RACHEL**  (*Wandering around the room alone. She is restless; she looks at one thing and another. Finally, quite to herself.*) Oh, God; I think you're losing your head. I think you're going stark raving insane and you've got no one in this ever-loving world, sweetheart, to blame except yourself. And maybe Joe. But then. . . . Are you losing it? Hmm? Let's see. (*She pinches herself firmly. For a full two seconds she considers the effect. Matter-of-factly.*) Ouch! (*Yelling toward the bathroom.*) Agnes? (*Waits.*) How long are you going to take, anyway?

**AGNES**  (*Off stage, from the bathroom.*) What?

**RACHEL**  I said, are you about through in there?

**AGNES**  In a minute.

**RACHEL**  You said that an hour ago. (*She waits for an answer, none comes. Rubbing her arm.*) What a stupid thing to do. That's no kind of test of insanity, anyway. That's for drunkenness or sleepwalking or disorderly conduct or something. How do you how if your faculties are ebbing away from you, anyway? (*Seriously considering.*) You go to an analyst, what does he do? You lie down on the couch, what does he do? Ha! No, a respectable analyst, what does he do? You lie—A quick little word association. You can't give yourself a word—well, why not? (*Sits quickly on the chair at the desk.*) Ready? Ready. Very well, when I say a word you come in with the very first word that pops into your head. Yes, I understand. Very well. (*Pause, tries for a split second to think of a word. Finally.*) Word. (*Immediately answers.*) Word! (*Blank pause.*) Dog. (*Absolutely blank for the count of six. Aside.*) Oh, for Christ's sake . . . (*Intense concentration. Mumbles.*) Dog. (*Breaking away, then finally.*) Jesus Chri—DOG! (*Pause. With the same studied intensity.*) CAT! (*Aside.*) For Christ's sake—well, that's it—cat. Keep it up. Cat. (*Same amount of pause between words, same intensity to each word.*) Rat. Mouse. House. Rat. Dog. Cat. Mouse. Louse. Bat. Pat. Fat. Louse. (*Breaking away.*) Fat louse, Jesus Christ. Rat, cat, mouse, louse, bat, house; you don't need an analyst you need an exterminator. You can't associate with yourself. Even words. (*Calling to no one.*) Joe! (*Sees the dictionary on the desk, puts it in her lap.*) Well, why not? As long as you don't know the word that's coming up. Now the first word that pops into your head. (*Answering herself.*) Yes, I understand. (*She opens the book, looks down, closes it. Flatly.*) Knickerbocker! (*Sighs slowly, then with redetermination.*) All right, I'll play your stupid game with you. Holiday. Take that. (*Opens the* book again. *Looks more closely. Reading.*) phen-a-kis-to-scope (*Pause. Looking at it. Continues reading.*) "An instrument resembling the zoethrope in principle and use. One form consists of a disk with the figures arranged about the center, with radial slits— (*Aside.*) Radial slits? (*Continues to read.*) Radial slits through which the figures are viewed— (*Becoming amused.*) —by means of a mirror." (*Closing the dictionary.*) But what's it *for?* Phen-a-kis-to-scope. Very well. (She *gets up, wanders to the dresser. As though she were thinking.*) Phenakistoscope. Ah, oh. Zoethrope! Naturally. (*Sitting at the dresser, the dictionary open in front of her, she quite casually opens the nail polish and pours an amount on one page, shuts the dictionary firmly, props it open again, like an easel against the back of the vanity. Studies it carefully from some distance.*) Ah . . . Oh, ah . . . A tree. (*Aside.*) A tree. That couldn't possibly mean anything. (*Looks back at it, studying.*) Ah. Ah. Your trouble is you have no imagination, Rachel. You're not nuts, you're just dull. Okay . . . Ah. An ostrich. That's a little better. An ostrich. Eating. (*Considering her progress.*) An ostrich, huh? That's vaguely phallic, you how. Well, vaguely. (*Shutting the book.*) That's the trouble with those things, when they start working you're in trouble. (*She gets up, carrying the book, rubs her arm.*) If you don't learn to stop pinching yourself. (*Calling.*) Agnes? Are you ever getting out of there?

**AGNES**  (*Off stage.*) What? I'll be out in a minute. Christ.

**RACHEL**  You said that an hour ago. (*She lays the book back on the dresser, wanders about.*) There's nothing wrong with you, Rachel, except you're given to talking to yourself—*driven* to talking to yourself. (*Falls down on her bed, stretched out, looking up blankly.*) Long pointless conversations before retiring. Well, doctor—it's this way. Joe turned out to be a rat. But then I think I knew that before he turned out. (*Props herself on one elbow.*) I was just sitting home saying to myself, Rachel, you have *got* to get yourself a new phenakistoscope. The one you've got is just a mess. The radial slits are all shot. And when the radial slits are shot, there's just no hope. For a phenakistoscope. Or anything else, for that matter. (*She sits on the side of the bed, face in hands, near the point of crying for just a second, then pulls out of it and gets up.*) Oh dear, oh dear, oh dear, oh dear. Joe. Joe. Joe where did you go? (*Pause.*) All the way to . . . (*Breaks off. Walks to dresser, sees dictionary.*) What have you been doing? Testing your sanity again, huh? What are you crazy or something? There's nothing wrong with you. (*Sees her reflection in the mirror. Pleased but critical.*) Five foot two. Five foot six, actually: Girls are bigger than ever. Lovely dark hair, fine hair. Opalescent skin. Lovely hips. Fine breasts. Nice legs. Nice, hell, great legs. Not bad ears; good hands. Slightly blah eyes, frankly; but then you can't have everything. (*Echo, breaking away. To herself.*) Can't have everything. What you are is probably a louse. A fool, of course, and a probable louse. Moral to a fault. And where you are a probable louse, Joe is a first-class, A-one definite louse without a doubt, and it is good to have a first-class definite louse out of your hair. (*She lights a cigarette.*) Four hundred and thirty-six dollars. (*Takes a puff; exhales.*) And thirty-eight cents. (*Wandering about.*) And several Government checks, like thirty, say. And about twenty-odd forgeries, and about four cars, and four hundred and thirty-six dollars and thirty-eight cents.

AGNES   (*Off stage.*) I'm out. What are you up to?

RACHEL   (*Without paying attention. To herself.*) Oh, God. (*Sees herself in the mirror.*) Girl, you are a mess. Just a mess. (*Pause. Agnes enters. Without looking directly at Rachel, she goes to her bed, picking up the dictionary on her way and tossing it on her bed. Agnes has a cold. She is carrying a box of Kleenex, a section of the* Times *folded open to the crossword, a pencil, a brush and comb, and anything else she can find. Her hair is wet, combed straight down.*)

RACHEL   (*To herself.*) Well, what do you expect with last year's phenakistoscope?

AGNES   (*Without looking up, goes to her bed.*) Are you going to take a bath or what?

RACHEL   Take a bath? When did you start saying, "take a bath"? Take a bath, take a haircut, take a shower—I don't how what you're coming to.

AGNES   I got a cold.

RACHEL   What's that got to do with anything?

AGNES   Well, I abbreviate when I got a cold. (*She situates herself on the bed with the paraphernalia about her, including a dish of peanut brittle.*)

RACHEL   (*Musing sadly.*) Four hundred and thirty-six dollars.

AGNES   (*Without looking up from the paper and brushing her hair.*) And thirty-eight cents.

RACHEL   I just wish I knew if I did the right thing.

AGNES   Look. A guy robs a store. If you turn him in, are you doing the right thing?

RACHEL   Do I know this guy or not?

AGNES   What guy?

RACHEL   Who robbed the store. In your hypothesis.

AGNES   Leave my hypothesis out of it. What difference does it make? He robbed a store you turn him in.

RACHEL   He didn't rob a store.

AGNES   Are you going to take a bath or what?

**RACHEL**  I don't think so.

**AGNES**  You going to stay up and read all night or what?

**RACHEL**  Four hundred bucks. God.

**AGNES**  If you're going to start brooding I'm going to bed.

**RACHEL**  If just once we'd say to ourselves—you do that, girl, and you'll be sorry for it later.

**AGNES**  Yeah. Not bloody likely. (*Blowing her nose.*) Jesus, I'm coming down with something.

**RACHEL**  (*Studying her.*) You know what you are?

**AGNES**  Yeah? Make it good.

**RACHEL**  Susceptible.

**AGNES**  Susceptible. You hook the dud and I'm susceptible. I got a lousy job in lousy Kew Gardens and a lousy date tomorrow for lunch and a lousy dentist appointment and a lousy boss and a lousy love life and a roommate who takes out her aggressions on me. And all you can say is I'm susceptible. I'm dying. Face it, Agnes, you got a lousy life.

**RACHEL**  I meant susceptible to colds. Or drafts.

**AGNES**  "Agnes Mulligan: This Is Your Life!" And the TV screen goes blank for thirty minutes.

**RACHEL**  Why do you always have a cold? You've had a cold since I've known you.

**AGNES**  Maybe I'm allergic to you. I wear low-cut dresses is why. Knew when I was nine, with a name like Agnes, I was in for a dumpy figure and a big bust and low-cut dresses and susceptibility to drafts.

**RACHEL**  Well, don't wear them.

**AGNES**  (*Almost always speaks as if she is talking to herself.*) If I'da had any brains I'd have changed my name.

**RACHEL**  Why don't you?

**AGNES**  What's the point of having a big bust if you don't wear low-cut dresses. (*She puts the crossword on her lap, picks up the dictionary. Then almost dreamily.*) What I can't wait for is a big house and about six handmaids and a big bed to sprawl all over. You know . . . I want to keep my figure—what there is of it. After I'm married, I mean. I really do. I want to look as nice as possible. God, I think that's important.

**RACHEL**  Oh, would you shut up?

**AGNES**  (*Has opened the dictionary absently during the last speech. She shuts it and looks at Rachel.*) What the hell did you do to the dictionary?

**RACHEL**  Oh. I made a Rorschach.

**AGNES**  (*Pause.*) Yeah.

**RACHEL**  I was checking my responses. What does it look like to you?

**AGNES**  (*Reopening the dictionary, unamused.*) It looks like I better know the meaning and derivation of all the possible words between "obsecrate" and "ocelot."

**RACHEL**  What does it look like, though? Do you get an ostrich?

**AGNES**  I don't get anything except mad. Jesus, Rachel.

**RACHEL**  I'm sorry.

**AGNES**  (*Pause.*) Good Lord. Nail polish, huh?

**RACHEL**  Yeah. I thought maybe I was going insane.

**AGNES**  And the simple act of pouring nail polish into the dictionary didn't confirm anything, huh?

**RACHEL**  Don't pester me. Do I eat peanut brittle in bed? I thought you'd never get out of that tub. Don't you know not to leave a screwed-up girl alone with herself for three-quarters of an hour? (*She has said it comically, but suddenly feels sad, puts her head in her hands again.*)

**AGNES**  Well, I was soaking. (*Notices her.*) Aw, come on, for Christ's sake.

**RACHEL**  I only want to know if I did the right thing.

**AGNES**  Look a hundred of that was mine. He was a bum, what can I tell you? He was a bum and a thief and you turned him into the Secret Service and now what are you conjuring up? Lonely Joe in a cell? Well, forget it.

**RACHEL**  You're not funny.

**AGNES**  He was a bum. (*Aside.*) Damn, I'm all over peanut brittle.

**RACHEL**  He was. Of course he was. But I had no idea he'd done any of that other.

**AGNES**  How long had you known him?

**RACHEL**  Three months.

**AGNES**  Well in three months you're supposed to know everything about the guy? Every bank he's robbed, for Christ's sake?

**RACHEL**  He hadn't robbed any banks.

**AGNES**  Federal bank notes passed totaling into the hundreds; you want to get technical, he's robbed a bank. A Federal bank at that. So you had fun; it wasn't worth it.

**RACHEL**  You're a lot of help. I think I'm going over the edge and you sit there complacently sticking to the blanket.

**AGNES**  (*Trying to wipe the blanket and Kleenex off her hands.*) This damn stuff. I'm growing fuzz. (*She sets the dish of candy on the table.*)

**RACHEL**  What will they do to him, do you think?

**AGNES**  (*Quickly, disgruntled.*) I think they'll hang him.

**RACHEL**  (*Getting up.*) Stop it! Now you just stop it!

**AGNES**  Hey, come on. He'll go to jail. He stole my dough and your dough and the Federal Government's dough and God knows whose else's dough and he'll go to jail.

**RACHEL**  I just couldn't believe it.

**AGNES**  Yeah, me too.

**RACHEL**  We really had fun, too.

**AGNES**  Well, don't think about it, okay?

**RACHEL**  We really did.

**AGNES**  She says we really had fun, I tell her don't think about it, she says we really had fun. Jesus. Listen. You know what happened to the fag bookkeeper sits next to me out at work? He picked up this guy. . . .

**RACHEL**  Agnes, I do not care what happened to the fag bookkeeper out at Standard Universal Plumbing.

**AGNES**  Standard Universal Fixtures. (*Pause. Firmly.*) There is no such thing as plumbing any more. (*Pause. Continuing.*) He took this guy he'd met up to—

**RACHEL**  Really! I don't—

**AGNES**  Look, do you think I'd trouble you if it wasn't pertinent? I'm not in the habit of telling you bedtime stories for the hell of it, am I? He picked up, good Lord, this guy! Apparently they just wander around till they see eye to eye with someone and then run right off the street and hit the sack, which, if you want to know my opinion, sounds a little capricious but not altogether impractical. Anyway, this big lug went home with him and "Stars Fell on Alabama," I suppose, or whatever the hell happens. Anyway, the next morning Henry waves good-by and two days later he sees this doll's picture in the paper—he'd been picked up for murder, my dear, of four or five fairies out in California and God knows how many more between here and there. Poor Henry almost died. He'd spent the night with this guy.

**RACHEL**  (*Pause.*) Fine! I'm sorry, I don't see the connection.

**AGNES**  You said you really had fun and you couldn't believe that Joe could possibly be—

**RACHEL**  We happened to have been going together for three months!

**AGNES**  And you didn't know a damn thing about him—

**RACHEL**  You think a one night fling is the same—

**AGNES**  And you'd had some fun and you didn't know beans about him—

**RACHEL**  I didn't just pass him on the street!

**AGNES**  No, you didn't just meet him on a street—

**RACHEL**  Like your bookkeeper—

**AGNES**  You met him at Bickford's.

**RACHEL**  (*Defiantly.*) Longchamps! Honestly. I happen to be in love with him. That's why I'm wandering around this damn stupid— wondering—why the hell. Oh, Christ. (*She sits back on the bed, stretches out, rolls over on her stomach, sobs once.*)

**AGNES**  (*Getting up.*) Oh, come on. Have a box of Kleenex.

**RACHEL**  (*Her face buried in the pillow.*) I don't want them.

**AGNES**  They pop up.

**RACHEL**  Go away. Why did I say anything? What had it cost me really? Nothing. (*Agnes goes to the desk, gets a bottle of liquor out of the bottom drawer, fixes two drinks—just liquor, no mix.*)

**AGNES**  Honestly. Here. Have a shot. Me too, it's good for a cold. If I'm going to be running around nursing a roommate all night. Me? I'm always nursing someone else's broken heart. Just once, I'd like a broken heart of my own.

**RACHEL**  (*Sitting up, takes the drink.*) You're great.

**AGNES**  I snore actually. Why don't you go to bed?

**RACHEL**  I can't. I don't think. You go on. . . . It isn't late, is it?

**AGNES**  No. I hate you like this, I pass up more good cracks.

**RACHEL**  I think maybe I should call in the morning.

**AGNES**  And tell them what? That he really didn't do it? Not here or in Denver or in Tucson? They knew twice what you did about him. (*Moving toward her purse on the vanity.*) I got a hangnail. Damn that typewriter.

**RACHEL**  I could drop the charges.

**AGNES**  (*Looking through her purse for a file.*) I doubt if they'd let him out for you. Besides, I don't know about you, but I'd be scared to death if he got out now.

**RACHEL**  I don't know what I should have done.

**AGNES**  Please don't worry about it. It's done. It's over, that's it.

**RACHEL**  (*Long sigh not looking at Agnes.*) Yeah. (*Rachel is sitting gloomily, looking off into space.*)

**AGNES**  (*Finding something in her purse.*) You collect coins? (*Pause. No response.*) I got a Tasmanian penny at Riker's yesterday.

**RACHEL**  (*Not listening.*) No.

**AGNES**  (*Temptingly.*) It's got some crazy fruit tree on it.

**RACHEL**  (*Not listening.*) No.

**AGNES**  (*Two fingers in the air, making a hand shadow.*) See the rabbit? (*Pause.*) You going to bed soon? Why don't you read something?

**RACHEL**  I tried it.

**AGNES**  Turn on the radio.

**RACHEL**  I tried it.

**AGNES**  What haven't you tried?

**RACHEL**  Oh, I'm being such a lunk. Really. Who's your lunch with?

**AGNES**  The boss's son. Tonsils. I told you about him. (*Nasally.*) He talks like that. And with a Harvard accent yet. He's got the kind of face, I swear as soon as it gets warm he's going to put on a funny pair of sunglasses. (*Pause.*) I feel I should sympathize with you, but honestly, Rachel, I've seen this happen I'll bet ten times since I've been living with you.

**RACHEL**  Not exactly this.

**AGNES**  And you say, "not exactly this" every time. It's a bore; you know what I mean?

**RACHEL**  All right. It's a bore. I couldn't agree more. How many boy friends have I had? Since you've been here? Not so many.

**AGNES**  I'm not your datebook. I don't know.

**RACHEL**  Since you've known me?

**AGNES**  I don't know. What am I?

**RACHEL**  Roger. Just after you moved in.

**AGNES**  Floyd. You'd just broke up with.

**RACHEL**  Then Roger.

**AGNES**  Then Val.

**RACHEL**  Tom. Then Val.

**AGNES**  And Marvin. What a loser he was.

**RACHEL**  And Joe. Six. God. It's just too much.

**AGNES**  In what? Nine months. Not even a year.

**RACHEL**  They were nice guys, though. All of them, really.

**AGNES**  Oh, charming. All. Burghers of Calais.

**RACHEL**  It's too much.

**AGNES**  It's an unearthly waste of time, you know? You know what you could do in nine months?

**RACHEL**  Very funny.

**AGNES**  I wasn't even *thinking* that! Jesus! I meant like get to know someone. Get married—get engaged, at least.

**RACHEL**  Well, with Joe it was nearly three months. (*Looks aside at the phone then reaches for it and sets it in her lap.*) Oh, God.

**AGNES**  (*At the vanity drawer, still filing her nails, she is not looking at Rachel. She drops her file.*) Fuck! (*Bends to pick it up.*) I've got to quit saying that. Jesus. (*Looking at Rachel now, who is very slowly dialing a number.*) Rachel. (*No response. Firmly, flatly.*) Rachel.

**RACHEL**  (*Not listening.*) What?

**AGNES**  (*Firmly, flatly.*) If you're calling your mother I'm moving out.

**RACHEL**  (*Not listening.*) What?

**AGNES**  (*Same inflection.*) I said if you're calling your mother I'm moving out. Out into the street, into the rain. I don't care; I'll be happier there. I'll catch pneumonia, I'll go to Saint Vincent's Hospital, I'll be happier there, believe me.

**RACHEL**  (*Putting the phone down.*) What's wrong?

**AGNES**  Nothing's wrong I've just had it with the Daisy Mae routine.

**RACHEL**  It isn't that bad.

**AGNES**  You are on that phone for one minute and you have an accent strong enough to paper the walls. And I've lived with one Southern girl and couldn't take that, but this nightly metamorphosis bit I don't need.

**RACHEL**   Well, maybe it would help. There are times when you feel like calling your mother; what's wrong with that?

**AGNES**   Well, then; call my mother. But you get a line from here to Dogpatch, Virginia, and I'm moving out. I can't take it. I don't intend to sit here and listen to it. The days of the Cotton Queen are over as far as I'm concerned.

**RACHEL**   It isn't Dogpatch; I wish you'd quit saying that.

**AGNES**   What is it?

**RACHEL**   Cullerton.

**AGNES**   (*Flatly.*) Cullerton. Virginia.

**RACHEL**   North Carolina.

**AGNES**   North Carolina. Jesus. How long did it take you to learn to lose the drawl?

**RACHEL**   How long? About five years.

**AGNES**   Five years. To learn not to drawl. (*To herself.*) Van Gogh didn't study that long to learn. Of course he couldn't drawl. (*Winces, turns to the mirror.*) I'm going to put up my hair. I wasn't going to, but if we're up for the night.

**RACHEL**   Go on to bed. I think I will.

**AGNES**   (*Looks into the mirror.*) Oh, Jesus. (*Looks away blankly. Count ten. Looks back blankly. Count ten.*) Agnes, you're a vision. (*To Rachel, without turning around. Rachel slides under the covers of her bed, opens a magazine, doesn't read it.*) You know, three years ago I had kinky hair.

**RACHEL**   (*Without listening.*) No kidding.

**AGNES**   I had it straightened. (*Pause.*) Ever since I've had straight hair.

**RACHEL**   Why don't you just let it be straight; it looks nice like that.

**AGNES**   No. What I'm not is Veronica Lake. I used to go to this beautician—this gal. Nearly killed me. Inside. She says, Agnes—she was Jewish, you know—Agnes, she says, I'll do wonders for you—you won't recognize yourself. Your own mother won't know you. For nearly a year, every week. She'd comb me out and reset me exactly the same. Agnes, I'll do wonders for you. I came out looking exactly the same as I went in. Solid year.

**RACHEL**   Why did you keep going back to her then?

**AGNES**   (*Begins to set her hair, rolling it onto large rollers and slipping a bobby pin onto the roller. This is a comically realistic process, done quite matter of factly.*) I don't know. It's just nice to run into a positive attitude once in a while. I finally quit. She called me up after a couple of weeks, wanted to how what happened. I didn't have the heart to tell her my mother still recognized me. I told the beautician I'd bought a wig. (*Rachel laughs.*) She tells me—oh, Agnes—you gotta bring it over. I do wonders with wigs. Your own mother won't recognize. . . .

(*Pause.*) You gonna stay up all night or what?

**RACHEL**   I don't know. (*She stretches out in bed.*)

**AGNES**   Why did you ask for the bathroom if you don't want to shower or something, huh?

**RACHEL**   Look—Agnes— (*Sitting up. Rather intense.*) Can we talk? Straight on this? So I can decide what I think for a minute, huh? Really, now—just straight for a minute or two and I'll be all right. I'll swear I don't know what the hell I'm going to do from here if I don't straighten myself out on this. I don't want to call Mom any more than you want me to, but I just want to—

**AGNES**   (*Getting up, she goes for a cigarette.*) Sure. Of course we can; talk to Doctor Muller. My fees are reasonable.

**RACHEL**   No, now—not even like that—just straight. So I know what I feel, or think or something! Sit down, now; stop flying around. See, I did like Joe and an awfully lot, too—

**AGNES**   (*She has lit the cigarette. She sits down on the side of the bed opposite the table.*) Fine. Okay.

**RACHEL**   Well, don't interrupt! God.

**AGNES**   Okay, okay.

**RACHEL**   While you wrinkled up in that damn tub I honestly thought I was losing my mind; you come back in here and I say, Agnes: I think I'm losing my mind, could you take a minute out of your life to listen to me and I get twenty minutes of Charlie Chaplin.

**AGNES**   Okay! (*Pause.*) So go on.

**RACHEL**   I'm sorry. It's just, Jesus. I don't know anything; I just can't seem to do something that doesn't backfire, boomerang in my face. Blow up right in my face. I do something heatedly, because I'm mad and it's the right thing to do, I know — and then the whole thing blows up in my face. They're practically ready to hang Joe and all because I turned him in for filching some money from us. Not that much, really, either; I didn't talk to him, I just turned him in. God knows what kind of fix he was in to take money from us. (*A rapid exchange follows between Agnes and Rachel.*)

**AGNES**   You want a cigarette?

**RACHEL**   I just . . . NO! God! I don't want a cigarette.

**AGNES**   Okay, so you don't want a cigarette

**RACHEL**   I just put one out. I have no urge for a cigarette at all. Thank you.

**AGNES**   I only asked, don't make a production out of it!

**RACHEL**   Well, I do not want a cigarette.

**AGNES**   Okay.

**RACHEL**   Is there anything else?

**AGNES**   All right, I said. *Christ!*

**RACHEL** (*Intensely.*) Well I'm trying to say something and little Miss Helpful Agnes butts in with -

**AGNES** Would you hand me the ash tray anyway?

**RACHEL** (*Takes the ash tray, slams it down on the bed beside Agnes. Very loud. Jerky.*) Christ! Here! Cram it!

**AGNES** I merely asked for the ash tray. (*Rachel looks away, disgusted. Pause.*) Any particular place you'd like me to cram it? (*Silence.*) Well, I'm waiting for you to go on.

**RACHEL** (*Still looking the other way. Quietly.*) Whenever you're ready.

**AGNES** I'm ready.

**RACHEL** (*Still not looking at Agnes.*) There's no point in me talking to myself. I could talk to myself by myself.

**AGNES** I was listening to you.

**RACHEL** (*Beginning to get tired, weary.*) Sure.

**AGNES** I was. I heard every feeble-minded word you said.

**RACHEL** Sure.

**AGNES** You want me to repeat it?

**RACHEL** No.

**AGNES** You said, "God knows what kind of fix he was in to have to take money from us."

**RACHEL** (*Silence. Then she turns to Agnes.*) Did I?

**AGNES** You did. You said you do something and it blows up in your face; boomerangs, orangoutangs, backfires. And you do what's right and an innocent guy – which is a lie – is going to get hanged – which is a lie, and, "God knows what kind of fix he was in to have taken money from us." One more word and you'd have said, "It's only money."

**RACHEL** Well, that's the stupidest thing I've ever said in my life then.

**AGNES** (*Gets up.*) I'm going to roll my hair.

**RACHEL** I can't even talk about him straight.

**AGNES** What it boils down to is he was a damn good-looking stud and you—

**RACHEL** Now, I resent that! For Christ's sake —

**AGNES** Well, a good-looking guy then. And you're damn mad that you misjudged him and that you won't have him around again. And on top of that you trusted him enough to leave him here for a few hours when he was short – and you have to admit that he was often short – and he took a month's pay from you. Now it's reasonable that you'd be pissed off. I would be too. I'd call the cops. (*She turns to the mirror and continues to roll her hair.*)

**RACHEL** I did.

**AGNES** Well, there you have it.

**RACHEL** (*Sitting up in bed. Pause. Quietly; defensively.*) It isn't just physical.

AGNES    (*Not turning.*) When someone says it isn't just physical, you can be pretty sure it's just physical.

RACHEL    (*Sliding back down into bed.*) I guess I am tired. I didn't sleep at all last night. Are you going to bed?

AGNES    Not now. I probably couldn't breathe anyway. I need a respirator.

RACHEL    How come?

AGNES    All night long I've been telling you I was a dying woman. I have a cold.

RACHEL    Oh.

AGNES    In my head.

RACHEL    (*Sleepy, from beneath the covers.*) Why don't you rub yourself with Vicks or something?

AGNES    Because I've got a luncheon date with the boss's son and I don't want to smell like Vicks. Even for him. I'll give him my cold first.

RACHEL    That's silly.

AGNES    (*Quite to herself.*) His soup would probably taste like menthol, for Christ's sake.

RACHEL    (*Flopping over on her other side.*) I think I'm going to sleep.

AGNES    (*Paying no attention.*) "Suddenly it's springtime." (*Drops one of the rollers.*) Fuck. . . . I've got to quit saying that. (*Looks at the roller; gets up and picks it up; goes back to the vanity.*) Get some sleep.

RACHEL    It won't look so bad tomorrow—I know. You know, though; you're probably right. I just miss him a lot and in a few days I'll see everything in a better perspective.

AGNES    In a few days you'll be knocked up by some stud named Herkimer probably!

RACHEL    (*Sitting up.*) I will not be knocked up by anybody. In a few days or nothing.

AGNES    Okay. I just meant, you've established a pattern by now. An orbit, so to speak and by Thursday you'll be head-over-heels mad for someone totally different. You'll pass the sun again, so to speak.

RACHEL    (*Under the covers again.*) I'm not that bad.

AGNES    Very well, you're not that bad.

RACHEL    At least my mother would have told me it would be better tomorrow. That's all I need to get to sleep probably.

AGNES    (*Gaily.*) It'll be exactly the same tomorrow. "The world it was the old world yet. And I was I; my things were wet."

RACHEL    (*Half sitting up again, disgusted.*) *What?*

AGNES    Nothing.

RACHEL    What do you mean, "My things were wet?"

AGNES    Nothing. It's a poem.

**RACHEL**  I know it's a—

**AGNES**  "Down in lovely muck I've lain; happy till I woke again. The world it was the old world yet and—"

**RACHEL**  "And I was I, my things were wet." So all right. What's lovely about a muck?

**AGNES**  He was drunk.

**RACHEL**  At Ludlow fair or some place, I know he was drunk. What's lovely about a muck?

**AGNES**  Well, maybe they pronounced it differently in Shropshire.

**RACHEL**  Very funny. (*Flopping back down.*) Are you coming to bed? I'm dead. I've just knocked myself out.

**AGNES**  Sure. You keep me awake all morning and ask me if I'm coming to bed.

**RACHEL**  (*Covered by the blankets.*) I'm sorry.

**AGNES**  Sure. You going to sleep or what?

**RACHEL**  (*A little muffled.*) I said I was. If I can.

**AGNES**  Well sleep it off. I don't know why you should worry any more about Joe than you did about whoever it was before. You've got to admit the pattern is evident there somewhere. Maybe you should really go to an analyst, you know? No joke. You probably have some kind of problem there somewhere. (*She turns to her. Rachel turns over. Agnes turns back to the mirror.*) I mean no one's normal. He's bound to find something. It might keep you away from dictionaries, you know? Jesus. (*Muffled noise from Rachel.*) Well, I say if it helps, do it. To hell with how funny it looks. God knows I'd like to find—I'm absolutely getting pneumonia. (*Gets up to get the box of Kleenex and carries it back to the vanity, talking all the while.*) I'm going to be a mess tomorrow. I probably won't make it to work let alone lunch. A casual lunch, my God. I wonder what he'd think—stupid Charles—if he knew I was putting up my hair for him; catching pneumonia. No lie, I can't wait till summer to see what kind of sunglasses he's going to pop into the office with. (*Turns.*) Are you going to sleep? (*Pause. No reply.*) Well, crap. (*Turning back to mirror.*) I may be tendering my notice, anyway. You've gone through six men while I sit around and turn to fungus. It's just not a positive atmosphere for me, honey. Not quite. You're out with handsome Val or someone and I'm wondering if the boss's skinny, bony son will come up to the water cooler if I. . . . (*Trails off, becomes interested in the roller. Now to someone as at dinner.*) No. No Stroganoff. No, I'm on a diet. (*Correcting herself.*) No. I will not admit that. Good or bad if he says Stroganoff and baked potatoes it's Stroganoff and baked potatoes. And sour cream. And beer. He's probably on a diet himself. He could fill out, God knows. (*Turning to Rachel.*) You know what Charles looks like? (*Pause.*) He looks like one of those little model men you make out of pipe cleaners when you're in grade school. (*Turning.*) Remember those? If I ever saw Charles without his clothes, he's so pale and white, I swear to God I'd laugh myself silly. He's Jewish, too. I'll bet his mother is a nervous wreck. I'll bet she thinks every woman on the block is pointing at her. Look, there goes Mrs. Schwartz; starving her children to death. Poor Charles. Shakes like a leaf. Of course Mrs. Schwartz wouldn't admit that either. No woman would admit her son was nervous; what's he got to be nervous about? The nerve of being nervous. My kid brother got an ulcer, my mother went to bed for three weeks, totally destroyed. Of course she spent about two thirds of her life totally destroyed. Upset—bawling. Weeks on end sometimes. My brother was great. He never paid the slightest attention to her; she'd get one of her spells and run off to bed bawling, it never bothered him for a minute. Off she'd go, the slightest provocation. Eric would say, "Mother's bedridden with the piss-offs again." I used to come home for a holiday or something and I'd say where's Mom and Eric would say, "Oh, she's bedridden with the piss-offs again." (*As if directly to someone, over lunch. Casually.*) You know, Charles, you've got nice eyes. You really have. Deep. I like brown eyes for a man. I don't like blue eyes, they always look weak or weepy. Either that or cold. You know? Brown eyes are warm; that's good. They're gentle. (*Quickly.*) Not weak, but gentle. (*Half to herself. Lightly.*) I used to want to have a girl; a little girl with blue eyes. For a girl that's good. So I used to always picture—God, idealize, really—very heavy-set, blond men. Swedish types, you know. (*Back to Charles.*) But a son I'd want to have brown eyes. That's better for boys. (*Looks at the sleeve of her robe.*) You think? (*Almost embarrassed.*) I don't know any more. Oh, yes; I got it at Saks. It was on sale, I believe. (*Breaking off, disgusted.*) Now, what the hell does he care where I got it? And it wasn't on sale, knucklehead. And it wasn't Saks. (*Concentrating on her hair.*) It was Bonds. Not that he'd know the damn difference. (*She drops a roller, it bounces across the floor. She picks up another without even looking after the first one.*) Fuck. (*Finishing her hair.*) I've got to quit saying that. (*This last said without listening to herself; second nature. She picks up a jar of cold cream, slowly, distantly, applies a dab to her lower lip. Pause. She sits still, staring off vacantly. A full thirty-second pause.*)

**CURTAIN**

# THIS IS THE RILL SPEAKING (June 1965)
*for David Starkweather in return for*
*YOU MAY GO HOME AGAIN*

## AUTHOR'S NOTE

I grew up in rural Missouri. When I first started writing stories they were all about the Ozarks, but I could never get the country on stage. I believe I had seen too many hillbillies depicted in plays, always barefoot, smoking a corncob pipe, lying down in the road with a jug or a hog, wearing faded gingham, the boys in overalls, the girls with their hair in pigtails. It was a block. I knew if I could once start I could capture the sound of my hometown people better that anything I had written so far. What was stopping me was the *look* of the thing. THIS IS THE RILL SPEAKING was a deliberate exercise to set down just the sound of the people, without thinking about how the play was to be done. A play for voices. I divided the 16 or so parts among 6 actors dressed in ordinary, nondescript clothes. I directed this one myself so I'd be sure nobody smoked a corncob pipe. The exercise cracked the block. While RILL was running at the Cino I began work on the much darker full-length THE RIMERS OF ELDRITCH.

One other thing. Jonny Dodd was answering the phone while RILL was running at the Cino. The conversation from his side always went: "Hello, Caffé Cino. (Beat) Lanford Wilson's THIS IS THE RILL SPEAKING. (Beat) Rill. (Beat) R–I–L–L. (Beat) I have no idea."

THIS IS THE RILL SPEAKING was first presented by Joseph Cino at the Caffé Cino, New York City, on July 20, 1965, with the following cast:

MOTHER / PEGGY: Alice Conklin
WILLY / ELLIS / EARL: Michael Warren Powell
JUDY / MARTHA: Claris Erickson
KEITH / TED / TOM / 2ND FARMER: John Kramer
ALLISON / MAYBELLE: Jacque Lynn Colton
MANNY / WALT / FATHER / 1ST FARMER: George Harris

The play was directed by the author, lighting by Earl Eidman, stage manager Richard Camargo.

The play subsequently toured through Europe with La MaMa Repertory Company under the direction of Tom O'Horgan and opened as part of the Six from La MaMa program at the Martinique Theater in New York on April 11, 1966.


CHARACTERS

(Grouped for each of six actors)

MOTHER / PEGGY
WILLY / ELLIS / EARL
JUDY / MARTHA
KEITH / TED / TOM / 2ND FARMER
ALLISON / MAYBELLE ROBINSON
MANNY / WALT ROBINSON / FATHER / 1ST FARMER


SCENE

The action of the play takes place on and around an elevated porch with a white railing. There are steps and a number of chairs opposite the swing. Scenes should be played on the porch and steps, at both sides of the porch, and in front. Lighting should be the scattered light of sun or moon through trees. The actors group and regroup, wandering about the set. The play is meant for six voices: three women and three men. All have moderately strong Ozark accents.

# THIS IS THE RILL SPEAKING

*Actions may be pantomimed, physical elements may or may not be used, i.e., there may or may not be a window, though the Mother will appear to be looking out of one.*

**MOTHER**   Well, there goes Walt Robinson, up to the post office. Willy, do you want to run and stop him?

**WILLY**   Run and stop him? What for?

**MOTHER**   You could offer to go for him, it'd be a good thing.

**WILLY**   (*Cutting in.*) What do you mean? He'll stay around the post office all day. It's the only thing he does all day long.

**MOTHER**   I suppose.

**JUDY**   Besides, who could be heard with him?

**MOTHER**   You shouldn't say that, Judy.

**WILLY**   He knows he's hard of hearing.

**JUDY**   Hard? He's never heard a word I've said to him, I don't think, and I yell my lungs out.

**MOTHER**   Well, you'd think they'd move a little closer to the square so he wouldn't have that hill to climb.

**WILLY**   It's the only thing he does.

**MOTHER**   I know.

**JUDY**   He doesn't even know what my voice sounds like, and I scream my lungs out to him.

**MOTHER**   Maybelle Robinson is over on her porch there.

**WILLY**   That's all she does. She spends her whole life there.

**MOTHER**   I suppose I should go over and keep her company.

**JUDY**   Why don't you talk to somebody younger? You're always talking to her. She never says anything worth hearing.

**WILLY**   I'm gonna go down by the river.

**MOTHER**   I don't know what to have for supper.

**WILLY**   They're tearing down that old bridge.

**MOTHER**   What old bridge is that?

**WILLY**   That old bridge by the fork.

**MOTHER**   There's no bridge there. You mean those rocks?

**WILLY**   It used to be a railroad bridge, years ago.

**MOTHER**   Who told you that?

**WILLY**   I don't know.

**JUDY**   Peggy should be coming over.

**MOTHER**   Peggy Harper is not coming over here.

**JUDY**   I told you.

**MOTHER**   I wish you wouldn't spend so much time with that girl.

**JUDY**   Peggy Harper is the nicest girl in the junior class.

**MOTHER**   That's not what I've been hearing.

**JUDY**   Well, I can't help it if you've been listening to Maybelle Robinson. I don't know what she has against Peggy.

**MOTHER**   She runs around half naked, and her fat as a tub. I'd think that girl would lose some weight or cover herself, one.

**JUDY**   Peggy is my friend and she can't help it if she has gland trouble.

**MOTHER**   Well, she could cover her bare legs; she looks like two sides of ham.

**WILLY**   She just eats too much.

**JUDY**   Well, she has gland problems.

**MOTHER**   Don't you leave the house in that halter and shorts either.

**JUDY**   What's wrong with a halter? It's more than a bathing suit.

**MOTHER**   I'm not going to have you talked about all over town.

**WILLY**   I'm going down to the river.

**MOTHER**   You stay away from the bridge if they're working down there. We don't need you knocked in the river and drowned.

**WILLY**   They're using the rocks to build a house, way up on the hill.

**MOTHER**   Young lady, don't you leave this house dressed like that.

**JUDY**   Peggy's coming over and we're only going to sit out on the back steps and talk.

**MOTHER**   Well, don't you leave your yard. Dressed like that.

**JUDY**   I'm not going to.

**MOTHER**   Willy, do you think your dad would mind if we had liver?

**WILLY**   We had liver last night.

**MOTHER**   We haven't had liver in a week. I don't think your dad likes liver really.

**MAYBELLE**   It looks like it's gonna do something.

**MOTHER**   Probably not till evening.

**MAYBELLE**   (*Curious; mysteriously; down the road.*) What's that a-coming up the street? Is that that junk man? I wonder what he thinks he's a-doing? What's he a-doing? Now he's stopped. Looks like something was about to fall off his cart. He's tying it *on* or *some*thing. Yes, it's gonna do something before long. You know Rachel Jackson had a girl.

**MOTHER**   When did she? Rachel Jackson a baby girl?

**MAYBELLE**   Yesterday afternoon and her over forty. Nobody even knew she was carrying it, fat as she is. You couldn't tell. And she didn't see fit to let a body know.

**MOTHER**   A baby girl. Where is she now?

**MAYBELLE**   Up to the hospital. Baby's in an incubator. Tiny thing.

Born a month early from what I hear. Blue as a turnip. They had to give it blood. Her mother ought to know better than to have a child at her age and as fat as she is. Little thing weighed five pounds even.

**MOTHER**  Rachel Jackson with a new baby girl and her with two boys out of school nearly.

**MAYBELLE**  It'll die.

**MOTHER**  Oh, you shouldn't say that. Five pounds isn't that bad. (*She "tuts" some.*)

**MAYBELLE**  Poor little thing. (*She "tuts."*] Blue as a turnip.

**MOTHER**  I'll be all right.

**MAYBELLE**  It doesn't have a chance from what I hear. It'll break that poor woman's heart.

**MOTHER**  It would that for sure.

**MAYBELLE**  Serves her right, fat as she is.

**MOTHER**  It'll probably rain by evening. Cool things off some. Today's gonna be a scorcher.

**MAYBELLE**  There he goes again. I guess he got that tied on. Whatever it was. Turning down toward Mrs. Stut's. Now, what business do you suppose he has down that way? Walt's hearing is getting worse; I swear I think it is.

**MOTHER**  I saw him heading up toward town.

**MAYBELLE**  I suppose he'll be up there all day long. That's all he does. Stands around with all those old men up there. Grunting around. Laughing. I don't know what he's laughing about, he can't hear a thing they're saying. I don't know what good it does him. He didn't hear the alarm this morning. Can't eat a thing but mashed potatoes.

**MOTHER**  I know.

**MAYBELLE**  Mashed potatoes and milk and some cully-flower. They took him off salt.

**TOM**  (*Young—fourteen; rapid exchange here.*) You hear about Ben?

**WILLY**  Yeah, I heard they called off his party. He didn't come to school.

**TOM**  His mom wouldn't let him have it. You know why?

**WILLY**  Mr. Hawkins said he got sick.

**TOM**  He got sick all right. He was home. You know why—his mom *caught* him.

**WILLY**  When did she?

**TOM**  Yesterday noon. He come home for lunch and was in his room and she came in without knocking.

**WILLY**  What'd she do? He should've locked the door.

**TOM**  She beat the tar outta him. He said he almost cried. And made him swear on the Bible that he wouldn't ever do it again.

**WILLY**  What did she do that for?

**TOM**  She said he'd go blind and go crazy and go to hell.

**WILLY**  That's a lot of baloney. You think he'll quit?

**TOM**  He said he had to: she pressed his hand right against the Bible and made him swear.

**WILLY**  What a mean thing to do. She wouldn't let him have his birthday party, I know that for sure—he didn't come back to school and Old Man Hawkins came in our class and said the party was called off 'cause Ben was sick.

**TOM**  He was sick all right. His mom's gonna make him go to work this summer. He said he didn't mind, he wanted to anyway.

**WILLY**  Boy, that'd be terrible to have your mom walk right in on you. He used to do it three or four times a day. Every day at recess I know.

**TOM**  Well, he won't any more.

**JUDY**  I wish they'd be a breeze and cool things off some.

**WILLY**  That'll teach him.

**JUDY**  Some anyway.

**WILLY**  Damn, I'll bet he looked surprised.

**TOM**  I don't know anybody else who does it as much as Ben does.

**JUDY**  It's not unbearably bad though, I suppose.

**TOM**  I don't at all.

**WILLY**  I don't either any more. I haven't in over a week.

**TOM**  *He* sure did, but he won't now.

**JUDY**  Dad said he can't remember a drier July in history.

**WILLY**  Did you go down to the bridge?

**TOM**  They're all finished. They hauled the last pile off this morning. I saw the truck go by.

**JUDY**  A breeze would be nice.

**KEITH**  (*Turning to her.*) I'm taking the muffler off the car tomorrow.

**JUDY**  Clevis will jail you if you do; you know how he is.

**KEITH**  I'll tell him it wore out and I'm getting a new one.

**JUDY**  John tried that and he got a ticket anyway. Clevis said he shouldn't have drove it till he got the new one then.

**KEITH**  They got somebody in jail.

**JUDY**  When?

**KEITH**  He may be out by now. He was probably just in overnight. We was talking to him last night. He's from Springfield. Lord, did he cuss out this town. Clevis would have put him up for a week if he could've heard him.

**JUDY**  Why did they jail him in the first place?

**KEITH**  Drunken driving. He said he wasn't, but you could tell he was.

**JUDY**  How could you tell?

**KEITH**  You could tell. We gave him a beer through the bars. He tried to give us a dollar for one can but we wouldn't take it.

**JUDY**  You could be jailed yourself for talking to him.

**KEITH**  There's no law. We shouldn't of had the beer, though. I just hope he doesn't slip and say something.

**JUDY**  He wouldn't.

**KEITH**  Well, he might, mad as he was. The Red Tavern in Nixa won't sell it any more. We had to go all the way to Rogersville to that place on the other side of town.

**JUDY**  It just looks like an awful lot of trouble for a headache to me.

**KEITH**  Tony was stopped last week—going around the square.

**JUDY**  Ummm.

**KEITH**  Clevis knew he was drunk as the Lord, but he didn't say anything. He's a nice guy, really, Clevis.

**JUDY**  Ummm.

**KEITH**  Billy Burt nearly knocked old Skelly down in the middle of Church Street yesterday. Old Skelly was standing in the road and swearing ninety-to-nothing, and Billy Burt just looked out and laughed.

**JUDY**  Ummm.

**KEITH**  He yelled back, "Why don't you watch where you're going, you old fool?" Clevis drove by and yelled to Skelly to shut up before he locked him up for disturbing the peace.

**JUDY**  What'd Skelly say to that?

**KEITH**  What'd you mean, what'd he say? Clevis told him to get the hell out of the middle of the street.

**JUDY**  I feel sorry for Skelly, someone like that. I really do.

**TOM**  (*Very rapid, darting exchange; lightly.*) Are you going to, too? Take it out.

**WILLY**  I'm not going to unless you do too.

**TOM**  Spit on it.

**WILLY**  What for?

**TOM**  It makes it slicker.

**WILLY**  I never heard of that.

**TOM**  Keep spitting on it; keep it wet. I'll race you.

(*The following two speeches are said simultaneously.*)

**MARTHA**  (*Calling.*) Carey. Car-ey?

**WILLY**  Okay, I'll race you.

**MOTHER**  Eat the crust too, Willy.

**FATHER**  Do what your Mother tells you.

**WILLY**  I am.

**MOTHER**  No, you're not. I can see.

**JUDY**  Keith said he's gonna take the muffler off the car next Saturday. Either that or tomorrow.

**MOTHER**  Not tomorrow, I'd hope. That's nothing to do on a Sunday.

**FATHER**   Well, if he wants to pay a fine that's his business. You just better see he don't go blasting past here, waking me up.

**MOTHER**   Judy, don't say things to upset your father.

**TED**   (*Very distantly whistles to a dog.*)

**JUDY**   Billy Burr almost knocked Skelly down in the middle of Church Street.

**WILLY**   He drives like a maniac.

**MOTHER**   He'll get his license taken away from him if he isn't careful.

**JUDY**   Oh, he will not. Honestly, Clevis was right there and saw the whole thing. He just laughed. Skelly was cussing to beat the band. Clevis said he'd lock him up for disturbing the peace.

**MOTHER**   Are you gonna eat that crust?

**WILLY**   I don't like it, I tell you. I'll get sick. Honestly.

**JUDY**   Skelly ought to be locked up himself, anyway.

**MOTHER**   He hasn't hurt anybody. I feel sorry for him.

(*The following two speeches are said simultaneously.*)

**TED**   (*Distantly, calling.*) Blackie? Blackie? Here, Blackie.

**FATHER**   You do, do you?

**MOTHER**   Judy, I wish you wouldn't say things to upset your father.

(*The following two speeches are said simultaneously.*)

**MARTHA**   (*Calling.*) Carey? You come in here to dinner now.

**WILLY**   May I be excused please?

**MOTHER**   Willy, they're children in China starving for want of a crust of bread. They're children in China that will die this very night for the lack of that crust of bread.

**WILLY**   Well, send it to them then; don't make me eat it.

**FATHER**   You eat that, young man.

**WILLY**   It'll break my teeth. Feel how hard it is.

**MOTHER**   Your teeth aren't that tender.

**MARTHA**   (*Distantly singing, over a bit.*) "Hush, little baby, don't say a word, Mama's gonna buy you a mockin' bird. If that mockin' bird don't sing, Mama's gonna buy you a diamond ring."

**KEITH**   (*Overlapping.*) Where you going so fast?

**ALLISON**   Home. Where would I be going?

**KEITH**   You always cut through the park?

**ALLISON**   I didn't see you, Keith Fellers, or I wouldn't have, smarty.

**KEITH**   Well, I saw you.

**ELLIS**   Do you feel any better now?

**MANNY**   I got to get home.

**ELLIS**   You feeling better?

**TED**   No. Worse if anything.

**MANNY**   I gotta get back home before long.

**ELLIS**   Drink another coffee maybe.

**TED**  No, I'll be sick again.

**MANNY**  You want to walk around the parking lot some more?

**ELLIS**  You need another black coffee.

**TED**  No. Come on. . . .

**MANNY**  Come on. Up you go.

**ELLIS**  You all right enough to go back in the café?

**TED**  I'll be okay.

**ELLIS**  You want a hamburger or something?

**TED**  Are you just trying to make me sick again? Don't talk about it.

**MANNY**  Some pie or something would settle your—

**TED**  —don't talk about it!

**ELLIS**  You didn't have any more to drink than the rest of us did.

**TED**  Well, I'm sorry.

**MANNY**  He didn't have as much. I don't even feel a buzz any more.

**ELLIS**  Look how white he is.

**MANNY**  Green.

**ELLIS**  I think he's passed out.

**MANNY**  I gotta get home.

**ELLIS**  We can't take him home like this.

**MANNY**  What are we going to tell his dad?

**ELLIS**  It's late already.

**MANNY**  I think he's passed out.

**ELLIS**  Teddy? Teddy?

**TED**  I'm okay. Stop shaking me around. Everything's spinning around.

**MANNY**  Are you going to be sick?

**TED**  I almost had the ground stopped moving around and you started shaking me around and started it all up again.

**MANNY**  He doesn't know what he's saying.

**ELLIS**  What are you going to tell your folks?

**TED**  I don't know, I told you.

**MANNY**  Well, look. We was out of gas way over past Nixa—

**TED**  No, no, no, I can't. . . .

**MANNY**  Why not? You got to say something.

**TED**  He'd never believe we ran out of gas. He'd never believe that one. Besides I've used that anyway.

**MANNY**  Well, a person can run out of gas more than once. It's a natural thing.

**TED**  He didn't believe it the other time.

**ELLIS**  Why not there was something in the gas line? And we thought we was out of gas and got it towed into Nixa?

**TED**  (*Feeling sick.*) Would you two quit talking about gas? Good God.

**MANNY**  Okay.

**TED**  What was we doing out past Nixa?

**MANNY**  Taking this girl home after the movie. Are you feeling better?

**TED**  A little.

**MANNY**  We better get back.

**TED**  I think I should try to eat something.

**ELLIS**  Oh, God.

**MANNY**  You said you didn't want anything.

**TED**  I think that would settle my stomach.

**MANNY**  Just a coke or something?

**ELLIS**  Are you feeling better? We gotta get home. You're looking better. You're standing a little better.

**TED**  Yeah, it'll be all right now.

**MANNY**  We'll get you another coffee.

**TED**  We won't say anything. I'll just sneak in.

**ELLIS**  Just so long as we get home before long.

**MANNY**  You'll be all right. Come on in.

**ELLIS**  We'll get you something to eat.

**TED**  Wait!

**ELLIS**  What's wrong?

**TED**  No, wait!

**MANNY**  Come on.

**TED**  I think I'm going to be sick again.

(*Ellis, Manny, Ted, Peggy, and Judy all speak at once.*)

**ELLIS**  Oh, my God, I knew it. Hell, we'll never get home.

**MANNY**  Jesus, watch out, then.

**TED**  Damn, I knew it. Oh, God.

**PEGGY**  That's lovely, it really is.

**JUDY**  And that's the living room. (*Continuing, dreamily but matter-of-factly; she and Peggy are sitting on the porch steps.*) And the bedroom will be all in white. White walls, of course, and white ceiling. And white lace curtains with some floral pattern in them: white on white. And there'll be a dressing table with a white pleated skirt around it in silk. And a white silk bedspread and the rug will—uh, the floors in the bedroom will be just natural wood. And I'll grow African violets on the window sill in the bedroom because it'll get the south sun. And I'll have a white Scotty dog or white yarn cat like Mrs. Carters makes on the bed and a few white throw pillows, set up against the bed pillows there.

**PEGGY**  Mmmm. That's lovely. It really is. White on white.

**JUDY**  All in white. And then the kitchen will be green—a pale green, you know, and yellow—very sunny yellow. And there'll be cabinets in pale green and the floor and walls will be yellow and the oven and stove and sink are all light green like the cabinets and the ceiling is very small checks. Just green and yellow checks. And the curtains—

there'll be two windows, one over the sink and one over the breakfast table—the curtains will be ruffled cotton. Just plain polished cotton. And they're checks. And that's the kitchen. And there'll be a stool to sit on. A high one. And that's green with yellow and green checks on the top, upholstered. And the counter—there's going to be a lot of counter space—and then that's violet—no yellow. Like the floor. (*Pause.*) And the bedroom is violet and light brown. The walls are three of them violet and the other one—

**PEGGY** (*Remembering gently.*) You did the bedroom in white.

**JUDY** Right. That's right. It's all in white. Everything in white. With natural floors. But not a cold white. Not that white. A kind of off-white.

**PEGGY** Cream.

**JUDY** No. More of an ivory.

**PEGGY** Mmmm.

**JUDY** And then the bathroom is all blue. Everything in blue.

**WILLY** (*Calling lightly.*) Tommy? Tommy? If I whistle listen—if I whistle once, it means I'm coming up for sure. And if I whistle two times, it means, maybe, and three times, I don't know yet. You got that? Once, I'm coming up, and two times, maybe, and three times, I still don't know for sure—and four times means I'm not coming up.

**MAYBELLE** Is that lightning bugs over there, or is that someone in your yard with a cigarette?

**MOTHER** No, it's lightning bugs. See, they're in the back yard thick.
(*Willy whistles twice—twice—three times—three times—twice, during the next line or two, keeping Tommy posted.*)

**MAYBELLE** Can you see if Walt's going to bed or is he still in there reading?

**MOTHER** No, he's still reading the Bible.

**MAYBELLE** He'll put his eyes out; he's not satisfied to be deaf. I'd call in to him for all the good it'd do. He should be in bed. It's past his bedtime. He's older than me eight years.

**MOTHER** I know.

**WILLY** (*Whistles one long note; beat.*) Tommy? Hey, Tommy?

**MANNY** (*Sober, manly, brisk, as if moving around a pool table.*) Shit, that was a easyun, you just lucked that one in, a beginner woulda made that'll. Thaell be the last for a while; shit, you just lucked out.

**EARL** (*Nineteen, very manlyesque.*) Four in the side.

**MANNY** Shit, you can't make that one. Better try the nine.

**EARL** Shit I can't.

**MANNY** Hell you can; I got six bits—two bits you can't.

**EARL** Shit, that's an easyun.

**MANNY** Shit it is; you better grease her up.

**EARL**  Watch this, shithead. (*Studies and shoots.*)

**MANNY**  (*Beat.*) Shit, you missed as good as a mile.

**EARL**  Hell I did. A little less English on thatun and it'd been just in there.

**MANNY**  Hell it would. Nine in the corner.

**EARL**  Four bits.

**MANNY**  Hell with you, too. You think I want to throw dough away? That's chicken feed.

**EARL**  Two bits.

**MANNY**  Hell, it's in there clean as a whistle. Watch this.

**EARL**  (*Quickly.*) Two bits?

**MANNY**  Hell yes. (*Studies and shoots.*)

**EARL**  (*Beat.*) We're even.

**MANNY**  Shit, that was almost in there.

**EARL**  Shit it was.

**JUDY**  Are you going to the movie tomorrow night?

**PEGGY**  When?

**JUDY**  Tomorrow night?

**PEGGY**  Oh, yeah. It's very good, actually. I saw it last year in Springfield. It's very good; I want to see it again. (*Beat.*) It's about this kinda island.

**JUDY**  During the war? I think I saw that one.

**PEGGY**  No, not that one. This one's in color.

**JUDY**  No, I didn't see that one then.

**PEGGY**  It's very good actually.

**1ST FARMER**  (*A man of forty-five or so; overlapping just a word, ponderously slow.*) So I said to him. If you cut it green. And just let it lay. An extra day or two more. Then, you're gonna get—now, mind, you're not gonna get forty bales an acre—any fool'll tell you that. Not with your lespedeza. But your legume *hay*. Will go farther next *winter*. And they'll milk *more*. Than if you went for your forty bales to the acre and have it dry in the bale on you.

**2ND FARMER**  (*Also a farmer; he has grunted approval at least five times during the above.*) Providing it don't get wet in the field.

**1ST FARMER**  Oh, yeah.

**2ND FARMER**  That's the risk there.

**1ST FARMER**  Oh, yeah.

**2ND FARMER**  If it gets wet in the field, then it's ruined sure.

**1ST FARMER**  That's the way I put it to him. I told *him*. You cut it green. When it looks fair. And providing the weather looks like it's gonna hold. You just let it lay an extra day or two more.

**MARTHA**  (*Singing again, faintly, simultaneous with the farmer.*) "If that diamond ring turns brass, Mama's gonna buy you a lookin' glass."

(*Martha continues to hum another verse.*)

**1ST FARMER** (*Continued from above.*) . . . And your lespedeza *hay.* Will be a sweeter *hay.* And they'll *milk more.* Than if you went for the forty bales an acre and have it dry in the bales on you. (*The song continues a while after this.*)

**KEITH** (*Overlapping the last of the song.*) You always cut through here, do you?

**ALLISON** I do not. Don't you stand so close either.

**KEITH** You been to prayer meeting or choir practice, I suppose?

**ALLISON** If you went to church at all, you'd know that choir practice was on Tuesday early evenings and prayer meeting was on Wednesday nights.

**KEITH** Do you want to go for a ride around?

**ALLISON** No, thank you, I do not. I thought you was going steady with Judy Atkins recently.

**KEITH** Well, I don't see her around right now, but you are.

**ALLISON** I hope you don't think that makes me feel beholden to you. Just because she's not around just now.

**KEITH** Besides, my hand might slip off the steering wheel and glance against your knee and you'd think you was being compromised or something.

**ALLISON** I know what you're after and I'd think you should know better than to try something like that with me. You may have a car and all, but that doesn't matter a hill of beans as far as I'm concerned.

**KEITH** Are you too holy for a little making out, are you?

**ALLISON** I happen to know Judy Atkins very well, and you better let me on by.

**KEITH** Does she talk about me to you?

**ALLISON** I would say she does, yes, she sometimes does. But don't ask me what because I'm not saying.

**KEITH** But it'll bet it just makes you squirm, doesn't it?

**ALLISON** No. It certainly does not. Make me squirm. What do you mean, it just makes me squirm? Let me on by.

**KEITH** You don't have to get so hot under the collar.

**ALLISON** I'm not getting hot under the collar or anywhere el—you just let me go on home now.

**KEITH** Why?

**MOTHER** (*Calling.*) Willy?

**ALLISON** Come on.

**KEITH** Why?

**MOTHER** (*Calling.*) Willy?

**ALLISON** Come on.

**KEITH** Why, she won't have to know. (*He puts an arm around her* *neck.*)

**ALLISON**  (*Pulling away, but rather reluctantly.*) That has nothing to do with it. Just keep your hands where they belong too.

**KEITH**  You're more amply built.

**ALLISON**  Judy is just thin—you keep your hands away.

**KEITH**  You want to drive up to Harper's Hill?

**ALLISON**  What would Judy think of that?

**KEITH**  She wouldn't know.

**ALLISON**  I suppose she goes up there with you.

**KEITH**  Did she tell you that?

**ALLISON**  I didn't say she told me everything. Besides everyone would see us going through town and on the highway.

**KEITH**  You'd like to, though, wouldn't you?

**ALLISON**  No, I would not.

**KEITH**  Sure you would.

**ALLISON**  I have to go home.

**KEITH**  I could drive you home after the hill.

**ALLISON**  No, thank you.

**KEITH**  I've seen you watching me.

**ALLISON**  I have not. I suppose you think if you're the basketball hero of the town and all, every girl is ready to just jump right into your lap; well, you've got another think coming.

**KEITH**  I know you have. I've seen you.

**ALLISON**  I haven't, I told you. I've seen you looking at me enough, and at every other girl around.

**KEITH**  Well, if you noticed that, you must have been looking.

**ALLISON**  Come on, I didn't say that.

**KEITH**  You want to sit in the car awhile?

**ALLISON**  No. I might sit here in the park, but not in your car.

**KEITH**  This is fine with me. Clevis might come by, though.

**ALLISON**  Nobody ever comes by here. I come through here every night and I've not seen anybody.

**KEITH**  I knew you would.

**ALLISON**  (*A bit more confused, intense.*) I have noticed you; I couldn't help noticing you. That doesn't mean anything.

**KEITH**  I knew you wanted to.

**ALLISON**  I didn't say I wanted to do anything except just sit and talk.

**KEITH**  All right we'll just sit and talk.

(*Everyone else is standing, looking off in different directions. They begin moving around, beginning slowly, becoming more urgent, faster and louder.*)

**ALLISON**  That's all.

**MOTHER**  Willy?

**KEITH**   ... Not all. ...

(*The lines flow one immediately after the other, building.*)

**PEGGY**   ... Fine. ...

**MANNY**   ... In the corner. ...

**ALLISON**   ... Yes. ...

**EARL**   ... Four in the side. ...

**KEITH**   ... Okay?. ...

**ALLISON**   ... No. ...

**JUDY**   ... No. ...

**MOTHER**   ... What?. ...

**WILLY**   ... What? ...

**JUDY**   ... Isn't it. ...

**MOTHER**   ... Will-y! ...

**WILLY**   ... What? ...

**JUDY**   ... Just. ...

**WILLY**   ... What do you want? ...

**JUDY**   ... lovely?!. ...

**MOTHER**   ... Come on, now. ...

**KEITH**   ... Okay?. ...

**PEGGY**   ... Yes! ...

**ALLISON**   ... Yes! ...

**PEGGY**   ... Yes, it is! ...

**FATHER**   (*Very loud.*) ... Willy! ...

**WILLY**   ... All right!. ...

**MARTHA**   (*Loud, sustained call lasting through Keith's "Take it easy!"*) Car—e-y!

(*The following short speeches are rapid, loud, urgent.*)

**ALLISON**   Keith!

**MANNY**   Hell you can!

**KEITH**   Take it easy.

**ALLISON**   *I love you so!*

**MARTHA**   (*Singing, beginning with Allison's last word and continuing through the next few speeches.*) "Hush little baby, don't say a word, Mama's gonna buy you a mockin' bird. If that mockin' bird don't sing, Mama's gonna buy you a diamond ring. If that diamond ring turns brass, Mama's gonna buy you a lookin' glass. If that lookin' glass gets broke—"

**WILLY**   (*Very softly, slowly rising in intensity.*) Tommy? Tommy? Listen. If I whistle once it means I'm coming up for sure, and if I whistle two times it means maybe and three times, I don't know yet. You got that? ... (*Fades at end.*)

**KEITH**   (*Cued by Willy's "whistle," very softly, slowly rising in intensity.*) Billy Burt nearly knocked old Skelly down in the middle of

Church Street yesterday. Old Skelly was standing in the road and swearing ninety-to-nothing and Billy Burt just looked out and laughed. . . . (*Fades away near the end.*)

**1ST FARMER**  (*Cued by Keith's "Old," begins not too soft, fades near the end.*) So I said to him. If you cut it green. And just let it lay. An extra day or two more. Now you're gonna get. Now mind, you're not gonna get forty bales to the acre. Not with your lespedeza. . . .

**MOTHER**  (*Cued by "said."*) Willy, there are children in China starving for the want of that crust of bread. They're children in China that will die this very night. . . . (*Keith's line should extend past the others a word or so, as the song ends.*)

**JUDY**  (*Immediately after the song, overlapping Keith's line just a bit.*) And the bedroom's all in various shades of violet. With violets printed on all the sheets.

**WILLY**  (*Answering back, as though from his bedroom, softly.*) You think Keith will like that?

**JUDY**  Oh, I'm sure. Violet's practically his favorite color.

**MOTHER**  (*Softly calling.*) You kids get to bed in there now. Judy, Willy, I don't want to hear another peep out of you two.

**JUDY**  I am.

**ALLISON**  We shouldn't've done that! Oh, God, I think I got my dress all— (*She stops before going up on the porch. Everyone circling.*)

**ELLIS**  You feeling better now? Hey, Teddy, you feeling better?

**MANNY**  What the hell are you gonna tell your dad?

**TED**  I guess that we ran out of gas on the other side of Nixa if he's awake.

**EARL**  You feeling all right?

**TED**  I'm okay, don't worry about me. I'll be all right.

**MAYBELLE**  (*On the porch; loudly, as though talking to someone deaf.*) Walt? Are you going to stay up reading all night?

**JUDY**  (*Calling softly.*) Willy? Are you sleepy? Are you asleep?

**MAYBELLE**  *I said are you going to come to bed now?*

**WILLY**  (*Sleepy, softly calling to Judy, as though from his room.*) No.

**WALT**  (*Loudly, as though talking to someone deaf; he is very old.*) I heard you. I'll be along.

**JUDY**  Have you decided what you're gonna be? Are you gonna be an artist like you said?

**MAYBELLE**  *You're gonna read and ruin your eyes.*

**MOTHER**  (*Begins to hum "All My Trials" very softly—a lullaby.*)

**WILLY**  I don't know. I been thinking I might be a writer like for the newspapers.

**WALT**  I heard you. I'm all right.

**JUDY**  I just want to be a good mother. A good wife and a good mother.

You know?

**WILLY** Uh-huh.

**MAYBELLE** *What are you a-doing tomorrow?*

**JUDY** How come you aren't going to be an artist? When did you decide?

**WALT** I'll probably go up to the post office if it's clear.

**WILLY** I thought I might be an artist on the side kinda. And if I write pieces for the paper too, then I could write pieces about *Nature*. And make people *really notice* Nature. You know?

**JUDY** That'd be nice . . . that'd be a very good thing to do.

**MAYBELLE** *Are you gonna hear the alarm?*

**WILLY** One piece I thought I'd write would be all about here. Only it'd be about the Nature around us all the time and that we never notice. You know?

**JUDY** Uh-huh.

**MAYBELLE** *There ain't no mail tomorrow, it's a Sunday.*

**WILLY** It would be just about the *wonders* of Nature. And I'd have a lot of characters and they'd all talk; only they'd all be things in Nature around us all the time. Like it would be a countryside. And the tree would talk and tell all about itself; like about its getting a new ring every year, you know?

**JUDY** Uh-huh.

**MAYBELLE** (*To herself.*) There ain't no mail tomorrow, it's a Sunday.

**WILLY** And the meadow would talk. And the brook would talk like a laugh kinda. And the hills would talk and the berry bushes like about the food they supply to wild animals and the wheat fields and things.

**MAYBELLE** There's nothing doing on a Sunday. You ought not to walk up that hill in this heat.

**JUDY** That's beautiful.

**WILLY** Just about all of Nature and all.

**JUDY** That's really lovely. It is. Wild animals.

**WILLY** And they'd tell all about themselves.

**MAYBELLE** *You hear?*

**JUDY** I sure do want to see it when you do it.

**WALT** I'll just go up a bit and see what's doing.

(*No one moves except Judy and Willy.*)

**WILLY** And I figure they'd each one have a little speech that they'd just say out directly about themselves like: "This is the rill speaking over here. They've been tearing down that old bridge down by the fork there. . . ."

**JUDY** What's a rill?

**WILLY** You know, like "I love thy rocks and rills."

**JUDY** Oh, sure. That's nice. Are you sleepy now?

**WILLY** Yes. Are you going to the movie tomorrow? Judy? Good night.

**JUDY**   Good night, Willy.

(*The others stir gently now, walk gently around.*)

**WILLY**   Good night, Judy.

**JUDY**   Good night, Mother.

**MOTHER**   Good night.

**WILLY**   Good night, Mother.

**MOTHER**   You two go on to bed in there now.

**MAYBELLE**   You come on in. (*She steps off the porch and stands motionless.*)

**KEITH**   (*Whistles to his dog, softly, distantly. He takes a few steps and stands motionless. The lights are quite dim.*)

**JUDY** and **WILLY**   Good night, Daddy.

**FATHER**   That's enough now. (*He stands motionless.*)

**JUDY**   Well, good night.

**FATHER**   (*After a brief pause.*) Good night.

(*Everyone is standing, quite still. The Mother continues to hum a few soft notes of the song. The light on the porch fades.*)

# DAYS AHEAD  (December 1965)

## AUTHOR'S NOTE

Neil again. I was in Boston as a playwright observer (a very useful program offered by The New Dramatists) on Frederick Knott's WAIT UNTIL DARK. It was the first time in almost three years that I had been out of town; actually, the first time in over a year that I had been above 14th Street. I think I was lonely, everything I wrote during that period was a little melancholy. I sent Neil a copy of both DAYS AHEAD and a semi–dumbness called SEX IS BETWEEN TWO PEOPLE. It was the first time I had missed rehearsals. I didn't see the show until the final performance. Neil, of course, had fathomed out that the play takes place on Valentine's Day and the beautiful set, with dried rosebuds and lace everywhere was a veritable Victorian valentine. Sorry about that alliteration.

DAYS AHEAD was first presented by Joseph Cino at the Caffé Cino in New York City as half of a double bill with the author's SEX IS BETWEEN TWO PEOPLE on December 28, 1965, with the following cast:

MAN:  Neil Flanagan

The play was directed and designed by Mr. Flanagan, with lighting by John P. Dodd.

## CHARACTER

MAN

## SCENE

A room. If furnished, furnished Victorian, with globe lamps and fringed table covers. One wall has obviously been built to divide the room in half; we cannot see what is on the other side of the wall. The visible half of the room should look as if it has been closed off for a long time, dusty, stale. A chair is the only real essential.

# DAYS AHEAD

*A man hurriedly enters. He has the look of a small businessman; you could guess he manages an antiques shop or clock shop or occupies a routine position in some strongly established business—bookkeeper, etc. He enters as though he has walked up several flights of stairs. He looks excited, expectant, and almost joyous. He is perhaps forty-five, with that indefinite look of the permanently middle-aged; he might be sixty. He is not senile, in any case, but is quite fastidious. He walks to the wall as soon as he enters, raps several times, as if it were a routine. He is quite happy with himself.*

**MAN**  My dear? (*He raps on the wall again, as before.*) Love? (*Calling to the other side. Almost embarrassed, as a child.*) I'm back; here I am. I know, you're thinking I've made a mistake and come a full day early; you're thinking, why, this is the thirteenth and not the fourteenth at all and, of course, you're right; I'm early, but I've made no mistake. (*Very pleased with himself.*) Can you guess? Well, here I am, standing here breathless, like a damn fool from all those stairs and so anxious I've not even sat down. When something marvelous occurs, I've always been like that. A day early, more or less, routine be hanged. Of course, who knows better than you; and it is marvelous! Can you guess? Can you tell I'm happy? But before, even before you knew me, as a student, away alone—never could wait. Christmastime, those times when I didn't go home and presents from uncles and aunts and all the family arrived, such excitement, with my studies piled up—still I couldn't wait. Never could. Christmas morning seemed so far away and what matter, because certainly they would never know, and what matter—so invariably—with all the gifts, wrapped so brightly as they were—invariably the curiosity always —always got . . . (*He has become quite winded, pauses now and takes a deep breath.*) Oh, really. I must sit down. Let me pull up the chair—those stairs, I'm afraid . . . (*He goes to the chair, brushes some dust off.*) Oh, my. (*Coughs slightly, still preoccupied with his thoughts, and begins to drag the chair to the wall.*) Invariably the curiosity . . . (*He coughs a little, finishes dragging the chair to the wall, and sits in it. He is not facing the wall, but the chair is situated alongside the wall, very close; his face should not be more than a foot from the wall. Sitting.*) There. Oh, my. And it seems more dusty than ever. (*Back to a kind of contented rapture.*) Oh, my dear, my dear. (*Adjusting himself in the chair.*) Yes, that's more like it. Now. I know you're anxious for news, love, so I'll tell you that first. (*Taking a very small note pad out of his pocket, the kind where the leaves fold over the top.*) But when you hear the revelation—and it is a revelation—why, you'll say, or rather you'll think—well, why didn't he tell me first off—why, hang the news, that's the best news I could have heard is what you'll say. (*Looking at the first page of the notebook.*) Well, let's see. There isn't all that much. It seems I'm always thinking nothing important happens; and then I get on myself for being so pessimistic and say, what exactly *has* happened? Write it down! Beth will want to know; you know how she cares about all those little things you think so trivial. And I press, I do—I press my mind for details that would be interesting, diverting, informative. And more often than not I have to conclude that as we grow older things that happen, things we would have found quite diverting, even scandalous some of them— well, not scandalous, eye-opening—seem—unimportant really. Ulti-mately—trivial. (*Light pause. He wanders some from the point from time to time, but all in the nature of being helpful.*) That's why it's so difficult to find something worthwhile, as we grow older. (*Consulting his book.*) The first month, a whole month—March—nothing. (*He turns the blank page.*) April, nothing. (*Turns the page.*) May, one note which seems now not as important as then. (*Wandering slightly.*) As usual April was the windy month—came in like a lion—May the wet one, June the balmy beginning of spring: the first sweetness. "May showers bring June flowers." Perhaps the other axiom pertains to some lower latitude, farther south. Or perhaps climatic conditions have actu-ally altered; that could be possible. (*Looking back at the book.*) The note for May is a gathering. Mrs. Fields. A small party, rather the same crowd. You'll remember three years ago I mentioned the Fields had done their living room over in rust. Rust everywhere. Sepia, she called it. Looked like rust; rust everywhere. Well, they have lately changed from rust to milky-green. Milky-green everywhere. Can you picture it? It makes one quite long for the rust back again. And that was May. (*Turning the page.*) In June I went walking; I left work early one after-noon and went into the park. The jonquils were gone, but there were flowering trees everywhere. A rain had come the night before, a soft rain, and every flowering tree had under it a perfectly circular, white. . . (*The word escapes him and he continues as if he had said it.*) . . . that was quite lovely. But as rain will, it had also washed away the scent al-together. The flowers smelled of rain; nothing more. I remembered there, when we walked in the park, or I tried to. I couldn't place it ex-actly—the park has changed in the years since. I thought, in the au-tumn the trees will be bearing fruit—sweet—and no one will be there to eat it. It'll rot there on the ground, in the leaves. It's a very sad waste, a useful tree in an arboretum. (*Turning a page for each month.*) July, August, September: no autumn again this year. One day the leaves are green and the next they're dead. Brown. Fallen. (*Turns the page.*) October. Well, news indeed! It isn't important. (*He puts the book away. Perhaps he has taken out a pair of gold-rimmed glasses to read the book, which he also puts away as he continues.*) Let me tell you. I've brought with me a fork. I looked around for something stronger; I couldn't find a thing. It seems you're always with me lately. (*The love and expectancy return to his face, to his voice.*) I think about you so often. It was lovely once. Of course we knew that. And I've always said that when I began to feel restless, discontent, it was my fault; I've always freely admitted that. It was some deficiency in me. I admit it. I admitted it then, didn't I? Twenty years ago. Haven't I every year? I don't know; it's so easy to say you've always known something, always said something, when you've felt it and not had the courage to speak. But I'm sure, fairly certain, I said it. Even then. Some deficiency in me. And you know as well as I what that can lead to. Doubting, mistrust, and I wouldn't have it! It would have led to arguments which you know I could not have withstood. Bickering, petty arguments over nothing, magnified grotesquely. I've seen no beneficial qualities in quarreling. Perhaps that was the lack. Who am I to say? But I felt you would have grown discontent. (*His hand passes over the wall.*) And this impromptu wall. I promised to keep you informed, and I have! (*Defensively.*) But each year, when I talk to you, I scratch the wall: it's almost as if unconsciously I wanted to see you again, isn't it? I've never mentioned it, but I rub the wall with my hand, fill my fingernail with plaster, all white; dig and chip. . . . Whatever it was in me that— (*Excited.*) Do you sense what I'm saying? Do you know already? I looked for something other than a fork, but it's all that's around. Whatever it was—that deficiency, I feel—I've outlived. I think if a restlessness still exists, I'm willing to chance it anyway. Do you know? (*He removes a fork from his pocket, and begins to dig, gently, unconsciously at the wall—just little jabs while he talks.*) It's been so long that I couldn't be sure. But lately, this year, more each day, I've been able to feel it. Memories are sweeter even than ever; you seem so much dearer to me every day. (*Digs.*) It's been long and I've been foolish—I know people would say that. That I've been foolish to ever expect to regain that first awakening love, that first sweet efflorescence. But it isn't memories! This year more and more, for the first time, I begin to see, more each day, how I want you now. How I look forward to days ahead, with your love. And that's what I was never able to do. Only doubts, misgivings that, if I'd have let them grow, would have destroyed us. But I saw that and said, no, no, we had a perfect love: if you're losing your trust, recognize it and don't let it happen. Do something. If you can no longer think about the future, and you once dreamed of everlasting love, don't give up the dream, find it again. (*He is digging at the wall, gently, regularly now.*) And I've—I've—Oh, God, do you know? That's why I couldn't wait; I had to come today, finally; as I said I would, and I've come back to you. I know maybe I was wrong to leave you alone. I've had to realize now that you might be—My dear, I didn't know what I was doing. I was passionate. I was losing the thing most precious to me; but I must have been right. You see now? Because I've come back. The doubts have waned and I love you. I've—I've had to realize now that you might be ill without my care—or you could have grown to hate me; even though I've kept my word. Everything that might interest you I set down day by day to tell you. Still I know you could reject me now. If you do, I'll understand it now. I've lived a lonely struggle on my way back to you; if you no longer love me, I'll let you go. Walk away free. That's the chance I have to be willing to take, dear, and I am now. I promise you. I've been alone these years, I can live without happiness if you wouldn't be happy with me. But if you can. If you can! We'll be always together. (*He pauses in the digging for a moment.*) I was not about to stand on the shore and watch you sail away with a widening breach coming between us. I would never have done that. (*He begins, more slowly.*) But you've come to realize that. Haven't you? Oh, love, love. We can be happy again together now. (*Continuing to dig at the plaster wall.*) We'll walk in the park! Through the walks in the arboretum—if you'll have me back. We'll walk by the river in the summer and crowd under the cool, sweating viaduct during a rain, and I'll buy you a little globe paperweight with a toy snowstorm like you told me you had as a child. Do you remember? And then, if you forgive me, we'll go to parties and dance in the street and you can take me to where you grew up as a young girl and we'll cry over the ugly apartment buildings that's taken over the wooded lots and hills where you played—again. All over again—if you'll accept me—and I'll never doubt now that I'm sure, and I am sure. If you only are, and if you are, we'll be so happy, love. (*A pause.*) Can you hear it giving away, the wall? (*The lights begin to dim, as he continues.*) We'll walk in the park. (*As the lights dim, his voice becomes softer and softer until he is no longer audible.*) Through the walks in the arboretum. We'll walk by the river in the summer and crowd under the viaduct for privacy; and I'll buy you a little globe paperweight with a toy snowstorm, like you told me you had as a child. Do you remember . . . ? (*The lights are gone.*)

# WANDERING  (March 1966)

## AUTHOR'S NOTE

While I was out of town observing WAIT UNTIL DARK, Ellen Stewart had to raise money for some crisis at the Cafe LaMama (back rent, bribing the fire department, occupancy license, something) and all the writers from Off-Off Broadway were asked to contribute a 2 or 3 minute play for a marathon benefit evening. By the time they reached me everyone was in rehearsal, and I was in the middle of something else. I gave them a sketch I had written for Second City while I was living in Chicago. (I never got up the nerve to send it to Second City.) A while later I felt deprived of the challenge to write a 2 minute play for a specific event. I wrote WANDERING to see what I might have done. It came in handy, because a month later there was a benefit for the Cino.

WANDERING was first presented at the Mark Taper Forum in Los Angeles in November, 1967, as part of an omnibus program entitled *The Scene*. It was later presented at the Cafe Au Go Go, in New York City, by Lyn Austin, Hale Matthews, and Oliver Smith, on May 8, 1968, as part of *Collision Course*. It was directed by Edward Parone; the designer was Michael Davidson; and the costumes were by Diedre Cartier. The cast was as follows:

HE:  Tom Rosqui
SHE:  Susan Browning
HIM:  Scott Glenn

## CHARACTERS

HE, SHE, and HIM are all about twenty five.

## SCENE

The stage, which can be very small, should have a bench to be used as chair, bed, couch, bench, whatever.

# WANDERING

*He and She are standing at attention, side by side. Him enters and sits. The actors should retire to the attention position when not speaking. Actions and props should be pantomimed, and the play should be done very rapidly without pause except toward the end, as indicated. The play runs through Him's life span of about forty years with several recaps at the end. Actions and characterizations should be very simple.*

**SHE**  Where have you been?

**HIM**  Wandering around.

**SHE**  Wandering around. I don't know why you can't be a man; you just wait till the army gets ahold of you, young man.

**HE**  They'll make a man of you.

**SHE**  Straighten you out.

**HE**  A little regimentation.

**SHE**  Regulation.

**HE**  Specification.

**SHE**  Indoctrination.

**HE**  Boredom.

**SHE**  You'll get up and go to bed.

**HE**  Drill, march.

**SHE**  Take orders.

**HE**  Fight.

**SHE**  Do what they tell you.

**HE**  Keep in step.

**SHE**  Do your part.

**HE**  Kill you a man.

**SHE**  You'll be a better person to live with, believe me. As a matter of fact your father and I are getting damn tired of having you around.

**HE**  Looking after you.

**SHE**  Making your bed.

**HE**  Keeping you out of trouble.

**SHE**  How old are you, anyway?

**HIM**  Sixteen.

**HE**  Sixteen, well, my God.

**SHE**  Shouldn't you be drafted before long?

**HIM**  Two years.

**SHE**  You just better toe the mark.

**HE**  How long at your present address?

**HIM**  Six months.

**HE**  Any previous experience as an apprentice?

**HIM**  No sir.

**HE**  Where did you live before that?

**HIM**  I was just wandering around.

**HE**  Not good, draft status ?

**HIM**  Well, I haven't been called but—

**HE**  We like fighters on our team, fellow.

**HIM**  Well, actually I'm a conscientious—

**SHE**  Sit down. Roll up your sleeve. Take off your shirt. Stick out your tongue. Bend over, open your mouth, make a fist, read the top line. Cough. (*The boy coughs.*) Very good.

**HIM**  Thank you.

**SHE**  Perfect specimen.

**HIM**  I do a considerable amount of walking.

**HE**  I don't follow you.

**HIM**  I don't believe in war.

**HE**  There's no danger of war. Our country is never an aggressor.

**HIM**  But armies, see, I don't believe in it.

**HE**  Do you love your country?

**HIM**  No more than any other, the ones I've seen.

**HE**  That's treason.

**HIM**  I'm sorry.

**HE**  Quite all right; we'll take you.

**HIM**  I won't go.

**HE**  Service is compulsory.

**HIM**  It's my right.

**HE**  You'll learn.

**HIM**  I don't believe in killing people.

**HE**  For freedom?

**HIM**  No.

**HE**  For love?

**HIM**  No.

**HE**  For money?

**HIM**  No.

**HE**  We'll teach you.

**HIM**  I know, but I won't.

**HE**  You'll learn.

**HIM**  I won't!

**HE**  You're going.

**HIM**  I'm not.

**HE**  You'll see.

**HIM**  I'm sure.

**HE**  You'll see.

**HIM**  I'm flatfooted.

**HE**  You'll do.

**HIM**  I'm queer.

**HE**  Get lost.

**SHE**  I'm lost.

**HIM**  I'm sorry.

**SHE**  Aren't you lost?

**HIM**  I wasn't going anyplace in particular.

**SHE**  That's unnatural.

**HIM**  I was just wandering.

**SHE**  What will become of you?

**HIM**  I hadn't thought of it.

**SHE**  You don't believe in anything.

**HIM**  But you see, I do.

**HE**  I see.

**HIM**  It's just that no one else seems to believe—not really.

**HE**  I see.

**HIM**  Like this pride in country.

**HE**  I see.

**HIM**  And this pride in blood.

**HE**  I see.

**HIM**  It just seems that pride is such a pointless thing; I can't believe in killing someone for it.

**SHE**  Oh, my God, honey, it isn't killing, it's merely nudging out of the way . . .

**HIM**  But we don't need it.

**SHE**  Think of our position, think of me, think of the children.

**HIM**  I am.

**SHE**  You're shiftless, is what it is.

**HIM**  I'm really quite happy; I don't know why.

**SHE**  Well, how do you think I feel?

**HIM**  Not too well really.

**SHE**  Where does it hurt?

**HIM**  Nothing to worry about.

**SHE**  Yes sir.

**HIM**  Thank you.

**SHE**  And that's all for the morning; Mr. Trader is on line six.

**HIM**  Thank you; send Wheeler in.

**HE**  How are you, old boy?

**HIM**  Not well, I'm afraid.

**SHE**  Don't be, it isn't serious.

**HE** Just been working too hard.

**SHE** Why don't you lie down?

**HE** Best thing for you.

**SHE** I know, but he was quite handsome; a gentle man.

**HE** Bit of a radical though; not good for the family.

**SHE** I know.

**HE** You're better off.

**SHE** I have a life of my own.  **HE** You have a life of your own.

**SHE** He was such a lost lamb.

**HE** Never agreed with anyone.

**SHE** Arguments everywhere we went.

**HE** What kind of disposition is that?

**SHE** I don't know what I ever saw in him.

**HE** You need someone who knows his way around.

**SHE** I do.

**HE** I do. (*A pause.*)

**SHE** I don't know why you can't be a man.

**HE** Keep in step.

**SHE** Toe the mark.

**HE** Draft status?

**SHE** Stick out your tongue.

**HE** You'll learn.

**SHE** What'll become of you?

**HE** I see.

**SHE** Think of the children.

**HE** Best thing for you.

**SHE** I do. (*A pause.*)

**HE** I see.

**HIM** I mean, that can't be the way people want to spend their lives.

**SHE** Trader on line six.

**HIM** Thank you.

**HE** Just been working too hard.

**SHE** I do. (*Pauses.*) Where?

**HIM** Wandering.

**HE** I see.

**HIM** They'll believe anything anyone tells them.

**HE** I see.

**HIM** I mean, that can't be the way people want to spend their lives.

**SHE** That's all for the morning.

**HIM** Quite happy.

**HE** Best thing for you.

**SHE** I do.

**HE** I do. (*A pause.*)

**SHE**  Where have you been? (*A pause.*)
**HIM**  Can it?

## BLACKOUT

# STOOP  (August 1969)

## AUTHOR'S NOTE

I have no idea where STOOP came from.  I'd forgot it existed.

STOOP was first presented as part of *Foul!* on the New York Television Theater (Channel 13), in November, 1969. It was produced and directed by Glenn Jordan with the following cast:

FIRST WOMAN:  Charlotte Rae
SECOND WOMAN:  Frances Sternhagen
THIRD WOMAN:  Barbara Carson

## CHARACTERS

FIRST WOMAN  About fifty. Stout. Resigned.
SECOND WOMAN  About sixty. Thin, a failing light voice. Resigned.
THIRD WOMAN  Somewhere in between.

## SCENE

The play takes place on the front steps (stoop) of a run–down city brownstone.

# STOOP

*They sit, staring blankly straight front, without energy or interest, but these attitudes should not be burlesqued, there just isn't much happening. They sit on the stoop of a run-down city brownstone. The Third Woman does not speak, nor does she show any interest in the other speakers. There should be a minimum of movement, fussing about. After a brief pause the First Woman sighs.*

**FIRST WOMAN**  I went to the doctor. (*Pause.*) I don't know. (*Pause.*) My back's been kicking up. (*Brief pause.*) I told him it's right through— (*She reaches back, laying her hand on her lower back, frowning, sighs, and returns her hand to her lap.*) He says you're doin' fine. Didn't once touch me. Says you're comin' along. (*Sound: A child is practicing on a piano very nearby. This will be the only neighborhood sound. Haltingly now we hear the first three notes of "My Old Kentucky Home" played on the piano. I'll indicate this with words— the notes should be all we hear. "Oh–the–sun–" [Mistake] Pause. "Oh-the-sun-shines-" [Mistake] At the first sound of the notes the second woman has glanced to her right. When the mistake is made she glances back front. No one will pay any attention to the notes now, except when indicated. The First Woman sighs:*) I don't know. I told him, I can't bend over. I can't pick up. He tells me stoop. (*Longish pause.*) I don't know.
**SECOND WOMAN**  (*After a beat.*) What's that smell, I wonder?
**FIRST WOMAN**  I imagine that's the new plant.
**SECOND WOMAN**  Worse than the old one. (*Pause. Piano [Off]. Haltingly: "Oh-the-sun-shines-" [Mistake]*) Harry didn't sleep a wink, was up coughing all night. (*Pause.*) My daughter called, her kids have been sick. I said don't try to come over; it's so dangerous traveling on the roads today. (*Pause.*) She said they're gonna come over Saturday. (*Pause.*)
**FIRST WOMAN**  (*Philosophically, but most of the lines are to be spoken philosophically.*) I think this Medicaid business has done a lot of harm. (*Pause. Piano [Off]. "Oh-the-sun-shines-bright-on-" [Mistake].*)
**SECOND WOMAN**  No, that's not the plant.
**FIRST WOMAN**  I imagine it's the river. (*First and second woman glance to their left and sniff. Sniff again. Look back front. Piano [Off] "Oh-the-sun-shines-bright-on-" [Mistake] [Mistake]. Pause. The following two lines are said simultaneously.*)

**FIRST WOMAN**   I told him if I could get—

**SECOND WOMAN**   I don't know why she wants—(*Pause.*) I don't know why she wants to come on a Saturday; that's the worst time. (*Piano [Off] "Oh-the-sun-" [Mistake] [Mistake] Pause.*)

**FIRST WOMAN**   I told him: If I could get up again when I stooped, I'd stoop. (Pause.) I don't know.

**SECOND WOMAN**   (*With a twinkle, and embarrassment.*) I went to the doctor last week. (*Pause.*) Every time I laugh I wet a little. (*She looks to the First Woman and smiles, a little ashamed. The First Woman laughs, the Second Woman laughs, they enjoy that a little. They turn back front. Pause.*) I wet a little then. (*They exchange a look as: Piano [Off] "Oh-the-sun-shines-" [Mistake.]*)

**FIRST WOMAN**   (*Pause.*) I don't know.

**SECOND WOMAN**   That smells more like smoke to me. I think that's the burning.

**FIRST WOMAN**   (*A little more energy—a discovery.*) That's what it is.

**SECOND WOMAN**   (*Overlapping a word.*) That would be it.

**FIRST WOMAN**   (*Overlapping a word.*) That's what it is.

**SECOND WOMAN**   (*Overlapping a word.*) That would be it. (*Pause. Piano [Off] "Oh-the-" [Mistake].*)

**FIRST WOMAN**   I bought a peach this morning. (*Pause.*) They got no taste anymore.

**SECOND WOMAN**   Um.

**FIRST WOMAN**   They're big though.

**SECOND WOMAN**   Um.

**FIRST WOMAN**   Taste kinda like a grapefruit.

**SECOND WOMAN**   Um.

**FIRST WOMAN**   Grapefruits don't have much taste anymore either.

**SECOND WOMAN**   Um.

**FIRST WOMAN**   Big though. (*Pause.*)

**SECOND WOMAN**   Um. (*Piano [Off] "Oh-the-sun-shines-bright-on-my-" [Mistake]. Pause. "Oh-" [Mistake] [Mistake] [Mistake].*)

**FIRST WOMAN**   (*Pause. Then reaching her hand to her lower back and frowning.*) It's right in through. . . .

**SECOND WOMAN**   It's your back.

**FIRST WOMAN**   (*Hand back in her lap.*) I think I pulled something. Or slipped something.

**SECOND WOMAN**   That's what it is; it's the burning.

**FIRST WOMAN**   They collected them late today.

**SECOND WOMAN**   Um.

**FIRST WOMAN**   Was there any— (*Piano [Off] [And at the sametime as above] "Oh-the-sun-shines-bright-on-my-" [Haltingly] "-old-" Pause. The two women wait, neither really indicating waiting, hold their* *breath maybe.* [*Mistake*].) —from our building this morning?

SECOND WOMAN  Oh, I don't go to watch anymore. They're getting so they don't pick up till nearly noon. Bodies laying all over the streets—now, that's not healthy.

FIRST WOMAN  They say it's not catching—so much any more.

SECOND WOMAN  Well. (*Pause.*) It's got rid of the rats.

FIRST WOMAN  Um.

SECOND WOMAN  I hate a rat.

FIRST WOMAN  Um.

SECOND WOMAN  Fixed their wagons.

FIRST WOMAN  Um.

SECOND WOMAN  Serves 'em right.

FIRST WOMAN  Um.

SECOND WOMAN  Any animal that'd play around in that river like that. (*They look at each other with a grimace.*)

BOTH WOMEN  Ugh! (*Pause.*)

SECOND WOMAN  Dirty little rodents. (*Pause.*)

FIRST WOMAN  If we had some water, we could boil up some tea. (*Pause.*) I hate that canned water. (*Pause.*) That can't be healthy.

SECOND WOMAN  Well—

FIRST WOMAN  I hear the radios might come back on. . . .

SECOND WOMAN  Um.

FIRST WOMAN  Before long.

SECOND WOMAN  Um.

FIRST WOMAN  Don't know why. (*Pause.*)

SECOND WOMAN  Um. (*Pause.*) Just when things were getting peaceful. (*Pause.*)

FIRST WOMAN  I don't know. (*Pause.*) I said I can't pick up. He says what's to pick up? Now, what kind of attitude is that? Don't pick up? (*Smiling. They look to each other.*)

SECOND WOMAN  Sounds like Mrs. Pringle. (*They laugh a little, smiling, turn back front, smiles fading. Pause. With a slight frown.*) I wet a little then. (*Brief pause. Piano* [*Off*] *"Oh-the-sun-shines-bright-on my old-Kentucky-home!" First Woman, Second Woman, and Third Woman, rather surprised, look off R. to the piano.*)

**END**

# SEXTET (YES)  (August 1969)
*For Beth and Harry*

## AUTHOR'S NOTE

The six people in SEXTET (YES) are people I worked for and with in Chicago. Their fascinating (to me at least) square dance of intertwined relationships was going to be the subject of a two act play, but the work kept getting more and more compact, more and more abstracted, until I found myself interested in the contrast of their sounds, the great differences in their personalities, more than I was in constructing any sort of realistic plot for them to cavort through. Also there was a strong Beckett influence at work here. SEXTET (YES) was written about the same time as SERE-NADING LOUIE, and some of the characters in this play overlap with that.

SEXTET (YES) was first presented by the Circle Theatre Company on August 9, 1969 and was directed by Marshall W. Mason with the following cast:

BILL:  David Stekol
BETSY:  Tanya Berezin
BOB:  Anthony Tenuta
BELLE:  Stephanie Gordon
BRENDA:  Beverly Gin
BERT:  Clyde Kelly

## CHARACTERS

BILL
BETSY
BOB
BELLE
BRENDA
BERT
All are middle-aged except BRENDA, who is in her twenties.


## SCENE

Six chairs are set in a row, against a dark void, facing the audience.

# SEXTET (YES)

*SET: They are seated at random on chairs, sitting up, waiting. Polite. At the beginning Bill speaks almost in answer to a question—and again when be begins again (on page 91 with "Occupation?") Voices rather removed, not too involved. All "Yes" quietly, as in "That is so, yes:" quiet confirmation. Backlit, very little light on their faces, but it grows during the play and fades toward the end as does the back light.*

**BILL**  The work? I don't—one of the offices midtown. A large silver building with tinted windows. I seem to remember the elevator doors made a "whoosh" when they opened in front of you and I lunched a good deal with clients and representatives and there was a train in the mornings and evenings and I forget their names but we played bridge on a masonite board that we balanced across our knees. (*Silence.*)

**BRENDA**  Oh, yes, Bill. Smallish eyes almost no lashes, yes. He sucked mints to sweeten his breath and used to meet me after work and we walked around the pond or galleries and sometimes pop concerts whenever he felt he could get away and it was either him or the other who used to always discover little eating places—ethnic places that only locals frequented.

**BERT**  (*Immediately.*) She was ravenous, said I went right through her, filled her up completely; said I moved with her like the tides moved with the moon, it was that natural.

**BOB**  (*Immediately.*) There was a fence that we used to jump the ponies over. Around the corral to get a run at it and over. My brother was a fair rider too; every summer we helped out. Up in Montana.

**BETSY**  The first time he was visiting and the others were outside on the porch; Bonnie, his wife, and Bill. Bill would have pissed.

**BOB**  Then we ranched for four years in Oklahoma.

**BETSY**  We could hear them talking about politics.

**BOB**  Oil wells right out on the pasture.

**BETSY**  I had had too much wine with dinner—

**BOB**  Fences around them.

**BETSY**  And was dizzy, so I lay down inside. He knelt by the sofa on the rug and talked to me and I smiled and answered and he leaned closer and closer over me, very close, a cyclops, and kissed me.

**BILL**  Brenda worked there or I wouldn't remember it at all.

**BETSY**  And we got up and went out to the others without another word.

**BILL**   She was so young.

**BETSY**   And when they left he shook my hand and we knew what it meant. What it signaled.

**BELLE**   When Barry was ill he said I want you to remarry. Because you'd be no use at all alone. He died so young. (*Silence.*)

**BERT**   (*Picking up interest/anecdotally.*) We were driving along a country road and her husband was telling a story; something about when he was a boy and she slipped her hand under my jacket. I'd taken off my jacket and had it folded in my lap, and I had on this white shirt and my chest was heaving and I'm staring straight ahead down this dirt road and her husband keeps on talking about when he was a kid. It was over in no time at all and then she started talking like nothing had happened and I'm gasping for breath and trying to zip up.

**BETSY**   Yes.

**BERT**   When we got out of the car I thought my knees weren't going to unbend.

**BOB**   We used to sing that—

**BILL**   Yes.

**BOB**   (*Singing lowly.*) . . . "He rides an old pony, he's just an old cowboy—my bones are of leather" I don't remember the words now— (*Continuing the music phrase.*)

**BOB**   Da-da-da-da-da-da-da-da-da-da-da. (*Muses.*)

**BILL**   She smelled of fresh air, she never perspired, except sometimes there would be moisture just on her temples. (*Bob's tune is done. Bill continues.*) Never was upset. When I couldn't meet her it drove me crazy and she took it in stride.

**BRENDA**   Yes.

**BOB**   (*Picking up.*) Then that part went: (*Singing slowly.*) "Come play the drums Slo-ow-ly Play the pipes lo-ow-ly, I'm an old cowboy, Da-da-da-da-da."

**BETSY**   I used to look deeply into his eyes, just gaze. And I'd move one shoulder, like you'd move to drop a shoulder strap only slowly. He loved the way I did that. When we were in public and I did that he used to look around to see who was watching as if he wanted to take me right there or what I'd done was so intimate he was almost embarrassed and he was always aroused by that. He'd press his leg against my leg under the table or if we were alone he'd move over and push me down into the bed.

**BILL**   She came to meet me once from an air-conditioned shop. I was in the sun and she came up, sliding her arm into mine and the coolness of the shop still around her was like a breeze.

**BRENDA**  He was like a father only one I could be with. Watching the ducks on the pond, he seemed really to enjoy talking to me—taking me to new places. He used to kiss me but it was as a father. That was enough and he accepted it—anything else would have been repulsive to me. He had a son my age, was wildly jealous that I'd ask to meet him, he hated him dreadfully.

**BETSY**  Yes.

**BELLE**  I'd kept my figure, especially my bust and legs. My legs have always been good, even after I began to get a tummy. And I worked, I though it rather courageous and I continued working after I married Bob. I kept Barry's name, professionally, people knew me by then. Bob never said anything, he didn't mind. Anything I wanted.

**BOB**  Yes.

**BILL**  (*As before.*) Occupation? As in with what was I occupied? And why? Or work. . . ?

**BERT**  Work? Where?

**BILL**  . . . career.

**BERT**  Yes, of course. . . .

**BILL**  There must have been something.

**BRENDA**  Oh, yes, Bill. I seem to remember him.

**BILL**  It was midtown of course.

**BERT**  An office.

**BILL**  A large silver building with tinted windows.

**BERT**  Altogether pleasant.

**BILL**  I seem to remember the elevators made a "whoosh" when they opened in front of you.

**BRENDA**  Smallish eyes, almost no lashes.

**BERT**  There was a train in the mornings and evenings.

**BILL**  I lunched a good deal; clients; I couldn't have cared less.

**BERT**  And I forget their names but we played a foursome of bridge on a masonite board we balanced across our knees.

**BRENDA**  Yes, he sucked mints to sweeten his breath which always tasted a bit of pipe smoke or plastic, you know that taste.

**BETSY**  Yes.

**BILL**  Yes.

**BOB**  It was her second marriage and my first. Barry had been an important executive at the agency, but never really in good health apparently. They had a nice house and she saw no point in moving and the taxes were high but you couldn't do better and I've always preferred the country. Bill and his wife lived close by.

**BILL**  Yes. And Bonnie and Bert.

**BERT**  Yes.

**BETSY**  Yes.

**BOB**  Yes.

**BELLE**  Yes. It was nice.

**BILL**  She meant more to me than any of them. The family, the job. It was a new life! It was like living again, all over again. All the things I never could remember doing. I worked like hell as a kid; worked on a ranch sixteen hours a day.

**BOB**  Yes.

**BILL**  Everything was her. Seeing her changed the weather. And I never touched her. There was no need. It wasn't like that. Of course . . . with my wife. . . .

**BETSY**  Yes. . . .

**BILL**  I imagined . . . (*Silence.*)

**BOB**  (*Standing, pulling at his seat.*) My legs cramp, after a while, sitting down. I get sweaty. (*Sits.*)

**BILL**  I married Betsy, I was a big deal young dynamo going places in the company and I was hot after her. The hots didn't last past six months.

**BETSY**  I used to say—

**BOB**  I married late—

**BETSY**  "Yes."

**BOB**  In life, I guess—

**BETSY**  "Yes," but that's all. He talked nonsense.

**BOB**  But I never considered myself a failure. Because I was content.

**BILL**  I'd asked about eight girls to marry me that year—was really hot to get settled and Betsy was the one who said yes.

**BOB**  I was easy to get along with.

**BILL**  I remember our honeymoon because it was the first I cheated on her.

**BETSY**  He's rough by nature but he was gentle; very patient with me. Actually he was gentler than I wanted him to be; but you can't say be rough with me, I just couldn't have. Bill was different, very cutting and rapid—short chops to the liver. Sometimes I thought he'd kill me. He couldn't wait to get it over with and I thought he'd never make it sometimes.

**BILL**  Yes.

**BERT**  Bill rode the train and I did too; only I came back earlier—Bill was all hours. So a couple of times a week Betsy and I went at it. Bill never knew, he would have pissed.

**BELLE**  I never fussed over a diet. I was never a large eater and luckily my skin was always good. Yes, I think early in life that's a matter of luck. We lived happily. Ideally almost. We had our lovely house on an acre and a half. And my children were grown up and off married and moved away. We enjoyed the house; I'd lived there for years, with

Barry, and I enjoyed my work. Bob had no children.

**BOB** We used to hold them in until we got down into the valley when there's a long level stretch then we'd give them rein. The trees by the river flying by. Even when we were ranching we'd find time nearly every day to take the horses out. Of course that's years ago.

**BRENDA** Yes.

**BILL** Yes.

**BOB** We were boys twenty-five thirty years ago. I met Belle because I was in the same field as her husband.

**BELLE** Yes.

**BOB** And she came sometimes to visit around, after he died.

**BELLE** When Barry was ill he said I want you to remarry. Because you'd be no use at all alone.

**BOB** He died quite young. Of course he'd been an important man at the agency.

**BETSY** Bill's an excellent provider and he's good with the kids. And work. Once a month it's jab jab jab and the rest of the time nothing. Bert talked nonsense. While we were doing it. The foulest things. I had to shut my ears to it and think of other thoughts. Walking through the snow barefoot or just being with him and him quiet. Or being bashed real good by some brute—something like that, sometimes that helped, really beat up—isn't it odd what crosses your mind? I hated him talking because I couldn't concentrate. Being good in bed requires concentration and I wanted to be good for him.

**BILL** We went to concerts; we expanded each other's possibilities. We opened each other's eyes.

**BELLE** He drove in to work and dropped me off. He worked at the magazine where Barry had worked and I was only a few blocks away so it was good. We always lunched together at the hotel.

**BOB** Yes.

**BELLE** And we had our table. People joined us there, it was like entertaining. It was more relaxed than it had been with Barry. And Bob was more thoughtful. Of course he never spoke up for himself! And he always re-figured the check and it was never wrong. And he was ponderous.

**BILL** Yes.

**BOB** Yes.

**BELLE** But he was a dear.

**BETSY** Yes.

**BELLE** Of course we fought like sin, we were both set in our ways before we were married. That always means some conflicts.

**BERT** (*Moving slowly into the rolling rhythm of sex.*) The first couple of times she complained that it hurt. She said it hurt her. But I took it very slow, hardly moving, and talking to her very soft, in the same rhythm that I was moving and after a while she began to relax and after a while I could begin to feel her stir, beginning to move against me as I moved and then she would begin to enjoy it, begin to breathe with me, breathe in and when she breathed out there was a little moan, involuntary, as if she didn't realize it was there, or didn't care.

**BETSY**   And I wanted to be good for him.

**BRENDA**   He always used to ask about my cross and I told him my dad or somebody had given it to me and he asked if I always wore it. I saw his brother once—a meek little guy who hunched his shoulders. It was laughable, no, that's unkind, it was unimaginable, to think they'd been young, and worked out west somewhere, riding horses.

**BOB**   I could never afford the things Barry had bought her. Steuben glass and antiques. Very expensive things. But I've always taken good care of what I had. With shoes thirty-five dollars a pair and everything priced to the sky.

**BELLE**   We had our difficulties but we cared for one another. We had a good life together. The two of us. He was unlike his brother. Unlike Barry. But he cared for me.

**BOB**   Yes.

**BELLE**   And I cared for him.

**BILL**   (*Longingly. Slowing down considerably.*) I wanted to take her up into the country. To see her running through the woods! And we'd have walked deep into the woods and come into a clearing, no larger than a small house of soft chartreuse grass and she'd lie down on that virgin place and we'd both know that's why we had waited. We had waited for this place in time and we'd lie down naked there in the woods with the sun coming at a slant through the trees, stripping us, and when she'd bend over me that delicate gold cross she wore would fall on my face and she'd move from side to side dragging the cross across my cheek and over my upper lip and I'd open my mouth for it. And I'd move my chest under her, back and forth and the wiry hairs on my chest would cause her nipples to grow hard and goosepimply, and finally she'd stretch out her body against mine. Warm. Scalding and smooth against me and a breeze would stir all that soft green over and around us and would cool us together. . . . (*Silence.*)

**BOB**   (*To: "Play the pipes lowly, play the drums slowly, etc." Singing lowly, distantly.*) Do-do-do-do-do-do-do-do-do-do-do . . . do. . . . (*The lights fade.*)

**CURTAIN**

# IKKE, IKKE, NYE, NYE, NYE  (October 1970)


## AUTHOR'S NOTE

I was hanging out with Bill Hoffman and Neil Flanagan one evening, probably at the Cino, that's where we usually hung out. Neil and Jackie had been plagued with deep–breathing anonymous phone calls all week. I don't know if he didn't understand telephone perverts (unlikely, he understood most things) or just wanted to play one, but he suggested we write something for him. Oh, youth! Back then all any of us needed was a subject and we were off.

Bill Hoffman reads the ads in the back of sex magazines because he finds them hilarious. ("GWF desires to meet same, interested in rubber, broken glass and Chopin.") He wrote THANK YOU, MISS VICTORIA almost the next day. It's a deadly sharp play about a lazy corporate president's son who reads the ads in the back of sex magazines, calls one of the numbers as a lark, and meets more than his match. Neil was brilliant in it.

Months later I was raking leaves in the huge front yard of a friend's house in Sag Harbor; a good strenuous activity for anyone who is looking for an idea that will pull him away from a good strenuous activity. Remembering Neil's request, the whole of IKKE, IKKE, NYE, NYE, NYE came to me. I dropped the rake and went inside. It wrote itself in two or three days. When the first draft was finished, Neil was off somewhere and Michael Feingold, still at Yale, needed something to direct, so I sent it off to him. It was years before Neil finally did the play, somewhere in California. He said he was great in it. He probably was.

Regarding the title. When the LaMama troupe toured Europe (I went along for the ride on a Rockefeller grant) I noticed nannies in the parks of Copenhagen slapping their young wards hands and saying something that sounded like, "Ikke, ikke, nye, nye, nye!" Which I took to mean something on the order of, "Nasty, nasty, no, no, no. Put that down". I've been told what they were saying was nothing like that, and didn't mean that either.

As I said, we wrote quickly back then. When I finished the play it had no title. When I thought of IKKE NYE, I realized I'd have to go back and make the French maid a Danish maid for the title to make any sense. Alas, the play got out of my hands, I forgot about changing it, so it stands now, totally wrong linguistically, misunderstood, misspelled, and without even the intrinsic logic that would make it comprehensible. I wouldn't change it for the world.

IKKE, IKKE, NYE, NYE, NYE was first presented at the Yale Cabaret, New Haven, Conn., on January 13, 1972. It was directed by Michael Feingold with the following cast:

GRAHAM: William Gearhart
EDITH: Lisa Carling


**CHARACTERS**

GRAHAM  About thirty-five physically, a bewildered child.
EDITH  Same age, tall, stringy, frizzy, every woman to every man.


**SCENE**

Living room of an apartment, doors to bedroom and kitchen, a princess phone by the sofa. Walls green, no paintings.

# IKKE, IKKE, NYE, NYE, NYE

**EDITH** (*Enters, a seductive queen, does not look back to the open door.*) Oh, very well, but only for one drink.

**GRAHAM** (*Off.*) I really—

**EDITH** (*Not looking back.*) If you absolutely must— (*Sultry.*) But I will not let you press an advance. No, no, no.

**GRAHAM** (*Off.*) Actually, I—

**EDITH** (*Turning.*) Shut the door, Graham. (*Insinuating, vamp.*) And don't you dare lock it.

**GRAHAM** (*His face appearing at the door.*) Oh. You have a phone. (*Drawn into the room by it.*)

**EDITH** Well, of course everyone has a phone—haven't you a phone?

**GRAHAM** Oh, yes—Dad has a phone—we have two phones—

**EDITH** I have two.

**GRAHAM** At home—but he keeps a lock on them.

**EDITH** One in here. (*Insinuating.*) And one in the bedroom.

**GRAHAM** Charming evening, Edith.

**EDITH** Wasn't it? I love the theater.

**GRAHAM** Yes, so do I.

**EDITH** (*An enthusiast.*) The glamour.

**GRAHAM** Sitting in the dark.

**EDITH** Exactly.

**GRAHAM** Expectant.

**EDITH** Yes.

**GRAHAM** All those anonymous people around you.

**EDITH** The clothes. Emotions. Catharsis.

**GRAHAM** The lights dimming.

**EDITH** Beastly play.

**GRAHAM** Wasn't it?

**EDITH** Pure smut.

**GRAHAM** At least they didn't disrobe.

**EDITH** (*Tinge of disappointment.*) Yes, that was something.

**GRAHAM** (*Gazing at the phone.*) Novel.

**EDITH** I'm not going to give you anything rousing to drink.

**GRAHAM** Princess, is it?

**EDITH** Let's see, that's vodka and . . .

**GRAHAM** Oh. Anything. I don't actually.

**EDITH** I always think a glass of wine is the perfect (*Insinuating.*) nightcap. We don't want you getting stimulated.

**GRAHAM** No, I wouldn't want—

**EDITH** (*Whisking into the kitchen.*) I'll only be a second.

**GRAHAM** (*The moment her back is turned, he dives at the phone, dials a number at random, beside himself with desperate urgency—breathes five quick times into the phone when he gets an answer—slamming the phone down as Edith breezes in with a bottle of wine.*)

**EDITH** (*Insinuating.*) A nice deep burgundy.

**GRAHAM** (*Instantly.*) Nice painting.

**EDITH** What's that?

**GRAHAM** Ah—the walls—nice color.

**EDITH** (*Sultry and daring.*) "Hot! Lime!" I shouldn't have. Supposed to bring out the beast in men. Oh. You haven't a cork screw on you?

**GRAHAM** No, I—

**EDITH** Well, I can manage. (*She whisks out—Graham dives at the phone, and sits on it as she whisks back in immediately.*) Now, If you will officiate?

**GRAHAM** Oh. Ah, fine. Will I what?

**EDITH** (*Handing him the bottle and corkscrew.*) You know when I told the other girls on the switchboard that the mail boy had asked me out—they were green with envy.

**GRAHAM** (*Having difficulty with the bottle.*) I seem to have–

**EDITH** Would you like—

**GRAHAM** No, I can get it.

**EDITH** They all think you're headed for Big Things.

**GRAHAM** Well, Dad says that if I do well in the mail room he'll make me a Vice President.

**EDITH** (*Superior person. All knowing.*) We knew. We sensed it.

**GRAHAM** Some vice presidents have as many as three phones.

**EDITH** We listened in.

**GRAHAM** (*Pleased and envious.*) Do you?

**EDITH** Should I—?

**GRAHAM** No, I have it.

**EDITH** They'll all want to hear about it tomorrow. And I'm not going to tell them a thing.

**GRAHAM** I think being a telephone operator must be the most rewarding position any American girl or boy could possibly aspire—

**EDITH** (*Provocative.*) No matter *how* they pump me.

**GRAHAM** (*Pulling the cork.*) Got it.

**EDITH** (*Looks for glasses.*) Oh, I'll get them. (*She whips into the kitchen. Graham gets the telephone from under him in one hand, the bottle in the other. Dials. Breathes heavily three times. Edith comes in. He switches hands, and is breathing the aroma of the wine.*)

**GRAHAM** Excellent year.

**EDITH**  (*Off on a cloud.*) Oh, men! (*As Graham stuffs the phone behind the daybed.*) Men! . . . Men of the world! So knowledgeable. Debonaire! Gourmet! (*She extends the glasses. He pours as she stares rapturously at him—devouring the experience.*) Yes. Yes. Yes. A toast. A salute. A prosit. To vice presidents.

**GRAHAM**  And operators.

**EDITH**  (*Peering over the glass. Seductively.*) Double entendre. (*She drains the glass.*) I never drink anything stronger than wine. (*Pouring another.*)

**GRAHAM**  I never drink at all actually.

**EDITH**  (*Glancing about her kingdom.*) Yes. "Hot lime."

**GRAHAM**  (Puzzled.) Hot line? Did you say hot line? (*Excited.*) Hot line. Hot line!

**EDITH**  Lime. Lime.

**GRAHAM**  (*Working into a frenzy.*) Hot line.

**EDITH**  The fruit. The fruit.

**GRAHAM**  (*At sea.*) Fruit?

**EDITH**  Citrus.

**GRAHAM**  (*Frustrated.*) Fruit? Edith, what are you talking about?

**EDITH**  The paint. The walls.

**GRAHAM**  (*Exhausted.*) Oh. Oh, my God.

**EDITH**  Are you—?

**GRAHAM**  No, I'll be OK. The stairs.

**EDITH**  (*Provocatively.*) You'll get used to them.

**GRAHAM**  Actually I've never been in anyone's apartment before.

**EDITH**  Naughty deceiver.

**GRAHAM**  Not physically, at least.

**EDITH**  You're all alike.

**GRAHAM**  (*Still trying to get his breath.*) Hot line, I—golly—I—

**EDITH**  What was that about physically?

**GRAHAM**  What color do you suppose the hot line is?

**EDITH**  Red?

**GRAHAM**  Red. Oh, Oh, god—or orange.

**EDITH**  I'm wondering if I should slip into something provocative. (*Looks at him. Dead pause as he weighs the further advances against her absence from the room.*)

**GRAHAM**  (*With calculation.*) Why . . . don't . . . you?

**EDITH**  (*Boldly.*) Dare I?

**GRAHAM**  (*Changing his mind.*) Well, actually—

**EDITH**  (*Bolder.*) Dast I?

**GRAHAM**  I'd better be–

**EDITH**  I will. I'll only be a minute.

**GRAHAM**  Oh, take your . . .

**EDITH**  Pour yourself another wine, Graham. Enter the gates. (*She watches with heavy eyelids as he obligingly pours himself a second wine. She slips away into the bedroom.*) I shall return.

**GRAHAM**  (*Dials the phone with the same urgency. When he gets an answer, in a breathy, excited voice.*) What are you wearing? How big are your hello? Hello? Hello? (*Dials again.*) How big are your—hello? Huh? No, I—What are you wear—? No, lady it isn't—How big are— lady, will you shut up and listen this is important. (*Breathes five times, in the middle of a breath.*) Huh? Oh, God— (*Hangs up, desperately dialing again, hangs up and stuffs the phone away as Edith enters again, in a chenille robe, fuzzy slippers in the shape of an animal and a cigarette holder—her manner is Mae West or some like "brazen huzzy."*)

**EDITH**  That's better. What care I? (*Stuffing a cigarette into the holder.*) Pour me a drink. Light my cigarette damnit. (*He does.*) Such a boring day. Such useless despair.

**GRAHAM**  (*Glancing at his watch.*) My, look what time.

**EDITH**  (*Throwing herself into a chair, her arms dragging the floor, her head back, her eyes closed, her cigarette burning the rug.*) Time. Time! Time! (*The weight of the world.*)

**GRAHAM**  (*Tentatively.*) Edith. Ah—Edith. You're burning the. . . .

**EDITH**  (*Lifting the cigarette to her lips.*) Yes, time. You strong men. Know all! See all! Hear all! Why me?

**GRAHAM**  Why?

**EDITH**  (*Lost woman.*) Why me? Of all the women at Skidney, Scheindecker, Hornblower and Bicks? What was there?

**GRAHAM**  Well, actually—

**EDITH**  (*Bitter.*) Or was it just my turn?

**GRAHAM**  Oh, no. You're the only— (*With a wistful dream, trying to tell her something personal and beautiful.*) Well—ring-ring.

**EDITH**  I beg your. . . .

**GRAHAM**  I'm at home and I call in sick—I call the office. Well, the phones at home are locked, but I run down to the Head Cheese Deli on the corner and call the office and—ring-ring-ring.

**EDITH**  Who's there?

**GRAHAM**  No, you say—you have the earphones over your head and that curling black plastic mouthpiece in front of you and I call (*Edith is getting into the part.*) in and you say—ring ring.

**EDITH**  (*Miming the switchboard, serious. Musically.*) Skidney, Scheindecker, Hornblower and Bicks.

**GRAHAM**  (*Bit to the heart.*) Oh. Oh.

**EDITH**  (*Continuing, lost to him.*) I'm sorry Mister Mimford but Mister Scheindecker's line is busy, I can connect you with Mr. Bicks.

**GRAHAM**  Oh, Oh. . . .

**EDITH**  Skidney, Scheindecker, Hornblower and Bicks.

**GRAHAM**  Oh, the way you—oh, a voice like that comes over the phone once in six hundred and thirteen calls.

**EDITH**  (*The business woman.*) Well, I've worked hard, strenuous . . .

**GRAHAM**  (*Adrift, excited, happy, eyes closed.*) Ring ring ring ring buzz buzz buzz.

**EDITH**  Time consuming dedicating.

**GRAHAM**  Buzz buzz buzz buzz.

**EDITH**  Such a sweet child.

**GRAHAM**  Putty, putty, putty, putty. . . . (*Opens his eyes, sees her.*)

**EDITH**  Have another wine.

**GRAHAM**  Yes, thank you (*He pours the last glass.*)

**EDITH**  (*Suddenly ecstatic—to* the *four walls.*) Oh, men. Men. Men in my apartment! Entertaining. *Madame* DuBarry. *Madame* Pompadour.

**GRAHAM**  (*In the rhythm.*) Madame Bovary.

**EDITH**  (*Provocatively.*) Oooooooooooooooooooooo!

**GRAHAM**  I shouldn't drink.

**EDITH**  Men are beasts when they drink. Is that all? What a hostess you must think me. Don't go away. (*She flits out. Graham reaches behind the daybed, a little mellowly drunk. Finds the cord, follows it hand over hand to the wall outlet. Stands up blinking as she enters.*) Look what I found! Gin gin gin! (*A bottle in each hand.*)

**GRAHAM**  Gin gin gin gin. I can't stay.

**EDITH**  (*Pouring the gin into a glass and dropping in an olive.*) A little martini.

**GRAHAM**  I've actually never had . . .

**EDITH**  (*Finishes the martini.*) Oh, the businessman lunch. The cocktail parties. Stars! Balconies! Stairways! Chandeliers! Raintree County! (*Hands him the glass.*)

**GRAHAM**  (*Sadly drunk.*) Prosit.

**EDITH**  Devil.

**GRAHAM**  (*By now a boneless, wistful, sad child.*) Mother's a sweetheart, but dad put a lock on all the phones. For weeks my one goal was to liberate those phones.

**EDITH**  Radicals. Men. Guerrilla warfare. Big ape!

**GRAHAM**  (*Wistfully.*) Once a week mom used to slip me the keys and go out for the afternoon.

**EDITH**  (*Standing suddenly, furious.*) Oh, you Big Ape! (*Contrite.*) I'm sorry, you were saying . . . ? (*Sits, politely, listens.*)

**GRAHAM**  She used to take the station wagon into the garage for a grease job. But dad came home one afternoon with an ulcer and there I was with every phone in the house unlocked.

**EDITH**  What a sad childhood. (*She moves to the day bed, with him,* *motherly.*) Poor little rich boy . . .

**GRAHAM** He was even more angry because I'd tied up Monique and locked her in the closet.

**EDITH** Little Lord Fauntleroy.

**GRAHAM** Dad had hired Monique so I'd have a companion—

**EDITH** (*With only slight contempt.*) Men of the world. Gentlemen's agreement. How little I know of the bright lights. Long Island. Oyster Bay. The Great Gatsby.

**GRAHAM** (*Dreamily wistful still, drunk.*) But Monique didn't speak English and Mom wouldn't let her answer the telephone. If it hadn't been for that I think something might have developed between us.

**EDITH** (*Less veiled.*) Hush money. (*Her lip curling.*) New Jersey abortions. Connecticut recoveries.

**GRAHAM** Everything changed after that. I came to the mail room.

**EDITH** But with all those possibilities. Opportunities. Secretaries. Executive Suite. Barbara Stanwyck.

**GRAHAM** . . . Dad married Monique. Mom ran off with the grease monkey. Monique has never really understood me since I tied her up.

**EDITH** What does the European Woman know of brute strength.

**GRAHAM** Nothing important happened in my life until the day I heard your voice. . . .

**EDITH** (*Provocatively.*) Provocateur.

**GRAHAM** (*Wistfully, bouncing, imitation of her lilting voice.*) Skidney, Scheindecker, Hornblower and Bicks.

**EDITH** Roue. Rogue.

**GRAHAM** (*A sad, happy boy.*) And I knew you'd understand. (*He lays his hand fraternally on her knee.*)

**EDITH** (*Standing and screaming.*) Police! Police! Rape! Rape! (*Recovers herself immediately. Sits.*) Oh, *yes?*

**GRAHAM** (*With a lost frown.*) Ah. . . .

**EDITH** (*Briskly rising, buzzing about the room emptying ashtrays, the big sister.*) Well, just a sip more, Graham, and then you've really got to go. I have to roll my hair yet, and grease my face and trim my corns—

**GRAHAM** (*Completely drunk.*) Where's my glass . . . ?

**EDITH** There is an interesting show at the Modern Art tomorrow.

**GRAHAM** Oh, yes? Thank you.

**EDITH** Sometime in the afternoon, if you'd like to give me a ring.

**GRAHAM** Ring?

**EDITH** Ring.

**GRAHAM** (*Excited, jumping, to the air, no phone or mime of one.*) Hello. Hello. (*Breathes three times quickly.*) What are you wearing? How big are . . . (*On* the last line he has picked up the martini to his ear, spilling it over him.*)

**EDITH**  Graham!

**GRAHAM**  What? Hello? What?

**EDITH**  Look at your—

**GRAHAM**  (*Looking down.*) Oh, I'm sorry (*Pulls out a handkerchief from his pocket, spilling about a hundred quarters over the floor.*)

**EDITH**  What are you . . . ?

**GRAHAM**  (*Trying to wipe the stain from his pants.*) It must be the— (*Puts his hand on her shoulder to steady himself.*)

**EDITH**  Police! Rape! Police!

**GRAHAM**  May I go to the bathroom?

**EDITH**  In there!

**GRAHAM**  May I have permission to leave. . . .

**EDITH**  Just go, Graham! Go! (*He is gone, she is alone, furious, in a heavy trauma. Throws herself to a chair, almost immediately recovers and looks around with self-satisfaction.*) Sex and the Single Girl. Valley of the Dolls. Manhattan bachelor girl's apartment. Asphalt Jungle. African Queen. (*The phone rings. She looks at it. It rings again. She rises, walks to it.*) Skidney, Scheindecker, Hornblo—hello? (*Puzzled, sweetly.*) Hello? (*Irritated.*) Who is this? I said who is this? (*Slight shock.*) I demand to know who this is! Young man I'm not going to hang up this phone until you tell me who this is! (*Beat.*) What am I what? (*Pause. Indignantly.*) Practically nothing as if it were your concern. You got me out of the tub and I've just thrown on a black lace peignoir, but I don't see it's any of your . . . oh (*Pause.*) Oh! (*Shock.*) Oh! (*Sits.*) Listen, young man, my husband is a policeman and he's right in the next room and if I decide to call him in here—oh! None of your business! None of your bus—quite large. (*I won't discuss it attitude.*) Quite large—I don't know, large, milky white pendant cantaloupes. (*Looking about the room—these worrisome details.*) I will not prolong this—your what? (*Out of patience.*) Your what? Enunciate for God's sake, you sound like an asthmatic dwarf! (*Pause. Puzzled and irritated.*)  Your huge throbbing *what*? (*Listens. Registers shock.*) *Where*? (*Shock.*) Oh! Oh! Oh, you pig! (*Draws her feet up onto the sofa getting comfy.*) Hold it a minute I hear something. (*Listens with her hand over the phone, listens for something from the bedroom. Then private, into phone.*) Now, what was that last? Pig! Monster! To even suggest! Oh! Oh! Oh, smut! Oh, you, oh (*It gets worse and worse.*) Oh, what? Uhg! Oh, Oh, Oh, (*Exhausted, waving the phone in the air, her eyes have stopped focusing.*) Ah, ah, ah, oh! (*Back to the phone.*) Oh! Where? Where, though? Oh, smut. Oh. Oh, to *me*? Oh, smut. Ahhh. Oh. Oh. Hello? (*Diddles with the cradle, exhausted, but curious.*) Hello? (*Exhausted, waves the phone idly, forgotten.*) Smut. Smut. Smut. Oh, smut.

**GRAHAM**   (*Enters. Nice little boy. Stamp collector.*) Oh, Edith, I hadn't realized how late it was getting.

**EDITH**   (*Can't bear, can't see, done in.*) Smut. (*Looks around blindly.*) Smut.

**GRAHAM**   I have to be going. I've truly enjoyed the evening.

**EDITH**   Smut. Oh. Oh, smut.

**GRAHAM**   I'll give you a ring tomorrow. (*Getting into his coat.*)

**EDITH**   Ring? (*Phone to ear vaguely.*) Hello? Oh, smut.

**GRAHAM**   Now, thanks for the drinks.

**EDITH**   Smut.

**GRAHAM**   I'll tell daddy you said hello.

**EDITH**   Hello?

**GRAHAM**   Night.

**EDITH**   Night.

**GRAHAM**   Night night.

**EDITH**   (*After he has gone.*) Smut.

## BLACKOUT

# VICTORY ON MRS. DANDYWINE'S ISLAND  (1970)

VICTORY ON MRS. DANDYWINE'S ISLAND was first presented at the Circle Repertory Lab Theatre in January of 1981. The production was designed and directed by Rob Thirkield with the following cast:

MR. ORFINGTON:  Terrance Markovich
MISS COMPANION:  Toni James
MRS. DANDYWINE:  Kitty Muldoon
MISS LIVEFOREVER:  Maura Swanson
THE GARDENER:  Rob Thirkield

Sound (drums) by Dan Bonnell


## CHARACTERS

MR. ORFINGTON
MISS COMPANION
MRS. DANDYWINE
MISS LIVEFOREVER
THE GARDENER


## SCENE

The setting is a cottage among others on an island. A sitting room with doorways to the outside both Right and Left. A doorway to Mrs. Dandywine's bedroom Up Center. There are chairs for Miss Companion and Mr. Orfington with small serving tables beside them and an important and comfortable chair or, better, lounge, for Mrs. Dandywine.

# VICTORY ON MRS. DANDYWINE'S ISLAND

> *Mrs. Dandywine is on her lounge thinking. She is stout and over fifty. She speaks with an elevated pronunciation and a deep sonorous and slightly superior voice, choosing her words carefully. She might use a cane, but only as a prop. Miss Companion enters excitedly. Miss Companion is thin, half-grey and over fifty. She gets things done in a catch-as-catch-can manner and is both excitable and impressionable. The play should be treated in the exaggerated high style associated with an English comedy of manners.*

**MISS COMPANION**  Mrs. Dandywine! You know, of course, that I hate myself for disturbing you, but—

**MRS. DANDYWINE**  I thought you—

**MISS COMPANION**  —but—

**MRS. DANDYWINE**  Were sunbathing —

**MISS COMPANION**  —but—

**MRS. DANDYWINE**  I dislike you to do more than one thing at a time.

**MISS COMPANION**  But there is a man!

**MRS. DANDYWINE**  It is enough that you interrupt me in my meditation. I can not at all understand someone interrupting herself.

**MISS COMPANION**  He has appeared at the gate. (*Mr. Orfington enters. He is younger than the women but over forty-five. Stout and self-important, fastidious and in no way effeminate.*)

**MR. ORFINGTON**  Dear kind lady, do forgive this imposition in the middle of such a hot afternoon. I am Mr. Orfington from the city. Mrs. Hengerfeld said when I passed your way I was to offer her compliments. I am most anxious to please you.

**MRS. DANDYWINE**  I had not noticed that it was such a hot afternoon, Mr. Orfington. To be candid, and this is my house, I had not noticed it was afternoon. It is time for my rest. (*She rises.*)

**MR. ORFINGTON**  By all means take it.

**MRS. DANDYWINE**  It is very brief, but essential. If you care for refreshments, Miss Companion will arrange them.

**MR. ORFINGTON**  I wouldn't dream of leaving without speaking with you.

**MRS. DANDYWINE**  I enjoy comradeship but disallow advances. Most usually. I have never in my life known anyone named Hengerfeld, but I forgive your imposition. (*She exits u.c.*)

**MISS COMPANION**  Mrs. Dandywine is a person of rigid habits.

**MR. ORFINGTON**  I myself have no habits at all.

**MISS COMPANION**  May I get you something to drink?

**MR. ORFINGTON**  Tonic disagrees with me. Sugar and water and lime juice.

**MISS COMPANION**  Mrs. Dandywine does not tolerate her routine to be interrupted, but I live for interruptions. I find rude people more exciting than any others. Would lemon suit you or should I go to the market?

**MR. ORFINGTON**  This will do fine. I myself am an artist. A writer of journals. I am influenced by everything I read.

**MISS COMPANION**  Mrs. Dandywine is very sedentary. I don't admire people who do things. Since she never leaves the house I see in her so many possibilities. I find that mysteriously piquant. A postcard with undecipherable handwriting. Do you enjoy mystery, Mr. Orfington?

**MR. ORFINGTON**  Not at all. It makes me very uneasy.

**MISS COMPANION**  Then I had better not tell you of our little mysterious circumstance.

**MR. ORFINGTON**  Certainly not.

**MISS COMPANION**  Oh! (*Sigh.*) To be content! To be strong! I think a lack of curiosity is the mark of a mature man.

**MR. ORFINGTON**  I have a sound digestion and an unperturbable countenance. I practice it in the mirror. I always try to eat four full meals a day. I have no preference for food but I like to be occupied. I live for my work.

**MISS COMPANION**  Do tell me of your work!

**MR. ORFINGTON**  Certainly not.

**MISS COMPANION**  Oh, yes, do!

**MR. ORFINGTON**  No one sees it. I labor on it continuously, and enjoy talking of nothing else.

**MISS COMPANION**  Then do. Tell me about it. What is your subject?

**MR. ORFINGTON**  I talk of my labor. Not of what I labor on. It's nature is one of self-revelation. I find through ceaseless dedication I can completely alter my philosophy every few days.

**MISS COMPANION**  How tirelessly an artist must pursue his calling. And how little the world would mean without it.

**MR. ORFINGTON**  Change, reconstruction, revelation, alteration, hypothesis, experimentation. All that is necessary to my nature. Change is my stability.

**MISS COMPANION**  I do hope you will speak with Mrs. Dandywine. She will be so pleased with your attention.

**MR. ORFINGTON**  Your way of life here is pleasant.

**MISS COMPANION**  We cook, we sew, we mend. We do what is expected. I myself go out on seeing excursions to the market across the flats.

**MR. ORFINGTON**   I never notice anything.

**MISS COMPANION**   No one would want it of you. But we poor laymen–

**MR. ORFINGTON**   I have learned to focus my attention inwards. I can flatter anyone. I find they give me more. I'm not sure I have the right house. Is there another Dandywine on the island?

**MISS COMPANION**   Certainly not. Of course you do. Everyone knows of Mrs. Dandywine. She is a person of importance to society. She inherited a great deal of money.

**MR. ORFINGTON**   Then that is undoubtedly she. And what of Mr. Dandywine?

**MISS COMPANION**   Do you mind if I embroider?

**MR. ORFINGTON**   Not at all.

**MISS COMPANION**   Mr. Dandywine was Mrs. Dandywine's father. The Mrs. is assumed. Mrs. Dandywine felt the Mrs. to give her stature.

**MR. ORFINGTON**   Mrs. Dandywine is unmarried?

**MISS COMPANION**   Of course she's unmarried.

**MR. ORFINGTON**   (*Removing his hat.*) I'll stay to lunch.

**MISS COMPANION**   I'm so glad. We're having scrod.

**MR. ORFINGTON**   Food is of no consequence to me. (*There is a tremendous knocking on the floor.*)

**MISS COMPANION**   (*After a long pause. With pride.*) Our mysterious circumstance.

**MR. ORFINGTON**   I beg your pardon?

**MISS COMPANION**   I say—

**MR. ORFINGTON**   Yes?

**MISS COMPANION**   Our mysterious circumstance.

**MR. ORFINGTON**   I heard your sentence; it had no subject.

**MISS COMPANION**   The subject was the tremendous knocking.

**MR. ORFINGTON**   I noticed no knocking.

**MISS COMPANION**   I am in deep touch with the occult. I could see events that will happen in the future. I never try; such things overexcite me.

**MR. ORFINGTON**   I have never been in the presence of the supernatural. It would have no interest for me.

**MISS COMPANION**   I'm surrounded by presences. I am never lonely.

**MR. ORFINGTON**   Certainly not. To be lonely is damn stupid.

**MISS COMPANION**   (*Shocked by his language. Standing.*) Mr. Orfingstone!

**MR. ORFINGTON**   Orfington.

**MISS COMPANION**   (*Sitting.*) Orfington.

**MR. ORFINGTON**  (*Standing.*) Mister.

**MISS COMPANION**  (*As before. Standing.*) Mr. Orfington!

**MR. ORFINGTON**  My card.

**MISS COMPANION**  How exquisite.

**MR. ORFINGTON**  I get them by the gross. They are very costly. (*They sit.*)

**MISS COMPANION**  Would you mind if I did it as a sampler?

**MR. ORFINGTON**  Dear lady it would flatter me enormously. I always like for my taste to be admired.

**MISS COMPANION**  I admire nearly everyone's taste. I have none of my own. (*The Gardener appears at the door. He is old but not over sixty. More likely ageless. He hangs his head, drags his feet, never looks at anyone directly and speaks in a high monotone voice almost like singing, and his words are in a language we cannot understand.*)

**GARDENER**  Mum mum mum um.

**MISS COMPANION**  Excuse me, Mr. Orfington. Yes, I see you. You may come in.

**GARDENER**  (*Advancing a step into the room. More than shy he is self-effacing. Of course not looking at them. Looking everywhere else.*) Mum mum mum mum.

**MISS COMPANION**  This is Mr. Orfington, who has come to visit with Mrs. Dandywine, and to stay for lunch.

**MR. ORFINGTON**  How do you do ?

**GARDENER**  Mum mum mum mum.

**MISS COMPANION**  (*Aside to Mr. Orfington.*) He is our gardener; he is very shy. Yes?

**GARDENER**  Mum mum mum mum. Ah ah day flox mum mum mum mum hmmmmmmmmmmmmmmmmmmm? (*Ending on a long high questioning hum-whine.*)

**MISS COMPANION**  Certainly you should.

**GARDENER**  Mum mum mum mum. (*He retires. Fades out. Mr. Orfington continues to look toward the door with a puzzled expression.*)

**MISS COMPANION**  We don't understand exactly what he says, but we wouldn't dream of interfering, he's so sensitive.

**MR. ORFINGTON**  Anyone so dedicated to his work.

**MISS COMPANION**  Of course the island is salt flats. Nothing could possibly grow here.

**MR. ORFINGTON**  I hadn't noticed.

**MISS COMPANION**  No one would expect it of you.

**MRS. DANDYWINE**  (*Appearing in the doorway to her bedroom. Mr. Orfington stands.*) Well! I feel quite dreadful!

**MR. ORFINGTON**  You didn't rest well?

**MRS. DANDYWINE**  I never do. It is a social obligation. I couldn't possibly. People would rob me blind. I have not remembered Mrs. Hengerfeld, and I never forget a name. I am afraid I must ask you to leave.

**MR. ORFINGTON**  She was, I believe, a friend of your father's.

**MRS. DANDYWINE**  My father died of sympathetic labor when I was born. We mourn his loss.

**MISS COMPANION**  He was a very aristocratic man.

**MRS. DANDYWINE**  (*Sitting.*) You will stay to lunch.

**MR. ORFINGTON**  (*Sitting.*) I will eat everything before me.

**MRS. DANDYWINE**  You will stay the night.

**MR. ORFINGTON**  I will be honored to accept.

**MRS. DANDYWINE**  We will be happy of your company.

**MR. ORFINGTON**  You have an adequate library?

**MRS. DANDYWINE**  I talk incessantly, but I never read.

**MR. ORFINGTON**  I read a great deal and quite slowly.

**MRS. DANDYWINE**  Fortunately that will be no hindrance. I do not require people to listen and answers to my questions annoy me. There was a time when I read the newspapers with great alacrity; especially the obituaries. But hardly anyone of any interest is dying anymore. Miss Companion, you will make me one of what Mr. Orfington is drinking and refill his glass. You have heard of our mysterious knocking? It is a great comfort to me. Do you know my history?

**MR. ORFINGTON**  I must confess that I have no interest at all in other people's lives but if it would make you like me better I would undergo almost anything.

**MRS. DANDYWINE**  (*Leans back in her chair, closes her eyes and after a proper interval begins to recite.*) My history is my only passion. I was not, of course, born here. I was born away. No one was born here. To speak of. I remember great arguments among my relatives over my father's demise. Or rather over the money he left at his demise. My grandfather had been in the war and was killed when an automobile backfired outside the house on his ninetieth birthday. He mistook the explosion for gunfire, took cover in the hallway and was crushed by the fall of the clock. However, it was his clock. But that clock never ran after that. (*Pause.*) I remember great joy over a number of things I can't remember. There was a sense of eminent accomplishment and a time of confusion. I was of course proud enough to remain apart from personal contacts. I have always prided myself on my pride. (*The gardener appears in the door. She senses his presence and is very annoyed. She opens her eyes.*) Yes, what is it?

**GARDENER**  Mum mum mum.

**MRS. DANDYWINE**  Certainly not.

**GARDENER**  Mum mum mum mum.

**MRS. DANDYWINE**  Oh, very well, whatever you will.

**GARDENER**  Mum mum mum mum. (*He retires. Mrs. Dandywine recloses her eyes.*)

**MISS COMPANION**  Mrs. Dandywine doesn't allow movement when she tells her history.

**MRS. DANDYWINE**  (*Continuing.*) Then a sense of failure. I felt I had failed to allow failure. Then I overcame. Through will. I don't remember what it was I overcame, I remember only a sense of victory which has remained with me ever since. My achievement was—my accomplishment has been the victory.

**MR. ORFINGTON**  I live of course in the city. I depend greatly on the prejudices of my friends for entertainment. I think it is past my time for lunch.

**MISS LIVEFOREVER**  (*Off. Screaming in a high, hoarse voice.*) I won't have it. Cur! Varmint! Reprobate! Scum! Thief! It shall not happen!

**MISS COMPANION**  Oh, it is she. Dast we ask her in?

**MRS. DANDYWINE**  Certainly not.

**MISS LIVEFOREVER**  (*She appears in the doorway across from the one the gardener uses. She is dressed in evening clothes, but they are badly worn, and she is hysterical, red-headed, smoking, wildly made-up.*) I shall throw a mammoth cocktail party over the spot and trample it to juice, do you hear me!

**MRS. DANDYWINE**  Mr. Orfington, I don't believe you've had the pleasure. This is Miss Liveforever.

**MISS LIVEFOREVER**  (*Overlapping.*) You and your goddamned gardener. You will not get away with it. I'll flood your yard with horse piss. It will not come up. You're in it together but you will fail utterly.

**MRS. DANDYWINE**  Miss Liveforever, this is Mr. Orfington.

**MISS LIVEFOREVER**  (*Preoccupied but automatically.*) You must come to my soirees, casual dress, canapes and a simple claret— AHHHHHH! (*This last as the Gardener has appeared in the other door. The rest to him, though a force keeps her from entering farther into the room.*) Then if this is to be the culmination of our struggle I am not unprepared!

**GARDENER**  Mum mum mum mum.

**MISS LIVEFOREVER**  You may have gathered the strength of the earth but I have the hoards. The masses! (*Laughs.*) I'll stomp it to sap, I feel it growing—trying to poke its tender shoots through the—oh, how dare you! (*The other three are above noticing the struggle.*)

**GARDENER**  (*Without moving farther into the room.*) Mum mum mum mum.

**MISS LIVEFOREVER**  (*Trying vainly to push her way into the room,* *struggling against an unseen force.*) Ah. Ah. Ah. Ah.

**GARDENER**  (*Still self-effacing, without looking directly at anyone.*) Mum mum mum mum.

**MISS LIVEFOREVER**  Beast! For six years we struggle here. You— will—fall as I did. No one will ever—may your damn bulb be eaten by a thousand—ah!

**GARDENER**  Mum mum mum mum.

**MISS LIVEFOREVER**  BARACK BARRAACK!

**MR. ORFINGTON**  Are there pickles?

**MISS COMPANION**  I'll get them.

**GARDENER**  Mum mum mum mum. (*Lightning and thunder and the sound of a slapstick.*)

**MISS LIVEFOREVER**  BALACK BAARACK KAZRAK! (*Tremendous knocking on the floor.*)

**MISS COMPANION**  Did you hear?

**MRS. DANDYWINE**  Such a comfort.

**MISS COMPANION**  Sweet or dill?

**MR. ORFINGTON**  Either will do. (*Thunder and lightning.*)

**GARDENER**  Mum mum ah day oh.

**MISS LIVEFOREVER**  (*At the same time.*) SLAP CRACK MACK! (*They reach a stand off.*) Then we'll see!

**GARDENER**  Ah, day oh. (*Miss Liveforever exits. The gardener exits.*)

**MRS. DANDYWINE**  I really find that woman most ordinary. I fear she has no lineage at all.

**MR. ORFINGTON**  I find I can not be agreeable unless I am eating. I don't smoke. I've never smoked. (*The house shakes and knocks. Lightning and thunder.*) Though I enjoy smoked foods.

**MISS COMPANION**  It seems to be growing dark. I shan't be able to continue my sunbathing. (*A knocking on the floor.*)

**MRS. DANDYWINE**  Ah. These comforts.

**MR. ORFINGTON**  (*Taking a small book from his breast pocket and writing.*) Excuse me, but I've realized something quite interesting about myself.

**MISS COMPANION**  Mr. Orfington is a journalist.

**MR. ORFINGTON**  (*Continuing to write.*) Three times now since I've been in this room I've felt a distinct vibration on the bottom of my feet. I don't before believe I've fully incorporated the feet into my philosophy. This may have very important ramifications for me.

**GARDENER**  (*Appearing in the doorway.*) Mum mum mum mum.

**MRS. DANDYWINE**  What is it?

**GARDENER**  Mum mum mum mum. (*He exits.*)

**MRS. DANDYWINE**  Miss Companion, you had better go see. Such a dedicated man. He was here before we came. So handy. He never eats, so it is not necessary to have him at table.

**MISS COMPANION**   I shall return and prepare your lunch. (*She exits.*)

**MR. ORFINGTON**   I was not unmoved by your history.

**MRS. DANDYWINE**   I hoped for that effect. The fact is I'm not sure of its validity.

**MR. ORFINGTON**   I suspected it was more than likely fabrication. That is why I was not unmoved.

**MRS. DANDYWINE**   I am moved only by my own situation.

**MR. ORFINGTON**   I think such an attitude is important to superior people.

**MRS. DANDYWINE**   Miss Companion is necessary to me. She hates me secretly. I enjoy secrets. Other people's secrets. My own make me uncomfortable.

**MR. ORFINGTON**   Almost everything makes me uncomfortable.

**MISS COMPANION**   (*Re-entering.*) Odd. Very decidedly odd. He showed me where the ground is cracked and something appears to be pushing up.

**MRS. DANDYWINE**   Mushroom.

**MR. ORFINGTON**   I very much enjoy mushrooms.

**MISS COMPANION**   No, it was green.

**MRS. DANDYWINE**   The island is a salt fiat; nothing can grow here.

**MISS COMPANION**   It would seem to be a bulb of some kind.

**MR. ORFINGTON**   I am completely indifferent to horticulture. Though other cultures are indispensable to me.

**MRS. DANDYWINE**   I do not claim to understand these things.

**MISS COMPANION**   Tulip or hyacinth or narcissus.

**MR. ORFINGTON**   I can not live in the same environment as a hyacinth. Artists are sensitive to such things.

**MRS. DANDYWINE**   As I remember from my history, it is the correct season for any of that order.

**MISS COMPANION**   The entire yard seems to be flooded in horse urine, except where the bulb is growing.

**MRS. DANDYWINE**   Natural phenomenon is, of course, Miss Companion's concern.

**MR. ORFINGTON**   I think everyone should have an interest.

**MRS. DANDYWINE**   I myself have none. I find they occupy my mind. (*Thunder and lightning.*)

**MISS COMPANION**   There is a storm.

**MRS. DANDYWINE**   As a child, I was told to count the seconds between the lightning and the thunder. Each second was said to represent a hundred yards from the place where the lightning had struck.

**MISS COMPANION**   We must wait and try it if the storm continues.

**MR. ORFINGTON**   Such an experiment would not interest me. I am a man of letters. I never found it necessary to learn the numbers above five. I would appear to have five fingers on each hand which I refer to in my journals as two fives or, if including my toes, four fives. With the three of us I would say we have fingers in one bunch of five fives and one bunch of one fives. I do it quite rapidly. With the toes we are two groups of five groups of five and two groups of five.

**MRS. DANDYWINE**  I do not enjoy mathematics. (*Lightning and thunder, concurrently.*)

**MISS COMPANION**  I neglected to count. (*She begins to chop a green onion.*)

**MRS. DANDYWINE**  Perhaps it will re-occur. (*Lightning and thunder, concurrently.*) Well. No matter. (*Lightning and thunder.*) Odd. I don't suppose it works. I am not native to this island. (*The lights grow red.*)

**MR. ORFINGTON**  I am native to the city.

**MISS COMPANION**  Everything is growing red.

**MR. ORFINGTON**  Is it?

**MISS COMPANION**  Without my glasses.

**MR. ORFINGTON**  I never bothered with the names of the colors. I say something is strongly colored or palely colored. Or tinted. Which color it is tinted does not interest me. I would say the air is strongly colored.

**MISS COMPANION**  (*Looking out the window or door.*) It is the house across the street.

**MRS. DANDYWINE**  Miss Companion, if you continue to interrupt the preparation of dinner we will never be able to feed our guest.

**MISS COMPANION**  Mrs. Dandywine does only one thing at a time.

**MRS. DANDYWINE**  I beg your pardon, but I do nothing at all.

**MISS COMPANION**  Miss Liveforever's house has burned to the ground.

**MRS. DANDYWINE**  I do not enjoy all the recent activity on this island. If it does not abate I shall put the house up for sale.

**MISS LIVEFOREVER**  (*Off.*) You!

**GARDENER**  (*Off.*) Mum mum mum.

**MISS LIVEFOREVER**  (*Off.*) I saw that thunderbolt. Of all the underhanded, conniving—(*She appears in* the *doorway, her dress and hat badly scorched. More hysterical.*) I'm not bested. There are other islands. We'll see! Now it's up to you. He can't help you now. This will be your trial.

**MRS. DANDYWINE**  I know nothing of law.

**MISS LIVEFOREVER**  We'll see how you fare when he leaves.

**MR. ORFINGTON**  If you are referring to me, I have agreed to stay for supper and to stay the night.

**MISS LIVEFOREVER**  I have spies everywhere. I am never at bay.

**MR. ORFINGTON**  I am a journalist and sailing disagrees with me. I want very badly to be widely noted, however, and will do anything that will cause you to mention me at your next party.

**GARDENER**  (*Appearing at the other door.*) Mum mum mum.

**MISS LIVEFOREVER**  It will never bloom. Damn it now and damn it in its bloom. Damn damn damn.

**MISS COMPANION**  (*Shocked by her language.*) Miss Liveforever!

**GARDENER**  Mum mum mum.

**MISS LIVEFOREVER**  I'll go. But you've not seen the end of this. (*She exits. There is a flash of lightning, thunder and a scream of AHHHHH-HHHHHeeeeeeeee.*)

**GARDENER**  Mum mum mum mum. (*We see now he carries a suitcase.*)

**MRS. DANDYWINE**  Yes, of course; whatever you will.

**GARDENER**  Mum mum mum mum.

**MRS. DANDYWINE**  Mr. Orfington, will you do me the honor of going with him to see what it is? (*The gardener exits.*)

**MR. ORFINGTON**  I shall bend every effort. (*He exits.*)

**MISS COMPANION**  I've never before prepared scrod for a journalist. Life is one blessing after another. To be allowed to do so much.

**MRS. DANDYWINE**  I expect he will want to retire immediately after the meal. You and I will play our game of patience.

**MR. ORFINGTON**  (*Re-entering.*) Remarkable what the sun does to my skin. I think I've not given enough consideration to temperature in my temperament. Extraordinary man, your gardener. Beat me in seven games of chess running. Kept talking about his mums, though there wasn't a mum in sight. There was nothing in sight at all as a matter of fact. Did you realize that this island was a salt flat? Pointed to a flower. He did; the island is round. A round flat. I must make a note.

**MRS. DANDYWINE**  Not a flower. Nothing grows here.

**MR. ORFINGTON**  Bud actually.

**MRS. DANDYWINE**  Nothing blooms here.

**MR. ORFINGTON**  Left, you know. Walked down the road.

**MISS COMPANION**  These things excite me.

**MR. ORFINGTON**  Or across the road. By the road. Up the road!

**MISS COMPANION**  (*Suddenly raising the skillet in a revolutionary cry.*) UP THE ROAD!

**MRS. DANDYWINE**  Miss Companion, please. Occasionally she is expendable.

**MISS COMPANION**  (*Quieted.*) Anyone for an aperitif?

**MR. ORFINGTON**  Drink is always good.

**MISS COMPANION**  There is great nourishment in orange juice.

**MRS. DANDYWINE**  I can't imagine him leaving just as Miss Liveforever removed herself.

**MR. ORFINGTON**   I try to imagine as little as possible.

**MRS. DANDYWINE**   They were both here before we came.

**MR. ORFINGTON**   I notice as little as I can.

**MRS. DANDYWINE**   I don't think they ever liked one another.

**MISS COMPANION**   Such a bother to get another gardener.

**MRS. DANDYWINE**   I won't think about it.

**MISS COMPANION**   It is very unlikely we will find another who doesn't require food.

**MRS. DANDYWINE**   A bud you say?

**MR. ORFINGTON**   A plant of some kind—or shoot of some kind. With buds.

**MISS COMPANION**   Nothing has ever grown here.

**MRS. DANDYWINE**   I so dislike altered circumstances.

**MISS COMPANION**   I live for altered circumstances.

**MR. ORFINGTON**   Change is my nature.

**MRS. DANDYWINE**   It's best to ignore these things. Have I told you my history?

**MR. ORFINGTON**   Yes, as I recall, you have; though I don't remember it. I find I always like something better the second time I hear it.

**MRS. DANDYWINE**   Surprise has no place in my life.

**MISS COMPANION**   I had best go water it.

**MRS. DANDYWINE**   I do wish you would finish one thing before you begin another.

**MR. ORFINGTON**   I ignore people whose nature is different from my own.

**MISS COMPANION**   I shall. Oh, these never ending tasks. Such a pleasure.

**MRS. DANDYWINE**   Please do not bother me with them. (*Miss Companion exits with a watering can.*) Miss Companion finds many things to do. My history is my only passion.

**MR. ORFINGTON**   I have no passions at all.

**MRS. DANDYWINE**   (*Leans back, sighs, closes both eyes and recites.*) I was born on this very island. I am the only thing that grows here. I had no parents and they had none. There is a force that continually moves from the center of the earth to reach the atmosphere. (*Miss Companion tip-toes back in, taking her seat, closing her eyes.*)

**MR. ORFINGTON**   (*In the rhythm of the scene, but with his eyes open, his finger in his collar.*) I seem to be strangling.

**MRS. DANDYWINE**   I live here in the isolation of a small community. I read the papers but no longer read the papers.

**MISS COMPANION**   (*Eyes still closed.*) It's blooming.

**MRS. DANDYWINE**   Please.

**MISS COMPANION**   Extraordinary.

**MR. ORFINGTON**   I think my lungs are collapsing.

**MRS. DANDYWINE**   I learned many things from many things and learned to forget them.

**MISS COMPANION**   It isn't a narcissus. It's a hyacinth.

**MR. ORFINGTON**   I can not live in the neighborhood of hyacinths.

**MISS COMPANION**   Artists are sensitive to such things.

**MR. ORFINGTON**   (*Rising, turning red in the face. Tip-toeing to get his hat.*) It was one of the first realizations I had regarding my organic make-up.

**MISS COMPANION**   You must not interrupt Mrs. Dandywine's history.

**MR. ORFINGTON**   I will not be able to stay to lunch, and I will not be able to stay the night. Good day.

**MISS COMPANION**   (*Her eyes still closed. Murmured.*) Men are so extraordinary.

**MR. ORFINGTON**   Mrs. Dandywine, good day. (*He exits.*)

**MISS COMPANION**   (*Softly.*) Extraordinary man.

**MRS. DANDYWINE**   (*Continuing.*) Then through will I overcame. I don't remember what it was I overcame. I remember only a sense of victory which has remained with me ever since. (A *pause.*)

**MISS COMPANION**   (*A contented sigh.*) Victory.

**MRS. DANDYWINE**   My accomplishment has been. . . .

**MISS COMPANION**   (*A sigh.*) . . . *The* victory.

**MRS. DANDYWINE**   The victory. (*There is a knocking on the floor. Mrs. Dandywine sighs.*) Such a comfort. (*The lights dim out.*)

### CURTAIN

# THE GREAT NEBULA IN ORION  (October 1970)

## AUTHOR'S NOTE

I spent my first summer away from New York City in 1970 in a hot attic apartment in Sag Harbor, New York, while all my friends were discovering Woodstock, which they loved and I couldn't abide. At the end of the summer I bought a house in Sag Harbor. I've said it was the last great buy in the Hamptons, but I've put so much into restoring the dump I'm not sure that's quite accurate. I had just finished the first absolutely final draft of SERENADING LOUIE. (I'd been working on the play for more than three years.)

At that time the director of the Stables Theater Club in Manchester, England wrote that two women in his company had, quite on their own, worked on LUDLOW FAIR, and, though they might be "a touch long in the tooth" for the play, he liked their work very much. If I had a companion piece for them, or if I wanted to write one, he'd be interested in putting the two plays together on the main stage. So what I began with, essentially, was two shapes, or two types, just a little more mature than the pair in LUDLOW FAIR. I had written a short story called FUZZ ON ORION'S SWORD, about a woman coming to visit her gay brother in New York. That story includes most of Carrie's history and the monologue/reverie on her poet boyfriend. Louise came from a costume designer friend who sometimes assisted Scaasi, hybridized with a story, almost verbatim, about winning an acting award that the actress/producer of LEMON SKY, Haila Stoddard, told me once while she was preparing dinner, paring asparagus. (Don't ever turn down a dinner invitation if Haila is cooking.) Under the influence of SERENADING LOUIE, which had, in its first draft, a number of asides to the audience, and is about old college buddies, and LUDLOW FAIR and the gay brother in the original story, NEBULA is essentially the earlier "Fuzz" story, balanced with another woman of equal strength. It was the first thing I wrote in the new house, perched in the middle of piles of removed plaster and wallpaper higher than my head, and the last thing I'd write for almost two years.

I sent off the first draft with a long letter apologizing for the lousy typing, the hurried draft, promising to work on it if they could use it. Unfortunately, it was sent just as the famous six months mail strike hit England. I had no idea if they received the play.

After six months, the first word I heard from Manchester was a letter of thanks and a packet of very kind reviews. NEBULA had premiered only three weeks after the first draft left Sag Harbor. Aside: After consideration, I don't think it's the perfect companion piece for LUDLOW FAIR, the two plays are probably too similar in tone and movement.

THE GREAT NEBULA IN ORION was first presented by the Stables Theatre Club, Manchester, England on February 18, 1971, and was directed by Paul Hellyer with the following cast:

LOUISE:  Lisa Ross
CARRIE:  Paula Wilcox

The American premier occurred on the triple bill with THE FAMILY CONTINUES and IKKE, IKKE, NYE, NYE, NYE at the Circle Theater, 2307 Broadway, on May 21, 1972.  It was directed by Marshall W. Mason with the following cast:

LOUISE:  Stephanie Gordon
CARRIE:  Tanya Berezin

## CHARACTERS

LOUISE  A smart woman in early thirties. Rather direct.

CARRIE  A slightly plumpish and attractive woman the same age; rather wooly.

## SCENE

An apartment overlooking Central Park West and 81st Street, New York City. Living room, doors to bathroom and bedroom; bedroom door ajar. The set need not be represented completely, but can be sketched and properties can be minimal. The play would benefit from being set as close to the audience as possible in, perhaps, a three-quarter round area. There is a minimal kitchenette in the living room, and the apartment should convey the feeling of a woman with good taste.

# THE GREAT NEBULA IN ORION

*The apartment is unoccupied. There is a noise off. A voice says: "Oh, wow, I hope you don't mind. . . ." There is the sound of a key in the lock. Louise enters carrying several packages, bustling in.*

**LOUISE**  Man, oh, wow, have I ever got to go to the—make yourself comfortable. The john? (*Carrie enters behind Louise, rather tentatively.*) The can? What did—to the loo? What did we call—?

**CARRIE**  I don't really . . .

**LOUISE**  (*Overlapping*) —When we had to pee—we had a cutesypie, prim-assed euphemism—

**CARRIE**  I'm not quite. . . .

**LOUISE**  (*She has managed to set the packages down in several places and throw her coat across a chair.*) Well, in any case, I've got to!

**CARRIE**  (*Who tends to cling to her purse.*) It's a lovely. . . .

**LOUISE**  Make yourself comfortable, I'll only be a sec. (*She flies off to the bathroom door, closing it.*)

**CARRIE**  (*Alone. Looks to the audience, smiles, embarrassed, looks out the window. Calls.*) Is this the park?

**LOUISE**  (*Off.*) What's that?

**CARRIE**  (*Calling.*) I said was that the park? Is that Central Park? (*A pause as she listens, waits, smiling. The smile fades, to the audience.*) Well, obviously it is the park. This is a terrible mistake. I knew it was, coming up here. I have no idea why I—

**LOUISE**  (*Off.*) What? I'll be with you in a jiff.

**CARRIE**  Nothing. Fine. (*Quietly whispering to the audience.*) It's rather like being sent up in one of those balloons—like—well, not a balloon, maybe, but rocket or—in any case there's a theory about time being at a different wave length or some such, you know. And if you go to Mars, say, though you might return only two months older the trip would take several years and things on Earth would be completely altered—or some such thing. You know. Relativity. And here I am, it's all rather disquieting. (*Shrugs, making do.*) In any case.

**LOUISE**  (*Re-entering.*) What's that, sweet?

**CARRIE**  I said bumping into you like this.

**LOUISE**  Yes, a lot of catching up. You look super, by the way, and I won't hear anything except that I'm more ravishing than ever. You look a lot thinner—

**CARRIE**  Thank you.

**LOUISE**  (*To the audience.*) It's a girdle, right? In this day and age, do you believe it? Oh well. (*Turns back to Carrie smiling.*)

**CARRIE**  You do, you look wonderful. (*To the audience.*) It's almost tra—

**LOUISE**  What is?

**CARRIE**  No, darling—I was. . . .

**LOUISE**  (*Realizing this was said to the audience and not her.*) Oh, I'm sorry. (*She has measured water into a saucepan and set it on the stove, preparatory to making a chemex of coffee.*)

**CARRIE**  Quite all right. (*Continuing to the audience.*) Almost tragic to see someone whom you remember as so unusually striking and realize that—

**LOUISE**  (*Pouring the boiling water into the chemex.*) Coffee we decided, didn't we?

**CARRIE**   . . . that special . . . (*To Louise.*) Yes, please—just black, no sugar. (*Back to the audience, almost in a whisper.*) . . . thing that they had was a vitality and youthful bloom, and when that's gone. . . .

**LOUISE**  This will drip through and we can talk. (*To the audience.*) Black, no sugar, could you die?

**CARRIE**  (*To the audience, still whispering.*) What you really feel of course, because you don't feel time passing, you know, minute by minute—you don't feel as though you're ageing, and then you see someone with whom you were young and you see the age in them and feel sorry, not so much for them as for yourself.

**LOUISE**  Yes, well, I think I've finally gotten over that pretty much. Remember the trauma when we turned twenty?

**CARRIE**  Oh, yes. Blank many years ago.

**LOUISE**  Just fourteen.

**CARRIE**  Oh, God.

**LOUISE**  This coffee is going to be swill—I'm lousy in the kitchen.

**CARRIE**  You want help?

**LOUISE**  Lord, no. Nothing is organized, the place is a wreck, what kitchen there is. I have a larger space for my filing cabinets. You wouldn't be able to find anything.

**CARRIE**  (*To the audience.*) I used to wait on her hand and foot.

**LOUISE**  Of course you know what a klutz I am in the kitchen anyway. I've never been able to understand how I could be so relatively organized professionally and the reverse— (*Burns herself—not badly—she doesn't want to be in the kitchen anyway.*) Damn! Tell me about the children— (*To the audience.*) I can't. Just can not imagine Carrie— Carolyn Brown nee Smith, class of nineteen fifty—beep—I think even that gives away too much—make that nineteen beep-beep—cannot imagine her with children. She showed me their pictures. In Bergdorf's yet. Where I never go. You know we had that big scene: "Louise, baby," "Carrie darling! It's been ages !" And she says, you've got to see my two kids and whips out these practically eight-by-ten color photographs and wouldn't you know they're gorgeous! They're beautiful. I almost burst into tears right in the middle of Mme. Greis' God awful autumn—if ever you could just *wish* children into being without all the bother they're what you'd wish for. A dark boy, very straight and serious and an angel girl as blond as—demure, long thin hands, and a knowing look, at about age seven. . . .

CARRIE  They're angels—they really are. Five and seven.

LOUISE  Five and seven . . . (*They smile, amazed at the years, the moment turns first into a musing pause, then an awkward silence. Carrie takes a drink of coffee, smiles to Louise.*)

CARRIE  (*To the audience.*) The coffee's swill.

LOUISE  Would you rather have a drink? Let's lace it up a bit. I can't really make anything—and this is supposed to be so simple.

CARRIE  That's not a bad idea. (*To the audience.*) She said at work she's organized and I'm sure she is—that's—(*Louise is pouring brandy into her cup.*) That's fine—oh, my!

LOUISE  (*She has poured rather a lot.*) What the hell.

CARRIE  (*Quickly here.*) Yes, it's after twelve.

LOUISE  What's that got to do—oh, well.

CARRIE  (*Immediately back to the audience.*) She has really a marvelous position with—well, no names—one of the better dress makers—her own line. Really very successful. Beautiful clothes. She's always had a wonderful feeling for fabric. Weight, drape, and all that—

LOUISE  Yes. It's nice. (*She has poured herself a straight brandy.*) It's work—it's—

CARRIE  I mean she's really becoming rather a name.

LOUISE  Exhilarating sometimes and fun.

CARRIE  It makes me feel rather proud in a way, I suppose.

LOUISE  (*Taking a sip, proudly.*) Hmmmm.

CARRIE  (*To the audience.*) And then of course, well, I don't know . . . it's sad.

LOUISE  Sometimes I feel my clothes are rags. I mean I say that, no one else better; then other times I'm really quite proud. I sometimes feel like more of a businesswoman than a designer. I can't think of any other reason why I succeeded in such a dog eat dog business when so many other people oh, well, hash. What are you watching?

CARRIE  (*By the window.*) What's the building?

LOUISE  The green one? It's the Planetarium.

CARRIE  Have you ever been ?

LOUISE  Not actually. I understand it's quite ordinary.

**CARRIE** Damn.

**LOUISE** Beg pardon?

**CARRIE** Oh, nothing. I don't think I like it. Could I have a brandy, darling? I don't much . . . (*Setting down the cup.*)

**LOUISE** Of course, of course. It's better than anything to take the chill off. The coffee's awful, isn't it?

**CARRIE** No, no, it's quite good—I— (*To the audience.*) Why is that, I wonder? I guess it's just so absurdly simple to make good coffee—of course I couldn't cut a dress.

**LOUISE** (*Handing her the glass.*) Cheers. Is that OK or do you want rocks?

**CARRIE** No, this is fine. (*To the audience.*) That's funny—are you ever a little proud when someone—well, this isn't a good example, but some slang like "rocks" for "ice" and you know what they mean?—I mean it isn't my word for it—of course I don't usually drink—I mean, I'm not a drinker, so my first thought when someone says "rocks" is— rocks. But, well, if I happen to answer immediately like that—"No, this is fine," I'm always just a little proud. I mean when we were in school we didn't say rocks—we said—I don't know—up ?

**LOUISE** No, up is without—

**CARRIE** Salt? It was . . .

**LOUISE** I'll think of it—we used it all the time—

**CARRIE** Well, no matter.

**LOUISE** I'll think of it.

**CARRIE** (*She has managed to drink the pony of brandy by now.*) The way we talked. All that slang—you know I dread the kids growing up, because I know I won't understand a word they're saying. Remember the way we talked? (*To the audience.*) My, that's warm—I shouldn't have—well, that damn Planetarium.

**LOUISE** Another?

**CARRIE** Just a bit. (*Shrug to the audience.*)

**LOUISE** (*To the audience.*) Drinks like a sieve. Always has. Wouldn't admit it on a stack of bibles. Always was a prig. Good family and all that, you understand—churchmouse poor, but lineage out the ass.

**CARRIE** (*Lifting the glass.*) Where on earth did you get . . . ?

**LOUISE** I don't know. They're not really good—Victorian.

**CARRIE** They're lovely though.

**LOUISE** Aren't they? A little musty shop down in the village. I've had them for . . . (*Biting her lip, blinking, remembering the circumstances, suddenly almost in tears.*) Golly.

**CARRIE** (*Not noticing.*) It's a beautiful rug.

**LOUISE** Needs a good cleaning. How's David doing?

**CARRIE** (*Surprised.*) Oh! Marvelously. (*At a loss.*) He's . . . just built himself a workroom out from the house . . .

**LOUISE** (*Trying to be interested.*) Workroom?

**CARRIE** Shop. He does woodwork.

**LOUISE** God.

**CARRIE** Makes toys and things.

**LOUISE** Oh, God.

**CARRIE** No, he's very good at it. I don't know, it's a hobby. He had it in the basement, but—you can't imagine—

**LOUISE** I can imagine!

**CARRIE** I mean aside from the noise, the sawdust—it's much better away from the house.

**LOUISE** You have land then?

**CARRIE** We have nine acres—not land.

**LOUISE** (*To the audience.*) He's rolling in money, it's absurd. (*To Carrie.*) It must be wonderful for the kids . . .

**CARRIE** Oh, yes it . . . there are trees to climb and David's got David Junior a base—softball diamond, I suppose it is and a tree house—and Alice has a doll house and garden house. He's really marvelous with them.

**LOUISE** They're such angels.

**CARRIE** Do you hear from your brother?

**LOUISE** Sam? He's not one to write all that much. Neither am I for that matter. From time to time. Twice a year. I can always count on him to send me something embarrassing for Christmas. He was here a year ago.

**CARRIE** Has he ever mentioned a Richard Roth?

**LOUISE** Richard Roth. R. R.; Roth. I don't think, but then I never pay any attention to what he tells me. I don't know how he's remained single. I guess no one would have him.

**CARRIE** I thought he was nice.

**LOUISE** Sam? Oh, he's great. It really delights him that every woman comes equipped—and he thinks they're made that way especially for his own personal enjoyment. I think he's marvelous.

**CARRIE** Yes, I—ah— (*To the audience, embarrassed.*) I really don't think Louise has changed a bit. I—ah—

**LOUISE** (*Continuing.*) Of course he's damn good at it. Practice makes perfect—

**CARRIE** Ah-ha . . .

**LOUISE** —I know he taught me everything I know about sex.

**CARRIE** (*Exasperated, to the audience.*) Now, I mean *that* sort of thing. Even if it's true, you don't—

**LOUISE** (*Pouring another.*) Who's Roth?

**CARRIE** (*Stopping short.*) Oh. A friend. Of Sam's. One of his friends.

**LOUISE** (*To the audience.*) I'm a year older than Carrie and the year I left Bryn Mawr was the same year Sam came to Haverford which is just a long goodnight walk away. And Carrie had met Sam so they saw each other. They didn't date, God knows. Of course all Sam's friends were older. (*To Carrie suddenly.*) Oh! I've got to tell you. (*Pleased and delighted with this story.*) We were having lunch—a bunch of us girls—no one you know, I don't think. I mean we meet nearly every Friday. We have a table reserved for us. And the conversation never is rough, exactly, but we didn't really notice that we had a new busboy. A very young kid with his hair shaved off—it couldn't have been more than a quarter-inch long and big old ears sticking out from the side of his face—maybe fourteen years old. And the girls were talking while he's sitting water and butter around; no one's paying any attention to him and someone asked Berilla what she'd been up to and she said she'd been going to night school. Of course nobody was listening, really. (*Aside to the audience.*) This is an old joke, it's not going to be funny, particularly. (*Back to Carrie.*) But after about half an hour someone turned to Berilla and said whatever are you doing in night school? And the kid's taking off plates by now and Berilla said, "Oh, I'm just taking a course in intercourse, all you have to do is come." And. We laughed, a little. But this kid had never heard it before. I don't imagine he'd ever heard a woman—well, he bit his lip and set the dish back (*Laughing.*) on the table and made a beeline for the kitchen—his ears—those big old ears just burning. He thought it was the funniest thing he'd—he was so funny and sweet. We just collapsed. He came back flushed and biting his tongue, with tears in his eyes. Such a dear.

**CARRIE** He was probably as shocked as anything.

**LOUISE** Oh, yes! Shocked and surprised and so endearing. With those big old ears.

**CARRIE** He sounds sweet.

**LOUISE** Really wonderful. (*A long pause. Carrie gets up and walks a few steps away. To the audience.*) Well, she's shocked. I suppose with kids of her own. Well, crap.

**CARRIE** Humm? Oh, no. Not at all. I'm abstracted. I'm not really good company today. It's wonderful seeing— (*Breaking off, to the audience.*) I'm not shocked. I've had a few drinks and I'm pleasantly high. I've decided whatever it was I was shopping for can wait until. . . . (*Back to Louise.*) Is it warm in here?

**LOUISE** It is a little, I can—

**CARRIE** No, no, I'll just take off my jacket. (*She does, and in a minute, her shoes.*)

**LOUISE** That's a beautiful suit. Chanel?

**CARRIE**  Umm.

**LOUISE**  (*To the audience.*) I loathe it, right? But then I would. It's a beautiful suit. It's not the sort of thing I do. I drape, Chanel cut. It's a very complicated pattern; you take it apart the jacket alone is in about forty pieces. I mean she made the same damn suit for about fifty years, but what the hell, right?

**CARRIE**  Oooo. That's better.

**LOUISE**  Actually I love the damn suit but it's all wrong for her. That's real, you understand, notice the fabric; that's no rack copy. Money, my dears—

**CARRIE**  I have one of yours.

**LOUISE**  Do you, which?

**CARRIE**  Well, I would, wouldn't I? A black wool with white piping.

**LOUISE**  (*To the audience.*) Oh, God. Well, she could do worse. Actually it should look rather nice on her.

**CARRIE**  Oh, I love it. I didn't bring it with me.

**LOUISE**  (*To change the subject.*) Who's Roth?

**CARRIE**  Oh, well, if you don't know him.

**LOUISE**  I might. I never listen to Sam.

**CARRIE**  I don't think they were that close. I didn't really know him at school. I met him there with your brother, but after I went out to California. . . .

**LOUISE**  (*Fishing neatly.*) Wait, is this the guy you wrote me—God, that's years ago.

**CARRIE**  I thought I had. The poet.

**LOUISE**  A poet, right.

**CARRIE**  Or he was when he was at Haverford, but I met him again in California.

**LOUISE**  With David.

**CARRIE**  No, no, David doesn't know him. Before David. He was a really exceptional poet but with—one of those very intelligent guys with enormous gaps. Like he spoke Greek and Latin. Actually spoke—well, I mean he didn't go around speaking it, but he could and one time I remember I mentioned the Secretary of State and he'd never heard of him. Didn't know any of the Cabinet. And on art, painting at least he was absolutely blank. Never heard of the most obvious: Magritte, Gris. . . .

**LOUISE**  Mmmm.

**CARRIE**  But he was one of the most independent and impulsive and masculine and I don't know, one of—

**LOUISE**  Probably what you mean to say is he laid you.

**CARRIE**  —Well, I don't mean—

**LOUISE**  Without so much as a will you waltz, I know the type.

**CARRIE**  Well, as a matter of fact, but it wasn't that—that's neither here nor—oh, well, it's silly.

**LOUISE**  (*To the audience.*) She's a little tight-assed, but she loosens up. Not such a bad egg really; we had some great times.

**CARRIE**  (*Loosely.*) I am feeling easier. I don't know. I'm only in town for two days; I have a list as long as my arm, I run into Louise in Bergdorf's, of all places, I mean I haven't seen her in what?

**LOUISE**  Six.

**CARRIE**  Six, nearly seven years. We were really close in school, but I thought oh, my God—scratch that—oh, my gosh—I don't like that kind of talk when I go out.

**LOUISE**  Right, I couldn't agree more. (*To the audience.*) Bombed, right?

**CARRIE**  I hear enough of that kind of talk on the street. But I ran into her and thought—

**LOUISE**  "Oh, my God."

**CARRIE**  Right—no, and I'm not bombed either. (*Straightens.*) It just needs a little concentration.

**LOUISE**  You want another?

**CARRIE**  Ummm. And I thought I hope it goes all right, you know? You run into a great friend after a while and you find you have nothing to talk about. It's embarrassing. You feel like a fool. So I said it was a mistake to come up for a bit and here I am relaxing when I've got a thousand things to be doing. Have you kept up?

**LOUISE**  Pardon?

**CARRIE**  With the girls?

**LOUISE**  Oh, I get the—no, I haven't really. I get the paper. You're in a better position than—

**CARRIE**  I don't know why you think that.

**LOUISE**  Well, I—perhaps not.

**CARRIE**  No, of course I am, but—no. I haven't. I don't really—I mean I read about you from time to time and Ruth.

**LOUISE**  (*To the audience.*) An actress.

**CARRIE**  (*To the audience.*) Films. (*Suddenly dizzy.*) Oh . . . oh, I don't think. . . .

**LOUISE**  What's wrong?

**CARRIE**  I had a chicken thing . . . for lunch. I'm all right.

**LOUISE**  Sure? So how do you like Boston?

**CARRIE**  Well, we're outside Boston some. It's really lovely. A little— well, you know I *move* well in those. I was going to say I don't think you would like it much. It's all rather provincial; Garden Party; or you'd feel it was. It's really very sweet. You don't want me to tell you about my bridge club and—

**LOUISE**  Oh, you don't—

**CARRIE**  What? Of course. What else? And they'd never forgive me if I didn't bring back some juicy gossip about the fashions for the fall—

**LOUISE**  Oh, I'll tell you, you won't like it.

**CARRIE**  Oh, no.

**LOUISE**  I know it must seem glamorous. I'm not very damn glamorous but everyone seems to feel I must be. There have been some really wonderful times. There's an award. Probably you don't even know about it—it's in the trade—that I've managed to win. Twice actually. And that was a thrill. There's a presentation luncheon and I don't know—I never. . . . (*Full stop, thinking.*) Well. It wasn't that I never got along with mom, she's very—well, I should say that I'm quite like her. There was never any question of family pride or any such thing— we all of us—Sam too—all of us took each other for granted. It was a very casual sort of family. We weren't like families. I mean I had left home by the time I was eighteen which isn't really terribly shocking anymore, but, well, the first time she came to see me—she didn't call or anything and I was having this torrid three day affair with a what- was-he-a writer—oh, god—I mean for the newspaper. Worse, he wrote those daily horoscope things. Well, he was a Pisces and they're into that —and mom comes to the door—Pisces is in bed naked—mom comes to the door with a little overnight bag and a hat with feathers or a feather, and I answer the door—I've not seen her in a year—and she was broadminded, you know, but I said, "Oh, mom, sweet, how won- derful, darling, but there isn't a cube of ice in the house, could you run down to the deli? It's just on the corner." And mom said, "Oh, sure, of course." She didn't think a thing of it. I mean we got along. And she's a teetotaller. But really—at bottom—she wanted me to be different from what we had been. To have a family and not mess with a career. She didn't see much use in it; or why I was so caught up. Well, I had two smashing seasons in a row and was pretty much the toast of the town that spring and I guess everyone knew I was going to win this award. I know I did. But you can't really know it until you—I mean what it's like until you do. And all my friends were there, who have been of—well, they've been wonderful—and I was very young; the youngest designer ever. I still was the second year I won—and— everyone *stood*. (*She is very moved.*) They were—I just didn't expect it. I know I—I—got the award and everyone cheered and they all stood and all I could think—stupid—all I could think of, standing there with the award (*Crying suddenly, covering her face.*) was: If mother could be here, if she could see—she could. . . . (*Out of it.*) Silly. It was the last thing I expected to think at a time like that. I mean we weren't even close. She didn't even like me all that much. Well, this is silly.

You're right. (*Gets up.*) It isn't a good idea. (*Walking around.*) No, it's wonderful, it is. It's good to see you—I need—Yes, Central Park. Fifth Avenue on the other side. Whyever do you hate the Planetarium? I think it's kind of lovely.

CARRIE  (*Beat.*) That's very. . . .

LOUISE  Oh, we weren't even close. It's such a silly thing. At a time like that what comes over you. What you think. (*Beat.*) We haven't talked about school.

CARRIE  No.

LOUISE  Thank God. Whatever (*Undecided.*) happened to Phyllis Trahaunt?

CARRIE  (*But interested.*) I haven't a clue.

LOUISE  (*At random.*) She was going with someone I think. . . .

CARRIE  Oh, no. No. You *knew*.

LOUISE  I've wondered. She's one of the few women I've wanted to dress; she carried herself so well.

CARRIE  (*In a hush-hush tone, implying scandal.*) Oh, she was beautiful. For all the good. But she wasn't *going* with anyone. Never.

LOUISE  I heard she was.

CARRIE  I don't much think so from what I heard.

LOUISE  No?

CARRIE  She didn't much like the boys, I hear.

LOUISE  Oh, really.

CARRIE  I'm surprised you didn't know. She was in your class.

LOUISE  I guess I never really thought. We had a few classes together.

CARRIE  But she never dated. She was always in Philadelphia.

LOUISE  I just assumed she had family there.

CARRIE  I haven't heard a word of her.

LOUISE  Huh. Nor I. (*Pouring another.*)

CARRIE  None for me. (*Louise looks to the audience as if to say something serious, decides against it, corks the bottle. Carrie is looking away, deep in troubled thought. The tone of her voice, serious and troubled, comes from the blue.*) Louise . . . ?

LOUISE  (*Startled, seriously in return.*) What, darling?

CARRIE  Oh.

LOUISE  I'm sorry, that sounded so odd. I'm hearing oddly today.

CARRIE  Well, I've joined practically everything there is to join. I mean I know you aren't interested in politics or anything like that—

LOUISE  Well, more than I was, actually—

CARRIE  Oh, darling, I am glad. But I know I have my children and they are—well, I won't show you again—

LOUISE  (*To the audience.*) Small favor—no they're lovely.

CARRIE  And I have a wonderful home and David and the kids—

**LOUISE** And you've joined everything.

**CARRIE** I've even taken some night courses—not like your friend—

**LOUISE** Berilla, no; I'm sure. I don't mean—

**CARRIE** I know. I really, in spite of that, envy you. You're like some of the girls and I don't know how they do it. I know it's just an attitude, I mean a state of mind, but knowing that doesn't help, does it?

**LOUISE** It might, if I knew what the hell we were talking about.

**CARRIE** Well. . . .

**LOUISE** I mean they say the first thing an alkie has to do is admit he's hooked.

**CARRIE** Well, then, what I've got to admit is that I'm not. Hooked. Even with all my activities I really envy you—you're—

**LOUISE** Darling, I'll trade anytime.

**CARRIE** Well, see, though, that's—you wouldn't really, would you?

**LOUISE** Well no, not really. But then really neither would you.

**CARRIE** But I would. When I first saw you I thought you looked all six years older and probably so did I, and I didn't really want to think about it—and of course I know you're a wonderful success and that's probably never easy but you seem—engaged.

**LOUISE** Oh, I'm engaged.

**CARRIE** Well, I'm not much.

**LOUISE** What is it, David?

**CARRIE** No, I don't really think it's David. I'm afraid it's more me. David is the happiest married man I know of. (*Count six.*) Well, that's silly. It's not really anything. It's just seeing you again after all this time. You start thinking back about the times we had and those times. It's silly.

**LOUISE** Is there anything—?

**CARRIE** (*Irritated. Almost uppity.*) Oh, don't be ridiculous. That's ridiculous.

**LOUISE** What is?

**CARRIE** Well, weren't you going to ask me if I need help or something? What I need is about two less drinks.

**LOUISE** Or two more.

**CARRIE** I don't think. (*To the audience.*) well, now I *am* uncomfortable and I thought. . . .

**LOUISE** Have another drink then.

**CARRIE** No! Thank you.

**LOUISE** Have you been trying to solve the world's problems again?

**CARRIE** No, I don't crusade anymore. It would look rather hypocritical. David has so many very rich friends.

**LOUISE** And is no pauper himself.

**CARRIE** Oh, dear. I really had no idea when we were married. I mean I knew he had money, but I'd no idea. It's just that being around them you realize that actually the country isn't run quite the way you thought it—I mean, they're really very powerful people.

**LOUISE**  I'm sure they are.

**CARRIE**  And, well, the country isn't run quite the way you think it is. The way people are led to believe it is.

**LOUISE**  I don't really think people believe it is.

**CARRIE**  I mean it's worse than that.

**LOUISE**  How?

**CARRIE**  Well, it's all a sham. I don't actually think I should say anything. It's just things I sense. The way they talk. I only meant that I decided crusading wouldn't have much effect. I don't mean I drift and mope. I diet and run about from this to that. You should see my schedule, but I'm just not—

**LOUISE**  Engaged.

**CARRIE**  Well, my mind isn't. Or I'm losing it or something. I'm not all there is all. This brandy is something else.

**LOUISE**  A present, isn't it great?

**CARRIE**  I'm not so sure. (*She finishes it off as Louise looks at her.*)

**LOUISE**  (*Not too obviously.*) Richard Roth.

**CARRIE**  Huh?

**LOUISE**  I don't know. I think you may have written about him.

**CARRIE**  I thought I must have. (*To the audience.*) We used to write years ago. But you know, we slacked off and finally just dwindled down to exchanging Christmas Cards. (*To Louise.*) Dick never wrote a letter in his life.

**LOUISE**  Dick Roth. What's he up to now?

**CARRIE**  Oh, now, who knows? Removed to Australia the last I heard. That was years ago, I wouldn't have any idea now.

**LOUISE**  I don't know about poets.

**CARRIE**  Oh, he was great but he was a nut. Everyone reviewed his work, if that means anything. I didn't really know him when he wrote; I really met him in California. I've probably told you: he had these enormous gaps and he knew practically nothing about astronomy or any of that, so I guess it came as a shock to him. He read somewhere that the sun—you know, our sun—would burn up in about a billion years or two. Or whatever it's supposed to do: burn out or blow up, and he never wrote a word after that. I suppose he reasoned that anything that was written would simply always be around somewhere but if there was going to be an end to it all one day he didn't see any point. As I said he was a nut. So he left school and came out to California.

**LOUISE**  Why California?

**CARRIE**  Astronomy. Mount Palomar. I guess he got very interested in cosmology or something. He was really crazy about it for a while. You know he was one of those types that's never interested in any one thing for any length of time. I think for about a month he was even interested in me. His sister was ecstatic, apparently he'd never been interested in a *person* before.

**LOUISE** (*To the audience.*) After Carrie left school she went for a year out—

**CARRIE** A little less.

**LOUISE** Out to California.

**CARRIE** We used to sit out on the beach at night. It was incredible. You've never seen skies like they have. And the nights aren't really cold but you need a sweater. We used to build up a bonfire. There's tons of driftwood around on the beach that washes up and we dragged it in from everywhere. You could have seen it for miles out to sea. You aren't supposed to, but no one says anything. There was a group of probably twenty of us. Dick and I used to wander out down the beach—you couldn't get lost—and you could see the fire with little people running off and dragging up more wood all the time. I even learned a few of the constellations. They're really easy. I mean at first they're just stars, but once you start getting them placed in your mind the whole sky starts dividing up into patterns like a quilt. And you can't look up without seeing, recognizing, Andromeda and Orion and the bears and the seven sisters. It's amazing.

**LOUISE** I can't even find the Big Dipper.

**CARRIE** Oh, you could—there's a way—you just have to find Polaris— well, I mean, I couldn't either, but you learn. Orion is the one though, you've seen him, you just didn't know what he was.

**LOUISE** I don't imagine.

**CARRIE** No, you had to. He's the one that you say, I'll bet anything that's some damn constellation. This is Orion. See, there are three stars— (*On the table, with her finger, dot, dot, dot,*) big ones across. That's the belt. And here . . . (*To the audience.*) Do you know this? (*Back to Louise.*) . . . perpendicular to the belt there are three more, closer together and fainter. (*On the table.*) And that's his sword. And this—the center star in the sword is the Great Nebula in Orion.

**LOUISE** The Great Nebula in Orion.

**CARRIE** Or of Orion, whichever. Which isn't a star at all.

**LOUISE** Of course not.

**CARRIE** Do you know this ?

**LOUISE** No. (*To the audience.*) Crocked, right? Plastered.

**CARRIE** Well, it's very interesting. The Great Nebula is a lot of hydrogen gas that's lit up by a couple of stars behind it somewhere, and some by its own heat, because it's condensing. It's moving, like a whirlpool all the time and getting tighter and tighter—what was that?

**LOUISE** (*Who has uttered a polite "umm" at "tighter."*) Nothing.

**CARRIE** And hotter and hotter—and it will keep getting more and more compact and hotter and smaller—I mean it's vast—and tighter and smaller until it's so hot and compact—just a ball of fire, burning by itself—that it will be a star. And we could actually see that. I mean the center star, we could see that it was fuzzy; a big fuzzy spot. And Dick said that would be a star someday.

**LOUISE** A star is born.

**CARRIE** Oh, come on. I thought it was interesting.

**LOUISE** I think you had to be there.

**CARRIE** Well, in any case you can't see it in Boston. The sky is so hazy you can't even find the sword.

**LOUISE** In New York you're damn lucky to find the sky.

**CARRIE** Well, we can usually see the belt but no more. I kept wishing you'd come out there. I wrote you didn't I?

**LOUISE** I was working, darling, I couldn't. . . .

**CARRIE** But you'd have loved it.

**LOUISE** I went to California once and I didn't love it. I wasn't having a whirlwind courtship and marrying a catch.

**CARRIE** (*Brief pause.*) It was kind of a whirlwind, wasn't it? More whirlwind than courtship. We had two dates, David said will you and I said where's Boston and we were having breakfast with his mother. On the terrace.

**LOUISE** And you forgot about astronomy.

**CARRIE** Well, Roth had pulled his remove to Australia, just a few . . .

**LOUISE** Weeks?

**CARRIE** Days . . . days . . .

**LOUISE** Well, he sounds kind of silly anyway.

**CARRIE** But he was fun though. You really would have loved it. You weren't working at anything important.

**LOUISE** No, I suppose not actually; but it was nice. It was a good year all around. You should have asked Roth what sign the moon was in.

**CARRIE** Oh, he didn't know anything about astrology; he hated it. Of course by now he's probably gone totally occult.

**LOUISE** And New York at the time was—different. Charmed or something. I'd never been here and the girl I roomed with—here—this very apartment—we found it—she was new to the city too.

**CARRIE** She was Bryn Mawr?

**LOUISE** Yes. But I don't think you knew her.

**CARRIE** It's a very exciting city. I don't know though, with all the crime. Of course it's just as bad in Boston, but somehow anything that happens in New York is glamorized or something. Maybe more does happen here.

**LOUISE** (*Who has been adrift. Waking up, after a beat.*) What? I'm sorry, darling. What?

**CARRIE** Nothing, I was just rattling on. Listen, it's late. . . .

**LOUISE** (*Longish pause. Waking again.*) What? Oh, God, I'm sorry. (*To the audience.*) God that's embarrassing.

**CARRIE** (*Fishing into her shoes.*) That's all right I should go. Oooo.

**LOUISE** Have another drink.

**CARRIE** Well, I guess. I don't really want to shop. . . . I'm out of the mood. There's nothing I can't really get in Boston.

**LOUISE** You're here another day.

**CARRIE** (*Standing, walking about.*) It's really a lovely apartment. You have another room. It's bigger than I— (*Opens the door.*)

**LOUISE** Oh, don't go in there, darling. It's a mess. You know me. (*Carrie retreats, rather startled, just a little.*) It's just the bedroom.

**CARRIE** It's large.

**LOUISE** It's such a mess. Here. Cheers.

**CARRIE** Yes. (*They sip, Carrie sits back down, looking puzzled.*)

**LOUISE** I really am a terrible housekeeper. We're both going to be stone drunk in the middle of the afternoon and create a scandal. Boston Society Girl and famed designer arrested for etc., etc.

**CARRIE** I know. Think of the ladies clubs. Well, I suppose Boston has the best fish markets in the country, that's something. There and Maine, and we have a place in Maine. I really—I really hate fish, I—

**LOUISE** That's funny.

**CARRIE** I can't even walk down half the streets,

**LOUISE** Listen, I want to appear sometimes at work in overalls.

**CARRIE** What?

**LOUISE** I don't know, I think I'm a little fuzzy. What did you call that? The great fuzz in Orion—?

**CARRIE** (*Away.*) Belt. Er, uh, Nebula. The great nebula.

**LOUISE** I'd like to be there.

**CARRIE** Yes. (*Pause.*) David is very chowder; a chowder person.

**LOUISE** (*Reviving.*) Listen, why don't you write for a change now that I've—that we've re-established some kind of—now— (*Laughing.*) I don't know what I'm saying.

**CARRIE** I know I'm going to be very popular, having—I'll tell them lunch—with my famous alumna.

**LOUISE** Tell them to buy something.

**CARRIE** Oh, they will; they'll have to.

**LOUISE** I want to do a whole line for little girls. Your little girl is so adorable—women overdress their little girls, I'd love that. Call it the— what's her name?

**CARRIE** Alice.

**LOUISE** The Alice Line.

**CARRIE** She'd be very proud. (*Carrie has on her jacket, she stands now.*)

**LOUISE** (*Superficially, phony.*) It's really been fun, Carrie.

**CARRIE** (*The same.*) Hasn't it? I'm so glad I— (*Stops, biting her lip. Covers her eyes with her hand. Louise looks at her, painfully, Carrie sits down. Louise sits down beside her. Carrie is trying very hard not to cry.*)

**LOUISE** Carrie. Can I get . . . what?

**CARRIE** (*Shaking her head, not looking up. Weakly.*) No, nothing. (*Now looking at her.*) Louise, I saw her picture, Phyllis' picture in your—I'm sorry, I didn't mean—I didn't know . . . I had no idea . . . I'd. . . .

**LOUISE** (*Looking away.*) Well, we all have our. (*Biting her lip, Carrie begins to cry openly.*) You don't want to go back, do you?

**CARRIE** (*Breaking down completely.*) No. (*Sobbing openly, audibly, shaking her head:*) No, no, I can't . . . no. (*Louise begins to cry now too. They sit at opposite ends of the sofa. Carrie reaches out her hand, Louise takes it, grasping hard, tightly. They continue crying openly. Not looking at one another. Carrie withdraws her hand, opens her purse, blows her nose.*) Ma-maybe—(*They look at each other now, their faces bathed in tears, both with the same thought, trying to laugh, shaking their heads up and down in agreement.*) Maybe Richard Roth ran off with Phyllis Trahaunt.

**LOUISE** (*Who has said "Phyllis" with her.*) Yes, yes . . . (*wiping her face.*) Damn my face.

**CARRIE** What are we going to do ?

**LOUISE** I don't know, Carrie. I don't know. I've not known for six god-damned years.

**CARRIE** I know.

**LOUISE** Maybe David'll build us a little rocket ship in his workshop, huh? We'll fly off to your. . . . (*A motion with her hand, crying again.*)

**CARRIE** (*Crying, trying to laugh.*) Nebula.

**LOUISE** Do you think he could?

**CARRIE** No. No. (*They laugh.*) He's a terrible carpenter. He is.

**LOUISE** I suspected as much.

**CARRIE** (*Blowing her nose again.*) Oh, he only spends his time out there because he can't understand why I'm always in such a foul mood. I look like hell—Oh, I don't care. (*She stares off.*)

**LOUISE** You could ask his sister where. . . .

**CARRIE** No, I couldn't. She's married, I don't really know her. I couldn't anyway.

**LOUISE** I guess. . . .

CARRIE  Where did Phyllis . . . ?

LOUISE  Thin air, darling.

CARRIE  I'd forgotten how lovely. . . .

LOUISE  Oh, don't. Her parents wouldn't answer my *"enquiries"*—she was very honest with them, so they didn't think much of me. I stay in this apartment because if . . .

CARRIE  (*A long pause. Finally picking up her gloves.*) Well.

LOUISE  Oh, don't go.

CARRIE  The thought of that hotel room is a bit—

LOUISE  Stay. We'll fix ourselves up and go out to a film. Have some great fattening dinner—you can have the sofabed; it's miles better than mine. They floodlight the Planetarium at night it makes a great nightlight coming through the window.

CARRIE  I don't know if I need that. (*With some humor.*)

LOUISE  Take your pick. (*Carrie smiles.*) Good.

CARRIE  The thought of that hotel. . . .

LOUISE  Darling, the thought of anything.

CARRIE  (*Neither moves.*) I had such great ideas of changing the world . . . you remember. I always thought . . .

LOUISE  We're better off than most. . . .

CARRIE  They keep telling us.

LOUISE  Umm.

CARRIE  I worked so diligently, and believed so. . . .

LOUISE  Yes, didn't we.

CARRIE  (*With a sigh.*) Oh, God, Louise. . . .

LOUISE  It's all just a great . . . (*They sit, huddled in their separate corners of the sofa.*)

CARRIE  (*Pause.*) The ironic thing. . . .

LOUISE  (*Pause.*) Of course it's all. . . .

CARRIE  Any other woman would be. . . .

LOUISE  . . . Yes. . . .

CARRIE  (*A long pause. The lights begin to fade, very slowly. They hardly move, staring off, lost in mixed images.*) It's all such a. . . .

LOUISE  (*A long pause. With just a touch of humor.*) The terribly . . . ironic . . . thing . . . (*A long pause. The lights fade out completely.*)

## CURTAIN

# THE FAMILY CONTINUES  (May 1972)
*dedicated to the members of the Circle Theater Company and their director.*

## AUTHOR'S NOTE

Rob Thirkield, Tanya Berezin, and Marshall W. Mason started Circle Rep on July 14, 1969. They always throw me in as one of the four founders, and I did go with them to look at the large empty loft above a Thom McAn shoe store, but I was of little help the first two years. I was reeling from the spectacular five performance failure of THE GINGHAM DOG, my Broadway baptism.

During that first summer the Circle Rep company moved to Woodstock, N.Y., rehearsing THREE SISTERS the whole summer. I didn't visit them once. They wanted to produce LEMON SKY, but there was no one in the company to play the father. By the time they presented their first production, still the best Chekhov I've ever seen, I was shuttling back and forth between Washington, D.C. where the Washington Theater Club was in rehearsal for the premier of a new final draft of SERENADING LOUIE and Buffalo, where the Studio Arena was giving the first professional production of LEMON SKY. Several producers came to Washington to see LOUIE and decided it was too much of a downer to take to New York. LEMON SKY moved from Buffalo to a 500 seat house in N.Y., got to-dream-about raves and closed after seven performances.

Then I limped back to my friends and threw myself into menial labor, building sets, platforms, cleaning, etc. at Circle Rep, only to discover that not only had I not written anything in a year, but that I could not write anything. This massive writer's block lasted another six months.

In their second season Marshall decided to do GREAT NEBULA and IKKE NYE on a double bill. Since both plays have only two actors, I felt they employed too few members of the large company. Using a number of exercises Marshall had been working on, I wrote THE FAMILY CONTINUES to showcase more of the company, and give some of the other actors a challenge. Only after I finished it did I realize that I had writted something! With the success of that triple bill, the next logical move was to write the company a full length play for the following season. THE HOT L BALTIMORE opened at Circle Theater on February 4, 1973, moved Off-Broadway, and ran over three years.

THE FAMILY CONTINUES was presented by the Circle Theater Company, 2307 Broadway, New York City on May 21, 1972 and again October 12, 1972 in a new production. Members of the company appearing in one of the two productions include: Henrietta Bagley, Patricia Carey, Stephen De Fluiter, Bradford Dourif, Conchata Ferrell, Michael Fesenmeier, Victory Levi, Eliza Miller, Pinocchio Madrid, Sharon A. Madden, David Stekol, Antony Tenuta, Trish Hawkins, and Rob Thirkield. Mr. Dourif was Steve Jr. and Mr. Tenuta played Steve in both productions. The play was designed and directed by Marshall W. Mason.

THE FAMILY CONTINUES was written for the Circle Theater Company and should be considered a game, an exercise in swift characterization and ensemble co-operation. Of the two productions done at Circle the second, using only eight members of the company, seemed to me the more efficient. The text is printed here with minimal stage directions to encourage directors and actors to work as unfettered as possible: any decisive activity based on observed behavior is permissible either abstracted or mimed. There should be no furniture and no props used in the production. There can be a bench for the actors to retire to when not speaking. Take as many liberties with the text as you want. In the second Circle production it was felt that the first time eight people speak at once, not everyone could be heard clearly. The parts were done two at a time, then repeated all eight at once (and during the repeat the actors somehow formed a car, Steve and the Girl at School got in it, and suddenly the car ran into the kid—the actor playing the kid went flying through the air landing splat! on the floor while the Narrator called out Phase three. As the Circle company is more than usually acrobatic I don't encourage everyone to try it, but it was effective.) Try anything to illustrate Steve's life as it passes him by. I feel it essential for the piece to be done simply and with a sense of joy in creation. I can't see it benefiting from a "down" production. There is no pause in the continual flow of words, unless indicated: one line comes immediately on the next or, sometimes, overlapping some. After Steve Jr. is born much of the dialog is spoken completely overlapping. It is not at all necessary, or even intended, for all the words to be heard. Think always of the total rather than the parts.

We found when two people are speaking at the same time they have a tendency to raise their voices. This makes it impossible to understand either. When two people are speaking in a normal tone at the same time it is possible to hear and understand both.

One wide spot (or that effect) on eight actors who divide the twenty-six parts among them, all except Steve (and at the director's discretion the Narrator) playing more than one part. Some will play five or more.
L.W.

# THE FAMILY CONTINUES

*The Narrator, Steve, Mother and Father stand.*

**NARRATOR**   Phase one. Getting born, learning to walk, learning to talk, the family, meeting a playmate, going to grandma's.

**ALL**   (*Softly, as Steve appears, getting born.*) Ahhhhhhhhhh!

**MOTHER**   Ouch. Damn.

**STEVE**   Wow, that hurt. (*Tries to stand, takes a flop.*)

**FATHER**   Looks just like his old man.

**STEVE**   (*Managing to stand.*) Hi, there!

**MOTHER**   Isn't he the sweetest thing?

**STEVE**   My name is Steven.

**GRANDMA**   That's a turkey.

**STEVE**   Call me Steve.

**GRANDMA**   And that's a chicken.

**STEVE**   I said my name is—

**GRANDMA**   And that's a duck!

**STEVE**   A what?

**NARRATOR**   Phase two.

**STEVE**   What's yours?

**NARRATOR**   Going to school, getting an education—

**STEVE**   What's yours? (*Pause.*) What's YOURS?

**NARRATOR**   (*Continued.*) The family continues, learning to get along, getting into trouble, trying to belong, graduation.

**STEVE**   (*Disgusted, to no one special.*) This is crap.

**NARRATOR**   (*Repeating for Steve's benefit.*) Phase two. Going to school—

**STEVE**   (*Shading his eyes, into the light or toward the light control booth.*) Is he going to talk through the whole thing? Cause if he is this is crap. OK, OK, OK, that ain't his ball, that ain't his ball, that ain't his ball.

**NARRATOR**   (*Continued.*) —getting an education, the family continues learning to get along, getting into trouble, trying to belong, graduation.

**STEVE**   (*After the Narrator finishes, a beat. Disgusted.*) That ain't his ball; that's my ball.

**FIRST FEMALE TEACHER**   That *isn't* his ball.

**STEVE**   That ain't his paint box, either.

**MALE TEACHER**   That *isn't* his paint box, Steve.

**STEVE**   Yeah, and it ain't your book.

**STUDENT**   It certainly is.

**SECOND FEMALE TEACHER**   That *isn't* his book i-thur, Steve.

**STEVE**   You damn right it ain't and it ain't his girl either. (*Aside to the light.*) This is really crap.

**GIRL AT SCHOOL**   I have a right to decide for myself whose girl I am. I'm a person too, you know; and I don't think very much of a person like you.

**STEVE**   (*Continued—to the girl, the narrator and to the light.*) OK. Would you shut up? Shut her up. This is really—That ain't your car and I—shut her up. (*The girl at school shuts up.*)

**STEVE**   (*Beat.*) Ain't his car either, you're lying through your teeth.

**SECOND STUDENT**   It certainly is.

**STEVE**   It ain't his car and I ain't the one who wrecked it.

**ALL SPEAK AT ONCE:**

**MOTHER**   I don't know what to do with him, you don't seem to be able to do anything with him. It was just an accident.

**FATHER**   Don't look at me, you call that steak? That ain't no steak. That ain't even pork chops. And I don't know the little bastard.

**FIRST FEMALE TEACHER**   That *isn't* his car, Steve; only it certainly *is* his car and certainly you wrecked it. You stole it and you wrecked it.

**GIRL AT SCHOOL**   He isn't a respectable type of person and he doesn't respect other people as people and I have a right to go with people like my own people.

**MALE TEACHER**   I realize your family is not what it should be, and you haven't the advantages other young men do, but this recklessness can't be overlooked.

**SECOND FEMALE TEACHER**   Oh, that poor boy, that poor little boy, that he is lying cold in his grave when Steve is alive; that poor poor boy.

**NARRATOR**   (*Continuing past the others.*) Phase three. Enlistment and leaving home, basic training and two years service, killing his second person, drunk and disorderly, A.W.O.L., dishonorable discharge, getting out.

**STEVE**   (*Going past everyone, including the narrator; hearing nobody.*) It was a lousy car, what the hell was it doing with the keys in the ignition if he liked it so much. Oh, crap. And that boy ran right out in front of the car so he deserved everything he got, so don't expect remorse or nothing from an innocent victim who didn't have a chance in the first place. (*The Narrator has finished, leaving Steve talking alone, he realizes now that the Narrator has spoken. Glares at him.*) What was that? (*Beat.*) You. Yeah, yeah, come on, man. (*Under his breath.*) Crap, man.

**NARRATOR**  (*Calmly, as always, repeating.*) Phase three. (*Steve waits, glaring belligerently through this.*) Enlistment and leaving home. Basic training and two years service—

**STEVE**  (*Over.*) Yeah, yeah. (*Meaning, like so what.*)

**NARRATOR**  (*Continuing without a break.*)—killing his second person, drunk and disorderly, A.W.O.L.

**STEVE**  (*To himself, disgusted.*) What a lot of crap. . . .

**NARRATOR**  —dishonorable discharge, getting out. (*Waits a beat.*) Phase four.

**STEVE**  Aw, shit.

**NARRATOR**  The filling station.

**WOMAN DRIVER**  It just goes tinkle,

**STEVE**  Yeah, me too, lady.

**WOMAN DRIVER**  And then it goes crick crick.

**STEVE**  (*Continuous, until he trails off during the girl's speech.*) Your problem is you're driving around a piece of junk.

**MAN DRIVER**  Fill it up,

**STEVE**  (*Without stop.*) You pay eight thousand clams for a chrome—what *change*?—junkheap and—

**FILLING STATION OWNER**  (*Over.*) Steve, customer. Hop to it!

**SECOND WOMAN DRIVER**  (*Honking.*) Beep, beep, beep, beep, beep, beep, beep, beep, beep, beep.

**STEVE**  —expect the pisser to run too. What'll it be? Open the goddamned hood you want me to look inside the mother—blow it out your ass.

**FILLING STATION OWNER**  Hop to it, Steve.

**STEVE**  (*Without stopping.*) Cold enough to freeze the balls off a wooly rhinoceros and—(*The girl begins her soft interested prattle, Steve continues without hearing her until be realizes someone is talking.*)—the bitch wants—up yours too ya mother. This is all a lot of. . . . (*Trails off noticing the girl.*)

**GIRL**  (*Beginning above, over Steve.*) I first noticed you at the store cause everything you bought was canned or frozen and then I saw you hustling all around the cars and I thought the breath comes out of his mouth when he runs around the pumps and I can't tell if he's smoking or if it's really that cold outside and when I saw you at the store again and then here at the coffee shop I thought he really does have very beautiful eyes and really very beautiful hands.

**STEVE**  (*Whose belligerent look has faded to an attempt to communicate. Eyes averted, voice almost lost, be immediately shoves his bands in his pockets, or behind his back.*) Yeah . . . well the crap they try to pull around. . . . (*Looks up belligerently again.*)

**GIRL**  And I thought, I wonder if he's ever had a warm meal instead of wolfing those french fries and where does he live and. . . .

**THEY SPEAK AT ONCE:**

> **STEVE** Yeah, well, with twenty minutes off for lunch you're lucky to get that. The shit they feed you around here: coffee to go, sugar in a little bag. Drive in for their grease jobs on the coldest friggin' day of the year.
>
> **GIRL** (*Wistfully.* —does he have a steady girl and what would his voice sound like when he's not shouting at the drivers and trying to get out of washing the windshields and if he sleeps by himself.

**STEVE** (*Hearing the last.*) Huh? What?

**NARRATOR** Phase five.

**STEVE** (*Overlapping a touch.*) Yeah, yeah, we're way ahead of you.

**GIRL'S MOTHER** You work in a service station, then.

**GIRL** Very ambitious.

**GIRL'S FATHER** For the meantime maybe?

**GIRL'S MOTHER** Around the gas pumps and so on?

**GIRL** Mechanically inclined.

**GIRL'S FATHER** Yeah, I'm sure.

**GIRL'S MOTHER** Is that right?

**STEVE** Yeah, what of it?

**GIRL'S FATHER** (*With loathing.*) She's a good little girl.

**GIRL'S MOTHER** Such a rebellious little darling. Picking up stray cats; birds with—

**THEY SPEAK AT ONCE:**

> **GIRL'S FATHER** Developed almost overnight. Has no idea what a woman is for; doesn't know she's a grown up girl. Doesn't know what a man expects.
>
> **GIRL'S MOTHER** —broken wings, learning how to cook and bake and sew and taking a typing course so she could get a nice job and meet some better people or follow an office career.
>
> **GIRL** (*Alone with Steve.*) I've always liked your hair and the way you almost don't snore, just breathe very heavily and it sounds like something's bothering you—
>
> **STEVE** I don't know what you expect I don't know what you want. I don't know what you expect.
>
> **GIRL** —sometimes and then you'll suddenly smile, while you're still asleep and I don't know what to think. . . .

**STEVE** Man, this is such a pile of. . . .

**MOTHER** I just think she's lovely. She's a pretty little thing.

**FATHER** Looks to me like you got your mind already made up if you think you're ready. I personally—

**MOTHER** —Almost too pretty.

**FATHER** —don't think you're ready. I don't think you know what it's all about. I think you're still the little bastard that stole that car and ran over that poor little kid.

**ALL SPEAK AT ONCE:** (*Note: in the Circle Theater Production the two who were not speaking hummed the wedding march. Steve and the Girl—everyone, in fact, mimed a wedding ceremony.*)

**GIRL'S FATHER** Unheard of. Out of the question! I'll drag your ass through every court in the country if you think you can pull something like this.

**FATHER** I don't think you know a goddamned thing about a goddamned thing is what I think, if you want to know.

**GIRL'S MOTHER** (*Crying loudly.*) What? Oh, my girl. Oh, my god. Oh, my little girl, Oh, my god, Oh, shit. I've never heard of such shit.

**MOTHER** It isn't the right time. Later, after you get on your own feet; after you know more; after you learn. After all!

**STEVE** (*Beginning later—leading the Girl c., where they kneel.*) We happen to not care a damn if you like it or not because we don't intend to live with either of you. We'll live up over the garage till we can get a place and we'll do fine without either one of you mothers thank you very much. (*Speaking alone by now, kneeling with the girl.*) We'll just live over the goddamned garage and be a hell of a lot happier if you god-damned well decide to leave us to ourselves.

(*A second of silence.*)

**GIRL** (*Softly, eyes down.*) OK.

**NARRATOR** (*Immediately.*) Phase six.

**STEVE** Oh, knock it off.

**NARRATOR** Failing to make it.

**STEVE** What? Failings ass, fellow!

**WOMAN DRIVER** It just goes gasp and then it goes tinkle.

**STEVE** What? (*The filling station reforms.*)

**WOMAN DRIVER** It just goes tinkle.

**STEVE** Yeah, me too, lady.

**GIRL** (*At the same time as the filling station, with no one paying attention to her.*) I really expected you to take everything easier and not yell at everybody so, and even at yourself. I can't make any sense out of you at all. Sometimes I think you only married me to get away from home and I don't like that because I miss my folks but I don't think I would if you'd be more with me.

**WOMAN DRIVER** (*In immediate answer to Steve.*) And then it goes crick crick.

**STEVE** Your problem is you're driving around a piece of junk.

**MAN DRIVER** Fill it up.

**STEVE** You pay eight thousand clams for a chrome—what *change?*—

junkheap and—

**FILLING STATION OWNER**   Steve, customer. Hop to it!

**SECOND WOMAN DRIVER**   (*Over the following.*) Beep, beep, beep, beep, beep, beep, beep, beep, beep, beep.

**STEVE**   —expect the pisser to run too. What'll it be? Open the god-damned hood you want me to look inside the mother—blow it out your ass.

**FILLING STATION OWNER**   Hop to it, Steve.

**STEVE**   Cold enough to freeze the balls off a wooly rhinoceros and the bitch wants—up yours too ya mother! This is a lot of . . . (*Trails off noticing the Second Friend's Old Lady.*)

**FRIEND**   (*Overlapping Steve some.*) Don't let her get you down.

**SECOND FRIEND**   You should see my old lady.

**SECOND FRIEND'S OLD LADY**   I know a place you can really kick up your heels.

**STEVE**   She's all right, she's OK.

**FRIEND**   Don't let her get you down.

**STEVE**   She's all right, she's OK.

**SECOND FRIEND**   You should see my old lady.

**STEVE**   She's OK, she's all right. (*He straddles the girl and the Second Friend's Old Lady. Standing. This sexual act, since it represents Steve's relations with his wife and the Second Friend's Old Lady, is condensed into one treble coupling. It should certainly not be realistic. The important thing is to see Steve in over his head again.*)

**GIRL**   (*They talk at the same time, she speaks somewhat slower.*) It was a nice day, it was a pretty day, we're running out of bread and we're running out of sugar but it was so sunny and warm and when you're with me like this I think everything is just fine and I feel so secure and warm and soft and so close to you because I know you really do care for me and I know you don't really let the service station get on your nerves when you're with me like this and you really do love me and hold me and I really do love you and hold you who—oooo. Oh. Oh. Oooohhhhh!

**SECOND FRIEND'S OLD LADY**   (*Rattling it off.*) He won't come home what are you so worried about? We'll be quiet as little mice. I just dig you, I'm not falling for you, I just dig your terrific body; you're built like a school teacher I used to have and we used to do it in the basement of the gym after last period. Go to it! Talk to me! Say "You're better than basketball!" That's what he used to say. My husband is a shit, Steve. My husband is nothing! Oh, my god I think you're coming. Oh, my god, I think I'm coming. Tell me when you come. Yell out "Sally" that's my name, Sally! Like you was a dying bull. Don't worry about the old man that shit is hard of hearing—ing

—ing—argh—grang—aghhhhhhhhhh! (*The two girls reach this "climax" at the same time. Steve drops them both onto the floor.*)

**STEVE** (*Exhausted, panting, to himself.*) Oh, crap, man, I can't cut this crap. . . .

**NARRATOR** Phase seven.

**STEVE** (*Panting, holding up a hand.*) Hold it. Wait a second.

**NARRATOR** Phase seven—

**STEVE** (*Panting.*) Surprise me—

**NARRATOR** —The family continues, managing the station—

**STEVE** Managing! Get that? Manager! OK, boy—customer—hop to it!

**SECOND WOMAN DRIVER** Beep, beep, beep, beep, beep.

**NARRATOR** —getting born, learning to walk, learning to talk, the family, meeting a playmate, going to grandma's. (*The birth scene from the beginning is repeated as Steve Jr. is born.*)

**ALL** (*Softly, as Steve Jr. appears, getting born.*) Ahhhhhhhhhh!

**GIRL** Ouch. Damn.

**STEVE JR.** Wow, that hurt. (*Tries to stand, takes a flop.*)

**STEVE** Looks just like his old man.

**STEVE JR.** (*Managing to stand.*) Hi there!

**GIRL** Isn't he the sweetest thing?

**STEVE JR.** My name is Steven.

**GIRL'S MOTHER** That's a turkey.

**STEVE JR.** Call me Steve.

**GIRL'S MOTHER** And that's a chicken.

**STEVE JR.** I said my name is—

**GIRL'S MOTHER** And that's a duck!

**STEVE JR.** A what?

**NARRATOR** Phase two.

**STEVE JR.** What's yours?

> **STEVE** (*His dialogue is continuous now, over Steve Jr. and the Narrator:*) Wait a minute. Wait a—who's going to pay for the for the little bastard? Cause look, I want to show you what there is in the till, here—

**NARRATOR** Going to school, getting an education, the family continues, learning to get along, getting into trouble, trying to belong, graduation.

> **STEVE JR.** What's yours? (*Pause.*) What's YOURS?

**STEVE JR.** (*Disgusted, to no one special.*) This is crap.

**STEVE** (*Continuing—digging into his pocket, counting change.*) Cause this is what there is. Ten, thirty-five, sixty, sixty-five, seventy, eighty . . . a dollar five. . . . (*To the others.*) Oh, shit, man! Keep it down.

**STEVE JR.** (*Shading his eyes, into the light or toward the light control booth.*) Is he going to talk through the whole thing? Cause if he is this is crap. OK, OK, OK, that ain't his ball, that ain't his ball, that ain't his ball. . . .

**NARRATOR** (*Repeating for Steve Jr.'s benefit.*) Phase two. Going to school, getting an education, the family continues, learning to get along, getting into trouble, trying to belong, graduation.

**STEVE** (*After the Narrator finishes, a beat. Disgusted.*) That ain't his ball, that's my ball.

**STEVE** A dollar five, ten, twenty, a dollar forty-five, fifty-five, sixty, sixty-five, seventy, seventy-five, two dollars. Two dollars five, six, seven, eight. Two—oh—eight.

**FIRST FEMALE TEACHER** That *isn't* his ball.

**STEVE JR.** That ain't his paint box, either.

**MALE TEACHER** That *isn't* his paint box, Steve.

**STEVE JR.** Yeah, and it ain't your book.

**STUDENT** It certainly is.

**STEVE** (*Continued.*) Plus what I got in the service station which is mostly mortgages. Get a loan on this to pay for that, get a loan on that to pay for the other and the friggin' that is worn out before the friggin' this is paid for, and the bank says they can't give you a loan on the other to get a new this.

**GIRL** (*After Steve.*) I don't know what you're talking about half the time, I really don't.

**SECOND FEMALE TEACHER** That *isn't* his book i-thur, Steve.

**STEVE JR.** You damn right it ain't and it ain't his girl either. (*Aside to the light.*) This is really crap.

**GIRL AT SCHOOL** I have a right to decide for myself whose girl I am, I'm a person, too, you know; and I don't think very much of a person like you.

**STEVE JR.** (*At the same time.*) OK. Would you shut up? Shut her up. This is really—That ain't your car and I shut her up. (*The girl at school shuts up.*)

**STEVE** Ain't his car either; he stole the damn car.

**STEVE JR.** Ain't his car either, you're lying through your teeth.

**SECOND STUDENT** It certainly is.

**GIRL** He certainly did.

**STEVE JR.** Ain't his car and I ain't the one who wrecked it.

**STEVE** Stole the car and he's the one that wrecked it.

**ALL SPEAK AT ONCE:**

    **GIRL** I don't know what to do with him, you don't seem to be able to do anything with him. It was just an accident.

    **STEVE** Don't look at me, you call that steak? That ain't no steak. That ain't even pork chops. And I don't know the little bastard.

    **FIRST FEMALE TEACHER** That isn't his car, Steve; only it certainly is his car and certainly you wrecked it. You stole it and you wrecked it.

**GIRL AT SCHOOL**   He isn't a respectable type of person and he doesn't respect other people as people and I have a right to go with people like my own people.

**MALE TEACHER**   I realize your family is not what it should be and you haven't the advantages other young men do but this recklessness can't be overlooked.

**SECOND FEMALE TEACHER**   Oh, that poor boy, that poor little boy, that he is lying cold in his grave when Steve is alive; that poor poor boy.

**NARRATOR**   (*Continuing past the others.*) Phase three. Enlistment and leaving home, basic training and two years service, killing his second person, drunk and disorderly, A.W.O.L., dishonorable discharge, getting out. Phase eight. Getting drunk, ten years go.

**STEVE JR.**   It was a lousy car, what the hell was it doing with the keys in the ignition if he liked it so much. Oh, crap. And that boy ran right out in front of the car so he deserved everything he got so don't expect remorse or nothing from an innocent victim who didn't have a chance in the first place. (*Realizes the narrator has said something.*)

**STEVE**   WHAT?

**STEVE JR.**   What?

**NARRATOR**   Phase eight. Getting drunk, ten years go.

**STEVE JR.**   What was that? You, yeah, yeah, come on, man. Crap, man.

**STEVE**   Yeah, well, let me tell you that's the first realistic thing you've said with those two bitches on my back and that dumb bastard a-wol; reckless bastard, he doesn't know his ass.

**NARRATOR**   (*To Steve Jr.*) Phase three. Enlistment and leaving home. Basic training and two years service—

**STEVE JR.**   (*Over.*) Yeah, yeah.

**NARRATOR**   —killing his second person, drunk and disorderly, A.W.O.L.—

**STEVE JR.**   (*To himself disgusted.*) What a lot of crap. . . .

**NARRATOR**   —Dishonorable discharge, getting out. (*Waits a beat.*)

**NARRATOR**   (*Continued.*) Phase four.

**STEVE JR.**   Aw, shit.

**NARRATOR**   The filling station.

**STEVE**   Crap.

**WOMAN DRIVER**   It just goes tinkle.

**STEVE JR.**   Yeah, me too, lady.

**WOMAN DRIVER**   And then it goes crick crick.

**STEVE JR.**   (*Continuous as before.*) Your problem is you're driving around a piece of junk.

**MAN DRIVER**   Fill it up.

**STEVE JR.**   You pay eight thousand clams for a chrome—what *change?*—junkheap and—

**STEVE**   Steve, customer. Hop to it!

**SECOND WOMAN DRIVER**   Beep, beep, beep, beep, beep, beep, beep, beep, beep, beep.

**STEVE JR.**   —expect the pisser to run too. What'll it be? Open the goddamned hood you want me to look inside the mother—blow it out your ass.

**STEVE**   Hop to it, Steve.

**STEVE JR.**   Cold enough to freeze the balls off a wooly rhinoceros and . . . (*The Second Girl begins.*) —the bitch wants—up yours too ya mother. This is all a lot of . . . (*Trails off noticing the girl.*)

   **STEVE**   (*Beginning at the same time as the Second Girl.*) Goddamned racket is what. Fuckin' sellin' grease and gas, what the hell kind of part do you think you're giving me here. Screwin' thinking I didn't hear that? "Ten years go." Crap! I ain't got wax in my ears by a long shot. Gettin' drunk. You think you can pull that shit? (*To Steve Jr. and the Second Girl.*) Would you knock it off? Learn to learn. Listen and learn something why don't you. Shut up and learn a thing. Two dollars and eight cents. And a mortgaged gas pump. That fucking leaks man—is why. Shit, man! Crap!

   **SECOND GIRL**   (*Beginning above, over Steve Jr.*) I first noticed you at the store cause everything you bought was canned or frozen and then I saw you hustling all around the cars and I thought the breath comes out of his mouth when he runs around the pumps and I can't tell if he's smoking or if it's really that cold outside and when I saw you at the store again and then here at the coffee shop I thought he really does have very beautiful eyes and really very beautiful hands.

   **STEVE JR.**   Yeah, well, the crap they try to pull around. . . .

   **SECOND GIRL**   And I thought I wonder if he's ever had a warm meal instead of wolfing those french fries and where does he live and. . . .

   **STEVE JR.**   (*They speak at the same time.*) Yeah, well, with twenty minutes off for lunch you're lucky to get that. The shit they feed you around here: coffee to go, sugar in a little bag. Drive in for their grease jobs on the coldest friggin' day of the year. . . .

   **SECOND GIRL**   (*Wistfully.*) —does he have a steady girl and what would his voice sound like when he's not shouting at the drivers and trying to get out of washing the windshields and if he sleeps by himself.

   **STEVE**   (*Into the light.*) What is this shit? I can't hear myself think. Is this shit going to stay like this cause I was told that I would have the light, man. So if it is, you can cram it, fellow, is all I got to say to it.

**STEVE JR.** (*Hearing the last the girl said.*) Huh? What?

**NARRATOR**  Phase five.

**STEVE**  Yeah, yeah, five? How did we get from eight to . . . ? (*Fades off as the girl's family begins. He watches the scene trying to recall it.*)

**STEVE JR.**  Yeah, yeah, we're way ahead of you.

**SECOND GIRL'S MOTHER**  You work in a service station, then.

**SECOND GIRL**  Very ambitious.

**SECOND GIRL'S FATHER**  For the meantime maybe?

**SECOND GIRL'S MOTHER**  Around the gas pumps and so on?

**SECOND GIRL**  Mechanically inclined.

**SECOND GIRL'S FATHER**  Yeah, I'm sure.

**SECOND GIRL'S MOTHER**  Is that right?

**STEVE JR.**  Yeah, what of it?

**SECOND GIRL'S FATHER**  She's a good little girl.

**SECOND GIRL'S MOTHER**  Such a rebellious little darling. Picking up stray cats; birds with—

**SECOND GIRL'S FATHER**  Developed almost overnight. Has no idea what a woman is for; doesn't know she's a grown up girl. Doesn't know what a man expects.

**SECOND GIRL'S MOTHER**  —broken wings, learning how to cook and bake and sew and taking a typing course so she could get a nice job and meet some better people or follow an office career.

**SECOND GIRL**  I've always liked your hair and the way you almost don't snore, just breathe very heavily and it sounds like something's bothering you—

**STEVE JR.**  I don't know what you expect, I don't know what you want. I don't know what you expect.

**SECOND GIRL**  Sometimes and then you'll suddenly smile, while you're still asleep and I don't know what to think . . .

**STEVE JR.**  Man, this is such a pile of—

**GIRL**  I just think she's lovely. She's a pretty little thing.

**STEVE**  Looks to me like you got your mind already made up if you think you're ready. I personally—

**GIRL**  Almost too pretty.

**STEVE**  —don't think you're ready. I don't think you know what it's all about. I think you're still the little bastard that stole that car and ran over that poor little kid.

**ALL SPEAK AT ONCE:**

**SECOND GIRL'S FATHER**  Unheard of. Out of the question! I'll drag your ass through every court in the country if you think you can pull something like this.

**STEVE**  I don't think you know a goddamned thing about a goddamned thing is what I think, if you want to know.

**SECOND GIRL'S MOTHER** (*Crying loudly.*) What? Oh, my girl. Oh, my god. Oh, my little girl, oh, my God, oh, shit. I've never heard of such shit.

**GIRL** It isn't the right time. Later, after you get on your own feet, after you know more; after you learn. After all!

**STEVE JR.** (*Beginning later. Leading the Second Girl c., where they kneel.*) We happen to not care a damn if you like it or not because we don't intend to live with either of you. We'll live up over the garage till we can get a place and we'll do fine without either one of you mothers thank you very much. We'll just live over the goddamned garage and be a hell of a lot happier if you goddamned well decide to leave us to ourselves. (*A second of silence.*)

**SECOND GIRL** OK.

**NARRATOR** Phase nine. Old age and senility.

**STEVE** What? What was that?

**NARRATOR** —Phase six. Failing to make it.

**STEVE JR.** Oh, knock it off—What? Failing? Failings ass, fellow.

**STEVE** You're out of your goddamned mind. I said let me see that.

**WOMAN DRIVER** It just goes gasp and then it goes tinkle.

**STEVE JR.** What?

**WOMAN DRIVER** It just goes tinkle.

**STEVE JR.** Yeah, me too, lady.

**SECOND GIRL** (*Over.*) I really expected you to take everything easier and not yell at everybody so, and even at yourself. I can't make any sense out of you at all. Sometimes I think you only married me to get away from home and I don't like that because I miss my folks but I don't think I would if you'd be more with me.

**WOMAN DRIVER** And then it goes crick crick.

**STEVE JR.** Your problem is you're driving around a piece of junk.

**MAN DRIVER** Fill it up.

**NARRATOR** Phase nine.

**STEVE** (*Flying at the Narrator, struggling ineffectively with him.*) I said let me see that. Show me Phase six. I want to see—where is Phase six, god-damnit. Failing to make it. Show me failing to make it back there, because I got shafted you son of a bitch.

**NARRATOR** Phase nine.

**STEVE** No, you bastard you're not going to pull that shit on me. This is shit. I said this was shit, well, this is shit. I don't buy your Phase nine. And I don't buy your Phase one through eight. So you better answer me a few things here. (*Trying to push the Narrator away or down or off stage, to no avail.*) All right then, all right! You mother! Read it out, say it out so I can hear it. So

**STEVE JR.** You pay eight thousand clams for a chrome—what *change?*—junkheap and— (*Looks around for Steve to order him to hop to it, shrugs, goes on.*)

**SECOND WOMAN DRIVER** Beep, beep, beep, beep, beep, beep, beep, beep, beep, beep.

**STEVE JR.** —expect the pisser to run too. What'll it be? Open the goddamned hood you want me to look inside the mother—blow it out your ass. Cold enough to freeze the balls off a wooly rhinoceros and the bitch wants—up yours too ya mother! This is a lot of . . .

**FRIEND** Don't let her get you down.

**SECOND FRIEND** You should see my old lady.

**SECOND FRIEND'S OLD LADY** I know a place you can really kick up your heels.

**STEVE JR.** She's all right, she's OK.

**FRIEND** Don't let her get you down.

**STEVE JR.** She's all right, she's OK.

**SECOND FRIEND** You should see my old lady.

**STEVE JR.** She's OK, she's all right.

(*The Second Girl, The Second Friend's Old Lady, and Steve Jr. begin the coupling scene as before. In the middle they are interrupted as Steve pushes them to the floor. Steve makes a lunge for the narrator, several hold him back until he stops struggling. The others stand with their heads bowed, embarrassed, not watching Steve gasp.*)

**NARRATOR** Old age and senility.

**STEVE** Like hell, too. (*As someone starts to leave the stage.*) Where the hell do you think you're going? (*They stop. All stand motionless, not*

everyone can hear it now. (*To the others who pay no attention to this.*) Shut the hell up—say it so I can hear it.

**NARRATOR** Phase nine.

**STEVE** I don't hear it. I want to hear it. Shut up you dumb fucks! (*He pushes the trio to the floor.*)

*looking at Steve.*) You son of a bitch. You can cram the whole god-damn—shit, man. I was told that I would have a number of specific guarantees here. Well, shit, man. I'm not gonna sweat my balls off for— (*Everyone moves, startling him, then, they stop.*) where's the goddamned kid? You notice there's not a peep out of that mother.

**KID**   Here, Steve.

**STEVE**   (*Looking anywhere but at the actor playing the kid. As the kid is in Steve's deranged mind several actors can divide the part of the kid among them if it makes the point more easily.*) What was you, five years old?

**KID**   Eight years old.

**STEVE**   What was that, sixty years ago?

**KID**   Yes it was.

**STEVE**   Shit. You ran right out in front of me. Where are you?

**KID**   Just here.

**STEVE**   What is it? Worms and that crap?

**KID**   No, all that's over with. It just lasts a little while.

**STEVE**   Where the fuck you supposed to be, heaven?

**KID**   I'm in the ground, Steve.

**STEVE**   Then how the hell can you talk to me like this?

**KID**   I can't.

**STEVE**   All right, who needs it. I had things that—goddamn. (*Disgusted.*) Aw, shit, man. (*Hurt.*) Oh, man. (*He stops, puffing. Looks around. Everyone stands, heads bowed, embarrassed. The Narrator clears his throat.*)

**NARRATOR**   Phase ten. Passing away.

**STEVE**   (*Overcome, stunned, scared, brave.*) Aw, come on, man, shit. (*The others begin to turn and walk away, quite casually, no thought of him—they walk singly off stage. The light on Steve begins to fade.*) Man, come on. Aw, come on, man . . . (*Breathes deeply, holding it in, the Narrator leaves, the last to go. Steve looks toward the fading light, awed. Slowly.*) Come on, man . . . shit, man . . . come on, man. . . . (*The light fades steadily dimmer and is gone.*)

**CURTAIN**

# BRONTOSAURUS (1977)
*for Tanya*


## AUTHOR'S NOTE

Michael Powell's first job in New York City was assistant to a very up-scale interior decorator. My first job was in the office of the cheapest, tackiest furniture store in town. He dragged books on Antique furniture back to the apartment; I devoured them. I developed an absolute passion for American furniture of the 18th and early 19th century. I haunted antiques shops in the Village; I just looked and made a pest of myself, I couldn't afford to buy anything. The Antiques dealer in BRONTOSAURUS is a composite of the lady Michael worked for and two of the killer dealers who became friends of mine, each of whom seemed to despise every customer who entered his shop. ("Why is that vase so expensive? Because you don't know what you're looking at, sweetie.")

The dealer and her nephew are two of the most naturally conflicting characters I've come up with. One, whose entire life is based on aesthetics, and the other, her nephew, who would feel that the most beautiful Louis XVI chair was merely matter held in suspension until it could rot into the earth and be useful, organic material again. I began the play, got as far as discovering that the nephew was going to study theology, realized that I didn't know beans about theology and was going to have to do a mountain of research. I set it aside, then lost it while renovating my house, and found it two years later, where it had fallen behind a bookcase. Lucky accident. I hadn't been ready to finish it at the time. On reading the opening I understood that the nephew didn't know beans about theology either, in fact had his own religion, and I didn't have to know anything except the nephew's heart.

The satori, or "sudden enlightenment" experience, that the nephew relates, is the closest I can come to describing the experience as I received it, at the age of eight, as I rounded the corner of my grandmother's house in Lebanon, Missouri. I would have said that the shrub was a lilac (or *syringa vulgaris*, I've become a terrible garden snob), not a "bush", as the nephew calls it, but he has no interest in the specificity of such things.

BRONTOSAURUS was first presented as the opening production of *The Late Show* at Circle Repertory Company* in New York City, at 11 PM on October 19, 1977. It was directed by Daniel Irvine; the costumes were by Laura Crow; the lighting was by Gary Seltzer; and the stage manager was Andrew Mishkind. Sound was by Charles S. London. The assistant to the director was Nina Friedman. The cast, in order of appearance, was as follows.

THE ANTIQUES DEALER: Tanya Berezin
THE ASSISTANT: Sharon Madden
THE NEPHEW: Jeff Daniels

**CHARACTERS**

THE ANTIQUES DEALER  A woman, well dressed and attractive, possibly 45. This part could be played by a man in which case "aunt" should be changed to "uncle," but I would prefer a woman.

THE ASSISTANT  A woman about the same age or younger; or, if pressed, a man the same.

THE NEPHEW  A young man, perhaps 17 or 18; he should be presentable and not unattractive. Again this part could possibly be played by a girl with very few changes, but I think a boy is more appropriate. In no sex combination should there be any sign of sexual attraction between the character of the Dealer and the Nephew.

**SCENE**

The present. New York City. The stage is carpeted in one neutral color. The only furniture is a pair of simple antique side chairs, elegant and light. There is no suggestion of walls or of the antiques shop.The chairs are isolated by light, surrounded by dark. The scenes alternate between the shop of the Antiques Dealer and her apartment.

* The name was changed from Circle Theater to Circle Repertory when the company moved to Sheridan Square in 1973.

# BRONTOSAURUS

*The assistant sits, her back to the audience, polishing a silver candlestick. The Dealer stands, her hand resting lightly on the other chair, looking out.*

**DEALER** He's not coming. He's lost in the city. She said he's a sweetheart. I should have been warned then. A real little pussycat. Half pussy, half cat, more than likely. Pussy. Cat. A bell should have tolled. I'm an innocent. I have a virgin streak in me—somewhere. I still believe. No, I don't—what I do have is a desperate need to believe. I saw a movie with a talking plant from outer space that repeated over and—

**ASSISTANT** A talking plant?

**DEALER** A sci-fi movie with a talking plant that said "Feed Me!" And there I am. I'm an outer space plant-form demanding (*Tasting the word.*) nourishment. Feed me, sustain me, make me believe. (*Pause.*) Oh, he can move in. From his mother's description he's grown into more of a puppydog than a pussycat. What do I care? I've got to talk to someone. I'll more than likely turn the poor child into a faggot within a week. Everyone in this business is a faggot, including me. I'm a bigger faggot than any of them, come to—dear, God, it's all about survival. What you see is what you get. Say I who am myopic. And there you have it. No, it isn't a need to believe. It's just an enormous, welling hope. An unwashed hope that's so general and vast and unspecific that it engulfs details. Fogs up edges. God, I'm hopelessly infantile. I read somewhere—I'm always reading somewhere, still blithely skipping the words I don't know; not skipping, assuming. On the fly. I must be some kind of speed-freak, I think. Everything at a rush. Catch-as-catch-can. (*Pause.*)

**ASSISTANT** What? You read somewhere . . . ?

**DEALER** Something about maturity. Made me realize I was condemned to adolescence. Moral adolescence. Consigned.

**ASSISTANT** Good.

**DEALER** Umm . . . with its unbased assurance and vicious competitiveness, unconstructive criticism, unearned ennui. A welter of personal habits: all compulsive, all sloppy. And no behavior at all.

**ASSISTANT** Should it be? Earned?

**DEALER** (*Coming out of an abstraction.*) Should what be earned, love?

**ASSISTANT** Ennui. Or criticism necessarily constructive?

**DEALER** (*With decision.*) He isn't coming. He's four hours late. If she had told me which plane he was taking. . . . Wandering in this city for four hours, he's probably a drug freak by now. I can't wait around, I'm supposed to be seven places. (*Referring to the candlestick.*) That's coming out wonderfully. It'll tarnish in a day in this humidity. When my hair kinks I know I'll come into the shop and all the silver will look like nickel, the brass will be black and the copper will have begun to turn that nice aqua color. Lock up, love, pull the shade down if you stay late, and turn out the lights. (*As the Assistant stands and walks off, the Dealer turns the L. chair to face R., the lights change, shift to reveal the Nephew standing, head down, beside the R. chair. The Dealer continues, but with a change in her voice, more friendly.*) Don't hang your head (*The Nephew raises his head.*) and do try not to look so forlorn. (*The Nephew mumbles.*) And please don't mumble. And don't let me frighten you. I'm all protective coloration. Under the peafowl feathers is only a peafowl. Are you tired? (*Pause.*) You aren't going to be drab and lackluster and uninterested, are you?

**NEPHEW**  Probably.

**DEALER**  Yes, well, you would know, having lived with yourself for . . . what would you say if I asked you to fix me a Manhattan? (*She takes her jacket off and hangs it on the L. chair.*) It's been all rather long today and all rather exhausting.

**NEPHEW**  I don't know what a Manhattan is. I know what it is, but I don't know how to make one.

**DEALER**  Um. That would do. I would say fix it to what, or fix it yourself, or better still: absolutely nobody drinks Manhattans. What you probably want is a vodka stinger. Don't let me walk on you, because with the best of intentions, I nevertheless will. Which only means more than likely what I'd like—immaterial—what I would really like, actually the only thing I drink, is white wine. Wouldn't you?

**NEPHEW**  Where is it?

**DEALER**  Not "Where is it?" "You want it, what's stopping you, get it." Not where is it. (*Pause.*)

**NEPHEW**  I don't know where it is.

**DEALER**  What would you like? Have one with me.

**NEPHEW**  No. (*Pause. Or dead stop. The Nephew speaks in a simple, deliberate almost uninflected tone. His rhythm, pace and lack of irony in contrast to her, but we should feel a power and a danger in him.*)

**DEALER**  I'm uneasy with strangers. Relative strangers. Strangers who are relatives. I hope to God sis warned you about me.

**NEPHEW**  She said you knew everyone and lived in a beautiful apartment.

**DEALER**  Um . . . "apartment." She would. Yes, I pour through catalogues looking for plants that are city hardy. Everything I touch dies of an innate sense of my ignorance of their needs. Or more likely my feigned interest in their behavior. I've never deeply accepted that "The force that through the green fuse," etcetera, They don't die, but they would if I didn't have a cleaning lady with a concern. She talks to them. And I have a feeling that the moment I leave the room they whisper back to her. About me. I don't know everyone. I don't know anyone. I used to know everyone. You're in time to see your only aunt come unglued in the humidity. (*She leaves the lighted area. The following lines are spoken from the dark.*) White wine in the refrigerator for future reference, where it gets too cold; red on the shelf above, where it stays too warm. (*She reappears holding a glass of wine.*) Room temperature in France is about fifty-eight degrees. There's a simple way to calculate that in centigrade, but I only remember complicated things. (*She passes between chairs and sits on the L. chair.*) Should you notice a crack forming, I hope you won't be self-conscious about telling me. No, the Everybodys, who were Anybodys, that I knew I've watched the last few years slowly realize that they had wasted their talent creating a "fashion" which, by its nature, changed and left them helplessly *derrière garde,* and clumsy about adjusting to the current whims without it being heartbreakingly obvious. If one cared. You're to be in school. Where? I mean I knew, but I've forgotten.

**NEPHEW**  Here.

**DEALER**  I know here, love. Where here?

**NEPHEW**  New York University.

**DEALER**  Umm. Do you know what you'll be studying? What's your major? If one still majors.

**NEPHEW**  Theology. (*Pause.*)

**DEALER**  Did Margy show you your room?

**NEPHEW**  Yes.

**DEALER**  I can remove some of the furniture if it's too . . .

**NEPHEW**  No, it's fine. (*Beat.*)

**DEALER**  "Fine." It's been described as one of the ten most beautiful rooms in the city.

**NEPHEW**  I like the view of the park.

**DEALER**  (*A little annoyed.*) Yes, the window was there, I thought why cover it. The park is nice to look at but I wouldn't go into it without six strong sober adults, and I don't know any. Or at least not six. Theology as theory or philosophy or what?

**NEPHEW**  I'll probably be a minister eventually.

**DEALER**  Oh, dear . . . God. (*She sets wine glass down.*) Oh, why not? Dear, yes, why not? What denomination are we—or are you—your father, I suppose, our family wasn't much on—uh vaguely Protestant, I think. Not Presbyterian or Anglican I—

**NEPHEW**   Dad is a Methodist.

**DEALER**   Of course. I knew that. Do they drink? I mean do they approve of drinking?

**NEPHEW**   They say they don't.

**DEALER**   (*Wonders, but doesn't comment.*) I read somewhere that every ounce of alcohol you drink kills four thousand brain cells which are not regenerated. Contrary to what I read somewhere else. (*She picks up wine glass.*) I understand that rather than being a steady, every-night tippler, it's healthier, or less destructive, really, to go on a monthly all out binge. Which is worth considering if one is interested in being less destructive. Which maybe I am; despite appearances. (*More expansively.*) Nephew of mine, my house is yours. (*Gets up from chair and moves about the room.*) Please make friends. Bring them here. I like young people. I like people, though I don't seem to sometimes. "People," you understand, no specific person. Bring them here. The "apartment" is yours. It's been photographed for every classy publication from *Abitare* to the *Sunday Times Magazine* and in not one picture has there been a living soul. Large, flat colorless rooms in perfect order. Flowers on every table and lovely, longing, sad-looking rooms. I've never liked a single photograph. If you hate it here I'll help you find an apartment, but I hope you won't. And next spring maybe you can help me look for a house—in the country. It's past time. I don't want to live in the city. I've not found myself in the catalogues. In the winter I tell myself I have to be here for the shop, but I need a summer place where I can get away. Only I'm chicken. I want land but I see myself buying a lush seven acres and with my care watching it turn to burning desert around me. Within weeks. (*Pause.*) A young theologian. Or possibly a young minister. Well, why not? God, yes, why not? (*Pause.*) I like that. You don't apologize. All my friends are apologists. Laugh at their interests and they lose interest. Pretend indifference.

**NEPHEW**   I didn't realize you were laughing at me.

**DEALER**   You're squinting. Do you need glasses?

**NEPHEW**   No.

**DEALER**   They why on earth do—well, no matter. Your complexion can be left to a good diet. Do you eat well?

**NEPHEW**   I don't know.

**DEALER**   Do you have breakfast?

**NEPHEW**   No.

**DEALER**   Then you will. So will I. We'll all start the day as we're advised to.

**NEPHEW**   No. (*Pause.*)

**DEALER**   Well, it isn't something we have to discuss now.

**NEPHEW**  I don't have any interest in food. I don't care what I eat.

**DEALER**  Well, if you don't care then there's no problem.

**NEPHEW**  There aren't many things I like to eat.

**DEALER**  Well, I'll serve what I like and you can learn.

**NEPHEW**  No.

**DEALER**  Oh, surely you can.

**NEPHEW**  I don't like to eat much.

**DEALER**  To eat much or you don't much like to eat?

**NEPHEW**  I don't like to eat much.

**DEALER**  Is this ethical or physiological? I would think with God's bountiful gifts one would be ethically bound (*As the Nephew turns and leaves, the lights change to denote a shift from home to shop, and the Assistant returns carrying a small wine table or candlestand which she places between, and just D. of the two chairs.*) to enjoy the mysteries of *supreme de Volaille a la creme,* or *coquilles St. Jacques normande*—I wonder should I take that as moral indignation, physical revulsion, or tactical retreat?

**ASSISTANT**  He sounds shy. (*She sits on the R. chair.*)

**DEALER**  I have trouble distinguishing between shy and dull. Oh, young people! They baffle me. (*She sits on the L. chair.*)

**ASSISTANT**  I thought you had them pegged.

**DEALER**  Oh, I have them pegged. I know all the crap they're pulling through uninterest and disinterest and ignorance and indifference. I think they're quite right and completely wrong. I am just inadequate to dealing with it. I admire fiber. I don't understand flaccid people. Shy, retiring, flaccid—

**ASSISTANT**  —Fiberless—

**DEALER**  —He's a mess, of course. His complexion, his posture. He is either an aquaphobic, or he's hyper-sensitive to phosphates or he has an extreme gland disorder or he just does not ever bathe.

**ASSISTANT**  They forget.

**DEALER**  They do not forget, they enjoy their own smell. They get off on reeking. I might find it ascetically bracing if they thought it was the way God intended they should smell, but no. They get off on it.

**ASSISTANT**  Don't you?

**DEALER**  (*Abstracted.*) Yes, well, at that price . . . oh, it all means nothing. More than anything he gives me the feeling of being one of Tinguely's antique-looking, non-product-producing machines. Something useless and archaic and mildly amusing and above all something that makes a great deal of noise as it clanks around in its useless revolution. I learned once, some theory, that one can exhaust oneself pushing a great mass or object but if that mass doesn't move, then the effort does not constitute work. It's just exhaustion. Work equals mass times the distance moved or whatever. And I am—not lately working. (*She stands and gazes out the shop window L.*)

**ASSISTANT**   Have you gotten him to eat?

**DEALER**   Yes, and exactly what he damn well wants. Very stubborn streak. But I couldn't call it religious preference. No religion except perhaps his own dictates a diet of hamburgers, cokes and French fries.

**ASSISTANT**   And only that?

**DEALER**   An occasional *Snickers* bar. An odd *Orange Julius*. Our conversations [forced on my part, non-existent on his] are completely circular. He's been in school over a month, I ask him what he's learning [not just because I feel I should keep abreast of how my money is being spent] and he tells me yes, he is learning a great deal and I say what are you learning and he says, "Not what they're teaching." Which I suspect is true, in my case. So what are you learning that they aren't teaching? And he says, "How not to teach." How not to teach. (*She sets the empty wine glass on the table, passes U. between the chairs, turns, and looks at table and wine glass.*) Ah, well. That looks sweet. Calculated, but sweet. A little "Bloomys," but they do all right. It's just that he never seems to be out and he never seems to be in. He's always there and he's never home. I wonder what it was I expected of him? What did I need? Or was I just madly plugging all possible gaps?

**ASSISTANT**   That doesn't bear too close inspection.

**DEALER**   (*Riding on, not picking up the inference.*) —I find myself being annoyed because I suspect he's out but don't know. I find myself listening outside his room, trying to catch a light under his door. I hear him cough and think, my God, am I never to have any privacy? Probably the only reason I never married is because I am congenitally incapable of living with another human being fouling my nest.

**ASSISTANT**   It was your idea.

**DEALER**   Oh, but someone to bring life into my—laughter, joy. Someone who would listen, not someone who would only wait till I had finished. But then who knows. Who knows anything? (*Pause, she lifts the wine glass, looking at it critically: Taps her ring against the bowl and listens to ring.*) "How not to teach." (*Ring, listens.*) "How not to teach." (*Ring. The Nephew enters silently.*) "How not to teach." (*The lights changes to denote a shift back to the apartment. The Dealer turns to face the Nephew.*) Could you possibly state that as a positive?

**NEPHEW**   How to teach.

**DEALER**   Ah . . . that's quite a thing to learn. (*She sets the glass on the table.*) How would you teach? How would you teach me? I know nothing about Theology, but I've always been a willing pupil of just about everything. Teach me.

**NEPHEW**   I'm going to find a place of my own. (*Pause.*)

**DEALER**  Of course you are. I said you might. Though I hoped you wouldn't. But I don't suppose you'll really want my assistance in finding a place. We'd be at cross-purposes, wouldn't we? I'd be looking for some place clean and convenient and light . . .

**ASSISTANT**  Anything else?

**DEALER**  No, thanks, you'd better go. It's late. (*The Assistant goes. As she passes the Nephew, he crosses to stand by the L. chair. The Dealer faces the Nephew from behind the R. chair.*) Nephew of mine, you are a puzzle. Ah, well, maybe ministers are best a puzzle. When did you decide, by the bye? If that's something you decide?

**NEPHEW**  I said I wouldn't stay long.

**DEALER**  You did not. But not to stay and not to go. To be minister.

**NEPHEW**  It's something I've known.

**DEALER**  From birth.

**NEPHEW**  Since I was twelve.

**DEALER**  It came upon you suddenly.

**NEPHEW**  Yes.

**DEALER**  In a blinding flash.

**NEPHEW**  Not blinding.

**DEALER**  A figure of speech.

**NEPHEW**  A realization.

**DEALER**  That you were to be a minister. I wonder that other professions don't have these *"callings."* Imagine a bricklayer or a fireman coming to his family, his eyes glassed-over, saying: "Parents! I've *seen!*" Or "I've been called." I know that sounds cynical and pejorative, but that's only my voice. Over the years, quite independent of conscious design my voice has developed a cynicism I don't always feel. Or don't intend to convey. I am physically incapable of talking about anything involving, say, religion without it sounding as though I would like to take a bottle of lemon oil and a steel wool pad and rub it out. But I believe you understand that I do not necessarily like the sound or the impression I make.

**NEPHEW**  I know.

**DEALER**  I was sure.

**NEPHEW**  (*Straightforward.*) I was standing at the side of the house. I don't remember what I had been doing. I don't remember anything before, immediately before, or immediately after. I stood for a while and then I went inside. I was standing at the side of the house. I had come from around behind in the shade and was standing in the sun; not doing anything, not going anywhere, just standing at the side of the house in the sun. And the hand of God reached out and touched me. That doesn't mean anything. It's abstract, isn't it? But it's the easiest way of explaining the feeling. (*Dealer sits on the R. chair.*) I was standing there, not thinking anything that I would remember. There was a bush on my left and the corner of the house on my right. Instead of just stopping for a while and then moving on, while I was stopped I became aware that my body was changing, or something was happening, physically happening, inside my body. As if all my cells were changing at the same time. Some vibrating sensation through my body that raised me or made me feel like I was physically growing, like a—perhaps a chemical change was occurring. And I started to get scared, but instead of that happening it was gradually like I wasn't standing there anymore. For a moment it was like I had changed into a gas. I felt I was spreading, thinning out, being led over the world or shown the world. Thinning out to take it all in, to absorb it. Or I was shown what I was. I heard people speaking in languages that I understood but had never heard before, I heard bells —no, I didn't actually *hear* anything, but I seemed to *know* about bells in church towns, in the farm country around small towns where they make wine, in France; and people getting up where it was just beginning to be light, to go to work; people walking on streets, shopping, and small things growing in the wet and shade in rain forests. I didn't see them, I wasn't shown, them, I just knew them. Because thinning out, or whatever it was, I *became* them. An old lady who thought in a language different from the one she spoke, dying in terrible pain in the geriatric ward of a very efficient hospital; twins just being born in the Orient; a boy my age, in India, whose job was to carry the censer with incense, swinging it, in a Catholic church: I didn't know them, I *was* them. I was *they*. They were me. We were all the same stuff, the same regenerating impulse. I just thinned out to mix with it all or to realize what I was, what I had come from, and gradually came back to my own design, my own body. But, of course, I thought about it differently, because it wasn't mine. I wasn't me. I was them. I was they. Which is grammatically correct?

**DEALER** (*Pause.*) "I was they" is correct, but it sounds all wrong, doesn't it?

**NEPHEW** I've not tried to explain the experience before, but you asked—

**DEALER** —and it's so easy and such fun to talk about oneself.

**NEPHEW** —Something I should try to explain. It shouldn't be all that difficult. It happened. For all I know it's the experience someone has when they say God has touched them, or when the Indians experience Satori.

**DEALER** The Indians in India.

**NEPHEW** The Buddhists, yes.

**DEALER** I wanted to be sure we weren't into the Hopi or the Navajo.

**NEPHEW** After that I decided to study theology.

**DEALER**  It might as easily have been bio-chemistry.

**NEPHEW**  I don't think so.

**DEALER**  Of course not. And you decided to come here. Where I could help you.

**NEPHEW**  I think we all need help.

**DEALER**  That's encouraging. (*She stands.*) Would you like a glass of wine? (*A very long silence.*)

**NEPHEW**  No.

**DEALER**  I think I would. Dear me. (*She exits with empty wine glass, and says the following lines from the dark.*) It's so difficult not to be wildly cynical and experienced and cutting. I wonder why that is? The devil in us, I think. But I'll try to contain all that. (*She reappears with the wine glass filled.*)

**NEPHEW**  It's all right.

**DEALER**  No, I have all my negative impulses under control. I won't make fools of us this minute anyway.

**NEPHEW**  I mean I'm unshakable. You can't touch that. It's there. I couldn't touch that.

**DEALER**  I, of course, am shakable to the core. But what religious feeling I have, although I'm not sure your experience wasn't more humanitarian than religious—

**NEPHEW**  —Nor am I, but they're the same.

**DEALER**  Of course. What religious feelings I have have been sublimated into beautiful line. Into furniture and painting and those people who create them. The Protestant Ethic with taste. Maybe it should be the Protestant Aesthetic. And are you having your philosophy or whatever, your understanding, your experience confirmed? By your studies?

**NEPHEW**  Indirectly, yes.

**DEALER**  In the rain forest, I'm sorry, I may have misunderstood, that thing growing in the dark and damp. That was a plant?

**NEPHEW**  A fern of some kind.

**DEALER**  As specific as that. Then you were one with the plants as well as the mankind or personkind. But then, "the force that through the green fuse," of course. Touché. Where exactly do you wish to move?

**NEPHEW**  I never intended to stay.

**DEALER**  You have a number of idiosyncrasies for one so young, but the one that I find particularly annoying is that you do not listen to the question. I did not ask if you arrived intending to leave, I asked where you intended to go.

**NEPHEW**  I want to be with friends of mine.

**DEALER**  Now, see? One can be to the point and still enigmatic if one only tries.

**NEPHEW**  I never intended to stay.

**DEALER** You intended only that I should pay your expenses.

**NEPHEW** You said you would.

**DEALER** My dear young nephew, I am liable to say anything.

**NEPHEW** It would be easier for me if you did.

**DEALER** I damn well bet it would.

**NEPHEW** It doesn't matter.

**DEALER** Of course, nothing matters. (*She places glass on table.*)

**NEPHEW** I want to be with my friends.

**DEALER** I told you before you came. I told you as you were standing in the middle of my living room that first night—with your feet splayed and your arms hanging akimbo: bring your friends here. The house is yours. Find a delicate girl with long fingers who will set up a loom in the middle of the parlor and clack away all morning in the sunshine. Bring in an incipient and completely untalented rock group who will rehearse in the dining room, leaving beer cans on the Duncan Phyfe table. Lean back laughing and break the legs of the Federal chairs. Bring them here. These friends. All of your friends. Take a girl, or boy for all I care, into your room, and rip the bed apart. Get come stains and shit marks all over the sheets. Seat them cross-legged on the terrace and preach to them the miracle of Yoga. Use my house. (*She steps toward the Nephew.*) If you have friends why haven't they been here? (*Beat.*)

**NEPHEW** They wouldn't like it. (*Pause.*)

**DEALER** Yes. (*She turns away.*) As plants as people, of course. They wouldn't be happy here. Things don't thrive in order and beauty, they thrive in hardship and decay. These friends wouldn't be fertile, fecund, they wouldn't be happy here. It's too— (*A wave of the hand finishes the sentence.*) Yes, I think you have made it clear that that at least is your firm if misguided . . . and you of course do not yet know of the actual efficacy of happiness. Your philosophy makes everything appear so easy. But you would say it isn't easy, it's only true, perhaps, but then what isn't? Truth is very broad and very deep and rather subjective, isn't it? You have a simplicity that's impossible for us who are competitive and . . . all those vulgar things. I must be sounding wildly condescending, but as I said that's only sound. I'm always skeptical of anyone who has it all so worked out. (*Pause.*)

**NEPHEW** I listen to you but I don't know how to help you.

**DEALER** Maybe it's just that condescension runs in the family. But if there's something you don't know school won't be a complete waste. (*Beat.*) When I was a child, even younger than you if such a thing can be imagined, I thought I would go to heaven, and my dollies would go to heaven, and my doggies would go to heaven, but even I did not suppose that the ferns would go to heaven. But why not? If they've lived a good life. And make the journey without so much as a frost-tipped frond. Who would want heaven, after all, without the ferns?

**NEPHEW**  "Heaven" is here. "Heaven" is the future.

**DEALER**  Heaven is . . . ah. Heaven on earth? One day? (*No answer.*) With the aid of science? Or without science altogether? (*No answer.*) I think without. Heaven is eating roots and berries and having a knowledge of the wonder of it all, or the sameness of it all—all life, which is a kind of promiscuous protoplasmic soup. Everyone sitting around in the altogether with a mongoloid grin: that is undoubtedly the answer. What matters? Nothing matters. Enjoy it. Or the regenerating *stuff* matters. Something like that? (*No answer.*) I think that's marvelous for thirty-five people for six weeks in a warm climate. (*The Nephew crosses to behind the R. chair, as the Dealer approaches the L. chair.*) You see, we have what would be called in personnel training a personality conflict. We see things quite differently. Paradise for you occurred once in say, Tahiti. Where there was no disease and no hardship. And you see a vision of that continuing, if the white man had not fouled paradise. While I see—without the assistance of Magellan or Cooke—one day drifts to the sandy shores of Tahiti a . . . very . . . bad . . . co-co-nut. (*Pause.*) I can't get it out of my mind, purely my negative bent, that in the last few hundred years we have recognized that that life, that *stuff* we are all made from comes in some rather disturbing forms. Like the yellow fever bacilli and athletes' foot fungus. And I at least, am not going to be really content in a world without *Desenex.*

**NEPHEW**  Why do you think paradise would be a tropical island? It could be a desert.

**DEALER**  Will your desert heaven have politicians? Teachers, I suppose, you damn well bet, but—say, a form of government? (*Pause. He stares at her waiting. Finally—*)

**NEPHEW**  No.

**DEALER**  Would it have science?

**NEPHEW**  No.

**DEALER**  All those little boys who wear glasses and work in their basement on rockets and model trains at last liberated from an obligation to make a name for themselves. Would it have art?

**NEPHEW**  No.

**DEALER**  That, at least, is absolutely for the best, I'm sure. Though you may at last have discovered a model to prove art's inevitability. And no furniture or architecture or engineering. All that is . . . what? In religious terms? Vanity, isn't it? (*Pause.*) And there will be no death, but people will grow old and die.

**NEPHEW**  Not very old, I wouldn't think.

**DEALER**  Nor would I. But what does it matter as long as life continues. And no one will be unkind or egocentric or ego-anything because they will know what life is. How simple. But then all great ideas are all so simple. Einstein's theory of time is like that, a continuum, but you're right not to clutter up your— I wonder why it is that I can't make myself grasp the image of deifying the hydrogen atom . . . but I'm always wrong; forever envying those who are right. That's just vanity, again, of course. I came close to the light myself once. The experience of feeling as though I was only [or, forgive me, *supremely*] gas. When I was having a tooth extracted, as I went under, counting backwards from ten to one—I think I got as far as six—I thought for a moment that I was becoming a gas myself. But then I woke up with a mouth full of blood and a cup of tea in my hand, having missed the revelation—by one or two numbers. Had I hung on till four or three . . . but I'm a natural resister. Change, no, that's vanity too, of course. But I liken change to someone coming into my house when I'm away and moving all the furniture about. I can't seem to slough it off, all this vanity, all this world, and give myself over to it. To Christ or to someone or to some cause or to anything. Slough it all and be bathed in the blood of the lamb. How wonderful that would be. How free one would feel. How right. Damn. Go free! As with your experience, thin out and go free! God, yes. Free of it all! All this vanity! How grand and liberating. "How like a god." It must be what the skydivers feel. Or those who have determined on suicide. Or mental defectives who blubber in their bibs and smile . . . smile, my God that smile. The serenity on their faces makes them look forever young, which is what they are, of course. But I grew up. Vanity. And was guided into or decided not to slough it off quite yet, but fool that I am, to *contend* with it all for a bit. Never mind that I make nothing out of it. I am hopelessly *involved* with the world; vanity again. I do not feel, deep in my marrow, that I am one with my neighbor and the goldfish bowl, but it is to be hoped that that will come. Having never experienced Satori or received the call I must muddle around in the darkness as best I can, worrying about those mundane things like grease spots and liver spots and bills of lading and the price of psychiatry, vanity again. Without the light, I sometimes am hurtful of others and especially myself, and I find myself over-compensating for the sake of social grace and tending to make a spectacle of myself. I do at least recognize that those around me are aware that I am hanging over that goodnight by a thread, as are they, and the only comfort we have is knowing that each sees the other's pain and fear, goddamn, vanity again, but that comfort is what we live for. They know that I have not deceived, at least, anyone into becoming my friend; and have at least tried to influence no one. Living in my time, in our time, not yours, but mine and my generation's time—that last generation, we honorable brontosaurs who are the last to die: that generation that plugged away those last few weeks before everlasting life was discovered; those last mad hours before everyone drank a potion and lived forever like a giant redwood or Frodo in the Grey Havens—we are the nervous dumb brontosaurs who knew only that at the very least their lives would have a form: a shape, a beginning and a middle and for those who cared for it a progeny, and finally and blissfully, or regrettably an end. You can have engraved on our tombs, vanity again, that we bumbled glassy-eyed, those cute little dim brontosaurus eyes, through life's humiliating, predictable metamorphoses [I pray] with a semblance of grace and compassion at times— and in a rather difficult age for intelligent beings, as we were the first and the last to make the migration purely for the sake of the journey, being fully aware of the absurdity, the biological accident, or if you would, the biological miracle of it all. And we made the migration to its no doubt ignoble end for the sake of experiencing the accident. Or for the sake of experiencing the miracle (*She picks up the glass of wine.*) and with a good handful of valium but without an excess of ameliorating philosophical palliatives. (*Beat.*) You would say, of course, it doesn't end. That life does not have a form or its form has no form. That it doesn't change. That it doesn't "evolute." You would have been one hell of a wet blanket on the Beagle. (*Long pause.*)

**NEPHEW** May I go?

**DEALER** As you say, you never intended to stay. Fly to your secrets and giggle with your compatriots about the brontosaur, with its fat ass and little brain and dim eyes. Spread the Light. God knows they need it. No point in hanging around here and being silted-in just yet. (*Pause.*) Yes, go. You may go, by all means. You can't help me, you said so yourself. Don't let one failure trouble your future. You are more than likely not dangerous. Please, yes, go. (*He does not move. He is trying to find a way to help her.*) Yes, go. Leave. Damnit, leave my house! (*Pause. He leaves. She places the wine glass on the table and turns the L. chair so that its back is to the audience as in the opening scene. This action is accompanied by a shift in the lights to the setting of the shop. The Assistant enters, carrying the candlestick and a buff cloth. She sits in the L. chair, her back to the audience.*) I didn't even know the . . . he had friends. Oh, the smug, simpering, sentimental, asinine, sophomoric— Baptist! Methodist! Someone should steal his copy of *The Prophet* from his knapsack. Knapsack, I want you to realize. He arrived with an imitation leather two-suiter and left with an army surplus canvas bag. It takes no time at all to pick up the style. Though I don't believe he has friends with his "I am a rock, I am an island" phi . . .

(*Beat.*)

**ASSISTANT**   Can one be both?

**DEALER**   Huh? Oh, sure. Rock Island. That's the caliber mind we're dealing with. There's no talking with someone who has seen the light. Unless one has also seen the light. Is there a Dylan Thomas in the shop? Oh, never mind, I have one at home. And what good anyway, I mean the man was a bigger drunk than I. Though I'm beginning to wonder if I really understood why. Perhaps I was only humiliated at asking him to stay. Free them all. We earned it for them, didn't we? But what do they care? And what do I care? Who knows? Who knows anything? God, I wonder seriously if all reformers had aunts: did Luther have an aunt, do you suppose? Or Thoreau? But even Thoreau didn't say, "I am Walden Pond." Oh, he has no defenses. He can't sip a glass of wine and look knowing and telling and modestly arousing and throw up some smart-ass facade behind which he can quickly regroup and regain his composure. As can we. On a good day. (*Takes a sip of wine. Pause, looks at the Assistant.*) Oh, leave off, darling. That's as good as that is going to get. (*The Assistant rises. The Dealer takes the candlestick in exchange for her wine glass and the Assistant exits with the glass and buff cloth. The Dealer places the candlestick on the table and puts on her jacket. The Assistant returns with a candle which she carefully places in the candlestick. As she prepares to light the candle—*) You go on. I'll lock up. I'll pull down the shade if I stay late. (*The Dealer takes the matches from the Assistant, and the Assistant leaves. As she begins to speak. the Dealer lights the candle.*) So I go home to a quiet house and I bathe and sleep peacefully. So in the summer I find a house in the country and have workmen repair the roof and put in a new heating system, and I clear the weeds from the garden. I paint the rooms white and come into town for shades for the windows. So I walk out of Bloomingdales with the shades ordered and a new silk blouse in a bag under my arm: a cream silk shirt that goes with anything. So I come out of the air-conditioned and carpeted, quietly bustling store into the street. The sun is very bright on the taxis and the sidewalk, and the air is very hot and not moving much. (*Pause.*) So I stand for a minute, trying to decide if I want to go uptown to the apartment or if I'll walk to the shop or go directly back to the country. I stop there for a second in the heat. The curb of 60th Street is on my left as I face Third Avenue and a traffic light is on my right. I stop a minute and stand; not thinking of anything I would remember afterward, not aware of thinking of anything. Going nowhere. I stop for a minute and stand for a minute in the sun. And whatever is happening to me, I'm not afraid. (*A pause. She blows out the candle, turns to leave, turns back and watches smoke rise from candle. Lights fade to blackout.*)

# THYMUS VULGARIS (1982)

THYMUS VULGARIS was presented in staged reading form on June 4, 1981, as part of the One Act Play Festival of the Lincoln Center Theater Company in the Mitzi E. Newhouse Theater, in New York City; Richmond Crinkley, Executive Producer; Edward Albee, Artistic Director. It was directed by Stephen Zuckerman, the cast, in order of appearance, was as follows:

RUBY: Ruth Ford
EVELYN: Sharon Madden
THE COP: David Morse

THYMUS VULGARIS was subsequently presented by the Circle Repertory Company, in New York City, on January 10, 1982, as part of a triple bill entitled "Confluence." It was directed by June Stein; the set was by Bob Phillips; costumes were by Joan E. Weiss; the lighting was by Mal Sturchio; sound was by Chuck London and Stewart Werner; and the production stage manager was Kate Stewart. The cast was as follows:

RUBY: Pearl Shear
EVELYN: Katherine Cortez
THE COP: Jeff McCracken

THYMUS VULGARIS was given its premiere performance at the Lee Strasberg Theatre Institute, in Los Angeles, in 1981, directed by Daniel Irvine.

## CHARACTERS

RUBY  Somewhere between fifty and sixty-five. Not thin and with the bleached ends of a rather vivid hairstyle. She is in a blue slip or housecoat.

EVELYN  Between thirty and forty—probably thirty-five. Not thin, very like her mother. Her hair is a vivid color. She wears a very expensive bright yellow silk dress or slacks a size too small.

THE COP  In his twenties, none too bright, tall, well built and blonde.

## SCENE

The present. A trailer park in Palmdale, California. In the center of the stage is a raised platform perhaps two feet high that is the size and general shape of a small house trailer. The platform is furnished as a trailer might be, everything quite close together, and perhaps painted in only two colors—yellow and blue for a choice. There are plenty of counters to duck behind and vanish from sight. At rise there are perhaps a few pillowcases or laundry bags stuffed with clothes. All this need not be more realistic than is necessary to convey the subject. No roof, windows, walls, background, etc.

# THYMUS VULGARIS

*Ruby is suddenly discovered in the center of the platform. She immediately reacts to the audience—acute embarrassment. She starts to step off the platform, doesn't know which way to turn, quickly puts three or four things away, pillowcases stuffed with clothes, which gives her the chance to duck behind a counter out of sight. She grunts from the effort.*

**RUBY**  Oh, dear God. Oh, goodness. Oh, my goodness.

**EVELYN**  (*Calling from off.*) Momma? Momma? (*She appears, striding on.*) Momma, I'm here. (*As she makes it to the platform, yells off stage.*) It wouldn't kill you to have a step here. (*On the platform, in doorway.*) Momma, I'm here! Can you believe your eyes? (*Ruby has been bending over and is out of sight. She raises up now and looks at Evelyn blankly.*)

**RUBY**  Huh?

**EVELYN**  Oh, my God. Oh, no.

**RUBY**  What?

**EVELYN**  Look at you. Oh, God, Momma.

**RUBY**  Evie! It's my baby! Out of the blue!

**EVELYN**  Why aren't you ready? Momma, I don't have time to sober you up.

**RUBY**  I am stone cold sober. If you had bothered to inquire in the last two years.

**EVELYN**  On a day like today. Of all days.

**RUBY**  Not a drop in over twenty-six months.

**EVELYN**  Well, did you get my letter? (*Pause. Devastated.*) You didn't get my letter! Oh, Momma, it's a red letter day.

**RUBY**  Well, maybe that explains why you sashay into the trailer like this. Catching me before I have time to do. (*Sotto voce.*) This isn't for me, honey. I mean I don't even go to shows. I can't stand up here with the lights on me and everybody watchin'.

**EVELYN**  Momma, you just gotta let it roll right off your back.

**RUBY**  (*Sotto voce.*) When have we ever had people staring at us?

**EVELYN**  Momma, everywhere I go. You ain't said a word about my dress.

**RUBY**  (*To* herself.) Oh, goodness. (*Notices the dress.*) That's very pretty. That looks almost like silk.

**EVELYN**  Momma, that is silk.

**RUBY**   Oh, I wouldn't have silk. You have to take it to the professional cleaners every time you get a spot on it. But would you look how pretty she is!

**EVELYN**   (*Preparatory, to a major announcement.*) Momma, sit down.

**RUBY**   I will not sit down till I've hugged my baby. (*Running to her.*)

**EVELYN**   (*Being hugged.*) I can't believe you didn't know. I wrote you everything. It took me two hours to compose a letter. I wrote eight pages, Momma.

**RUBY**   (*Arms length.*) Of course she did.

**EVELYN**   Is this the same trailer or did you trade it for a smaller one?

**RUBY**   This is the same trailer you know.

**EVELYN**   I can't hardly move in here.

**RUBY**   God almighty, let me make us some coffee.

**EVELYN**   (*Same.*) Momma . . . sit down!

**RUBY**   (*Testing coffee pot.*) This is still warm. I'll just heat it up.

**EVELYN**   (*Announcement.*) Momma. I'm getting married!

**RUBY**   Ohhhhhhh. My little baby. (*Running to her, hugging her again.*) I almost didn't forgive her for catching me by surprise. And now she's getting married. You tell me, honey, while I do.

**EVELYN**   Momma, there's no time to do. Oh, you didn't get my letter. You don't know the particulars. I'll tell you in the taxi.

**RUBY**   I'm not going nowhere looking like this.

**EVELYN**   (*Noticing a foreign smell on her arm.*) What do I smell like?

**RUBY**   Taxi to where?

**EVELYN**   Hollywood.

**RUBY**   Hollywood? Hollywood is in Los Angeles. You know how much it is to taxi from Palmdale to Hollywood . . . ?

**EVELYN**   I know how much it is. I just did it. It's forty-one dollars.

**RUBY**   Oh, my God! That's a cleaning lady for two months. I wouldn't have to turn my hand.

**EVELYN**   You ain't ever gonna have to turn your hand again, Momma.

**RUBY**   Normally this place is spotless, honey. If I'd known.

**EVELYN**   I waited at Ed and Nora's place for you. I tried to call you; I couldn't understand why nobody was there. I wrote it all down. I said for you to get there early so we could have a talk.

**RUBY**   Who is Ed and Nora, honey?

**EVELYN**   They're Solly's dearest friends.

**RUBY**   And who's Solly?

**EVELYN**   He's my intended. He's my man.

**RUBY**   Oh, my.

**EVELYN**   He's my grapefruit king. What is that you got growing all around the trailer? I just walked through it and I've got its smell all over me.

**RUBY**  Oh. That's thyme.

**EVELYN**  That's what? (*Beat.*)

**RUBY**  Thyme.

**EVELYN**  It stinks like I don't know what. Smells like medicine. Is that a drug?

**RUBY**  Honey, that's an herb.

**EVELYN**  Well, some drugs come right from herbs. It smells like *Vicks VapoRub*.

**RUBY**  It's used in cooking.

**EVELYN**  Forty-eight dollars a half-ounce, I bathed in *Mon Plasir*, I smell like someone doped me up for coming down with the croup.

**RUBY**  (*Looking off.*) I should maybe trim it off the path—neaten it up. —What is that? Is that a cop?

**EVELYN**  Oh, no. What have you done now? Good Lord, yes. That's a highway patrolman. Don't let him see you.

**RUBY**  (*Overlapping.*) What did you do that you'd be wanted by the highway patrol?

**EVELYN**  Momma, the only motor cop I've seen in a year is the one Solly bribed to get us to the airport on time.

**RUBY**  Would they follow you from Hollywood?

**EVELYN**  They don't follow me, Momma, unless they want my picture—Oh, he's coming here.

**COP**  (*Enters, looks for a place to go up, finds it, stands in the door.*) Excuse me.

**RUBY and EVELYN**  How do you do? Hello. What can we do for you?

**COP**  Is this the Bentley ur—uh—trailer? I'm looking for a Mrs. Ruby Bentley.

**RUBY**  No. No.

**EVELYN**  No. No.

**RUBY**  This is the Gonzales residence. We don't know a Mrs. Bentley.

**EVELYN**  (*Annoyed with Ruby, but making do.*) See—no—habla—anglay.

**COP**  They said over there that this was the Bentley trailer. I got a . . .

**RUBY**  People in this particular trailer park don't really know other people in this particular trailer park too good.

**EVELYN**  We're mostly just prominent citizens who are innocent bystanders.

**COP**  Well, see, I got this urgent . . . (*He notices the audience and freezes.*) Oh, my lord.

**EVELYN**  You got a what? (*Snaps her fingers in front of his face. The Cop stands transfixed.*) Well, that's done it.

**RUBY**  (*Sotto voce.*) This isn't gonna turn out good, honey. This isn't for people like us.

**EVELYN**  Look at him.

**RUBY**  This ain't right for me either. I'm okay for a person, honey, but I'm no good for a character.

**EVELYN**  Momma, we're not people like us no more. In the last year, Momma, I've made a complete three hundred and sixty degree turn. Everywhere I go. I've signed autographs.

**COP**  (*Coming out of it, slipping on a pair of sunglasses. From here on, he is "acting" and very badly.*) Well, uh, you see, I have this urgent and important official police business communication with a party by the name of Bentley.

**RUBY**  We're very sorry we can't help you.

**EVELYN**  (*Nudging him out.*) You call again, though, any time.

**RUBY**  Any time. Such a nice, strong, clean looking young man.

**COP**  Yes, well, actually six feet four. Naturally blonde. A hundred ninety-five.

**RUBY**  And such a nice smile. That's always so important in an occupation where you meet people.

**EVELYN**  Momma.

**RUBY**  You work close by, do you?

**COP**  Right here in Palmdale, Miss. Uh Mrs . . . uh . . .

**EVELYN**  Sanchez.

**RUBY**  And you drive a motorbike.

**COP**  Yes. It's a Honda brand bike.

**EVELYN**  You're the real article, no doubt about it. It's been fun.

**COP**  Honda is a . . . good bike. I get good . . . mileage. Good check-ups.

**EVELYN**  That's fine. Goodbye now.

**COP**  Well, I better not stay from my appointed rounds. (*Backing out.*) It's been a privilege.

**RUBY**  Oh, yes. There's always a demand for someone of your vocation and appearance on the uh . . . media.

**COP**  Yes, ma'am, I appreciate the exposure—er—uh—the time.

**RUBY**  Any time. You never know.

**EVELYN**  Any time.

**COP**  Yes, ma'am. I appreciate it, ma'am. (*Falling off the platform. Backing out.*) Good day . . . good day.

**RUBY**  Sorry, we couldn't be more help.

**EVELYN**  (*As the Cop backs out saying "Good day, ma'ams."*) Good lord, I thought he was gonna unbutton his shirt.

**RUBY**  Goodbye. (*Sotto voce.*) Some of them, especially men, I think it kinda goes to their head. (*The Cop is finally gone.*)

**EVELYN**  (*In a flurry.*) Throw something in a bag and let's get out of this soup can before he gets wise to whatever you've done.

**RUBY**  Honey, I ain't like that no more. I'm completely changed.

**EVELYN**  Cops don't inquire at the homes of people who are completely changed.

**RUBY**  I am innocent of wrongdoing for over two years. I've become a conscientious citizen.

**EVELYN**  Momma, conscientious citizens don't live in a trailer at the smack damn edge of the desert. Ten more feet that way, you'd be parched by noon. People who have changed don't have their trailer crawling over with a cooking herb that smells like Vicks and motorcops, Momma. And any minute, he could be coming back. I'll phone for a taxi while you put something on (*Takes the phone book.*) and let's blow this joint. Taxi, taxi—taxidermist, dear God, right in Palmdale, it just makes you creep. (*Dials. Ruby is putting on a white blouse.*) Momma, don't wear white; either one of us shows up at a wedding service in white, the roof would fall in on the church. (*Phone.*) Yes, I . . . uh . . . (*Hangs up.*)

**RUBY**  Didn't they answer? (*Pause.*)

**EVELYN**  Of course they answered. They're a taxicab company. That's how they get their business. I hung up. What do I care if that cop comes back? I'm just sittin' here with my momma.

**RUBY**  Honey, your momma doesn't really feel up to being busted just today. Your momma isn't as spunky as she used to be.

**EVELYN**  I hung up because that girl was gonna say what was my destination. And I don't want to hear that right now. Aww, Momma, I wrote you such a beautiful letter. I wrote you like poetry—that's how moved I was to be writing to you after all this time. I know you think I'm just terrible and selfish and heartless—off God knows where—but sometimes I get so moved—just thinking all the things I'd like to tell you and do for you. Only I never go ahead and tell 'em to you or do 'em for you. I really always have been full of wonderful and beautiful things. Sometimes I think of myself as an untapped person. I have so many things in me that are beautiful. Only for some reason I never seem to be able to let anyone see.

**RUBY**  They're just blind if they can't see.

**EVELYN**  I really have such wonderful . . .

**RUBY**  You don't have to tell me, honey . . .

**EVELYN**  . . . poetic . . .

**RUBY**  I always have known that. And now she's getting married. (*Pours coffee.*)

**EVELYN**  Well . . . (*Pause.*) I maybe better call Ed and Nora and see if Solly's got there.

**RUBY**  Where is he supposed to be?

**EVELYN**  Oh, Solly's got these two wonderful friends in Hollywood.

**RUBY**  Ed and Nora.

**EVELYN**  Yeah. We're meeting at their place. They got a real nice place. I was there and Ed was there and Nora was there and the preacher— but when Solly didn't come and you didn't come, I said I'd go looking for you.

**RUBY**  Well, he's there by now.

**EVELYN**  Oh, I don't want to know. If he is or not. If he's showed or not. I want to believe. It's been wonderful believing. I don't know how you can stand being cooped up in here like this.

**RUBY**  Well . . .

**EVELYN**  I mean, I guess you get used to it.

**RUBY**  Oh, well, no. I get bruises easily.

**EVELYN**  I get that from you, then. 'Cause the least thing. (*Drinks coffee.*) That's the first thing I've had in my stomach all day from worry.

**RUBY**  You seem to have put on a little weight since I saw you.

**EVELYN**  What are you talking about? I've never been in better shape in my life. This is how Solly likes me.

**RUBY**  Do you think he found out? Is that what's got you upset?

**EVELYN**  Upset? Me?

**RUBY**  All red and trembling.

**EVELYN**  Momma, I'm flushed with happiness. I'm trembling with joy!

**RUBY**  You never could see yourself . . .

**EVELYN**  Found out what?

**RUBY**  What?

**EVELYN**  That he found out what?

**RUBY**  About your . . .

**EVELYN**  You mean my work? (*Ruby nods gratefully.*) Momma, I met him at the . . . "Club."

**RUBY**  At the where?

**EVELYN**  At the . . . "Dance Hall." (*Beat.*) The . . . "Place." (*Beat.*) "The house." He was a regular customer. Momma, it's the love of the century. We've been in columns.

**RUBY**  My goodness.

**EVELYN**  In newspapers.

**RUBY**  Oh, my goodness.

**EVELYN**  I'm not the person I was, Momma.

**RUBY**  What did they say?

**EVELYN**  (*Digging in her purse, hands Ruby two or three newspaper clippings.*) They said: Bliss! They said: The love of the ages. They said: Romeo and Juliet. They said: Grapefruit King and Showgirl! "Showgirl"? Twelve times if it was once I drag-ass up to that two-bit Sands for an open call for the chorus. Six times if it was once to Caesar's Palace for an interview for cocktail waitresses. They said I couldn't walk. I won't tell you what they said I walked like. I mean they aren't even polite to a person. They said I had too much personality.

**RUBY**  Well, of course you do.

**EVELYN**  Not nice, Momma, they didn't mean it nice. Fourteen times to the Circus without even one callback and once—once!—Solly takes me to eat a steak at some gussied-up clipjoint and I'm a "showgirl." "Beauty" they called me.

**RUBY**  Well, you are.

**EVELYN**  If it had happened to someone else, it could make you believe. "Hope," the girls said. They said it gave them hope. It was like Cinderella they said. Only different. Solly comes . . .

**RUBY**  What are you saying his name is?

**EVELYN**  Sol. Sol.

**RUBY**  I want to get it right for when I meet him.

**EVELYN**  Sol. Like the sun. Like Ol' Sol. Like Bam-De-Sollay. Like (*Singing.*) "Don't know why, there's no sun up in the sky . . ."

**RUBY**  "Stormy weather . . ."

**EVELYN**  Only there is a sun up in the sky and he's my Sol.

**RUBY**  Ol' Sol.

**EVELYN**  See, Solly had been coming around for six months, maybe— and he's dropping a hundred on one girl and two hundred on another girl—

**RUBY**  Where's this?

**EVELYN**  At the . . .

**RUBY**  At the "club?"

**EVELYN**  At the club.

**RUBY**  I bet they were impressed.

**EVELYN**  Why?

**RUBY**  With someone like that comin' there every . . .

**EVELYN**  No, no, Momma. This is Las Vegas, this is a class operation. The maids make twenty—thirty bucks a night just from change that falls outta these guys' pants. It's a class operation. This last year has been upward mobility all the way. This club was not dealing in nickel and dime tricks.

**RUBY**  It was a class operation.

**EVELYN**  All the way. And then Solly saw me . . .

**RUBY**  Did you know who he . . .

**EVELYN**  Momma, it's a small town. Everybody knows everybody. He was like I told you.

**RUBY**  He was a regular.

**EVELYN**  The girls called him—well, they had their pet name for him, 'cause of his difficulty.

**RUBY**  What was that?

**EVELYN**  No, Momma, it was a disrespectful name; it was . . .

**RUBY**  I mean his difficulty.

**EVELYN**  (*Pause.*) Well, everything changed after me. Just imagine that with me there wasn't any difficulty any more. Old Solly was a new man.

**RUBY**  You made a new man of him.

**EVELYN**  Or, he was like a man for the first time.

**RUBY**  Oh. (*Beat.*) How did you manage . . .

**EVELYN**  So in a manner of speaking, I was his first.

**RUBY**  My . . .

**EVELYN**  It was like magic.

**RUBY**  It was like a fairy tale.

**EVELYN**  Some of the girls said something very similar to that, but they were being vindictive. It's a cut-throat business.

**RUBY**  It was like Cinderella.

**EVELYN**  Only different. That's what they said. The Grapefruit King . . .

**RUBY**  And Juliet.

**EVELYN**  (*Pause, dreamily drinks coffee.*) In fifty-seven years you haven't learned to make coffee.

**RUBY**  Forty-nine. (*Pause.*)

**EVELYN**  (*Looking at the phone.*) I'm scared to call.

**RUBY**  You're looking more yourself.

**EVELYN**  (*Smelling the air.*) What did you call that stuff?

**RUBY**  It's thyme. Like you heard of thyme honey?

**EVELYN**  You try to make honey out of that—

**RUBY**  You don't do it, bees do it. There was a bunch of different herbs, but now it's just thyme. It sort of took over. We got a favorable climate for it. We had all the Italian ones, but they didn't do so good. They started out good, then the thyme just grew right over them.

**EVELYN**  It doesn't have no look to it at all. Can't you get rid of it?

**RUBY**  I would, only it reminds me.

**EVELYN**  It's got the looks of a weed.

**RUBY**  There ain't no weeds, honey, the weeds got crowded out and there ain't nothin' but Thymus Vulgaris. That's what they call it over in Latin.

**EVELYN**  Where?

**RUBY**  You know, like that language in church. All the herbs got an informal name and a formal name; and its formal name in the Latin language is Thymus Vulgaris. I mean I didn't know but . . . Mr. Gonzales told me. I knew all of them; but I don't remember now.

**EVELYN**  I bet.

**RUBY**  It just means thyme, common thyme, like you cook with.

**EVELYN** Well, it's named right then, 'cause I ain't seen anything deliberately grown that looks or smells more common than that does. (*Beat.*) I think I'm scared to call Ed and Nora.

**RUBY** Do you know their number?

**EVELYN** Oh, sure . . . I remember things . . . Solly never does. He's got business worries. (*Dialing slowly.*) What does it matter? When I saw you I knew what it was. It was like the whole Cinderella didn't happen. Like the whole upward mobility didn't . . . he wanted you to come visit with us. I told him how wonderful you was. Wouldn't that be nice? With a garden and a swimming pool and maids?

**RUBY** Maids?

**EVELYN** Everybody I know now has maids, Momma. Ed and Nora's got three or four. Solly's got six or eight. It's funny, you think you won't know how to act. You think all that help is just gonna get in your way, but after a few minutes it's no different than a waitress bringin' you coffee. (*On the phone.*) Hello? (*To Ruby.*) This is one now. (*Phone.*) Is Nora there? This is Evie. (To *Ruby.*) See? She's going to get her. They do their thing and you do . . . (*Phone.*) Hi, honey. (*To Ruby.*) Hold my hand. (*Phone.*) Oh, yeah—she was here, just like always. She was workin' in the herb garden. (*Beat.*) He hasn't?

**RUBY** He hasn't?

**EVELYN** And you ain't heard?

**RUBY** They ain't heard?

**EVELYN** Well, we're here . . . having a cup of coffee. Why don't you jot down the number? Then you call if you hear. Valley 6-84 . . . (*To Ruby.*) What is that; is that a three or another eight?

**RUBY** Let me get my glasses.

**EVELYN** Well, it's your number—never mind, it's a three. (*Phone.*) It's a three. Three four. Yes, I imagine he got stuck in traffic. [My ass.] Well, we're having a nice visit. I haven't had a visit with Momma in a long time. Not in a long time, we ain't visited; that's true ain't it, Momma? Bye-bye. (*She hangs up.*)

**RUBY** I can't really swim anyway.

**EVELYN** Neither can Sol. He's got it for his friends and business associates. That's what he's like . . . I swear I don't know how you can breathe with that stuff choking you. Did you plant it or did it take over?

**RUBY** No, it was planted. Then it took over.

**EVELYN** I expected you to notice something in the columns—

**RUBY** I hardly had a chance to read them.

**EVELYN** Read that one.

**RUBY** I been lookin' for my glasses.

**EVELYN** Well, it say, "Sol—Maidblest—Soretti"—that's the way they do it in columns, they put the grapefruit name in the middle of his name. Maidblest is his grapefruit—and Miss Evelyn Blare—

**RUBY**   Maidblest is his grapefruit?

**EVELYN**   That's not what I'm trying to show you.

**RUBY**   I know Maidblest. They're a popular grapefruit.

**EVELYN**   Oh. Momma. Forty-two states. Out of a possible fifty.

**RUBY**   They're a good grapefruit

**EVELYN**   He's very conscientious about them.

**RUBY**   Well, he ought to be.

**EVELYN**   But just look: It says "Miss Evelyn Blare." "Sol - Maidblest - Soretti and Miss Evelyn Blare were seen" - then it says where all we were seen.

**RUBY**   Where?

**EVELYN**   Well, they're all different.  Wherever it was that night.  They were following us around for statements.  That isn't important.  It says Miss Evelyn Blare.  My rightful name.

**RUBY**   I thought you were usin' . . .

**EVELYN**   All those other names Solly made me throw away.  He said, just throw them away.

**RUBY**   I thought some of them were catchy.

**EVELYN**   So did I, but he didn't want me catchy, he wanted me presentable.

**RUBY**   I always thought Evelyn was such a pretty name.

**EVELYN**   I wasn't gonna tell him, but I figured after the way we met, what was I gonna lie about.

**RUBY**   She used to come on the radio and play the violin.  Evelyn and her magic violin.

**EVELYN**   When his mother found out we was getting married, she cried.

**RUBY**   A lot of mothers don't like that.

**EVELYN**   No, for happiness.  We called them with the news.  We was gonna call you, but I couldn't find your number in the book, so I wrote you a letter.  Only you didn't get it.

**RUBY**   Well . . .(*Sadly sheepish.*)  you looked in the book under Ruby Bentley, didn't you?  And when you wrote, you wrote to me under Ruby Bentley.  Something addressed to the name of Bentley wouldn't find me here no more.

**EVELYN**   Huh?

**RUBY**   Well . . .living here all by myself . . .time on my hands . . .

**EVELYN**   Momma!

**RUBY**   But it wasn't no good.  I was just foolin' myself.  I was livin' in a Cinderella world like you.  It wasn't real.  But you should have seen how I fixed myself up.  Every day.  You wouldn't have known me.

**EVELYN**   What did he take?

**RUBY** It wasn't like that, honey. He didn't even drink. It was like my last fling. I didn't want to tell you, only I didn't know how to explain my heavy heart.

**EVELYN** Momma, you ain't gonna ever have a heavy heart again.

**RUBY** Honey, it broke this time. I'm too old for it. Promise you won't think bad if I tell you something.

**EVELYN** What?

**RUBY** I won't tell you if you're gonna think -

**EVELYN** Momma, how could I ever think bad of you? Haven't I been to every one of your weddings and never been anywhere but on your side every time?

**RUBY** Well, it's over. This one did it. It was his first and my last. He was real excited. He had to teach me how to write my new name - he had a beautiful handwriting.

**EVELYN** What?

**RUBY** Well, I wasn't bending the truth to that patrolman. This is the Gonzales trailer, now. It looks beautiful in writing; let me write it for -

**EVELYN** I know.

**RUBY** He was nineteen.

**EVELYN** Oh, God.

**RUBY** He drove in on a motorbike and he took me by storm.

**EVELYN** Oh, dear God.

**RUBY** We planted tomatoes and herbs and grape vines and all kinds of Italian things. Only they never came up, and he drove off.

**EVELYN** That isn't an Italian name, that's a Mexican name.

**RUBY** Oh, I know, honey, but . . .he dreamed. He was a real dreamer. You should have heard what this place was supposed to be like. He was such a worker. He planted the plants, and then I think he got discouraged.

**EVELYN** Momma, your whole life since I've known you has just been one sad story after another.

**RUBY** He liked my golden hair. Since he left, I've just not had energy to do for myself. He just took all my energy with him when he left. This year I've just sat around.

**EVELYN** What else did he take?

**RUBY** He wasn't like those others, Evelyn. He'd been to school down at the extension of the Junior College. He'd had a full year of classes at the college before he gave up. And if he hadn't gotten discouraged about this place, he would have had it looking better that it ever did.

**EVELYN** *Vicks VapoRub.*

**RUBY** Well, that's why I can't do nothin' about it. He said it was a favorable climate for it. Like Italy. And honey, he spoke English better than me. But the thyme is the only thing that reminds me.

**EVELYN** Momma, as far as I'm concerned, I've come here none too soon. You don't want to let yourself go. You have to have a grip on yourself. That's the one thing we've always had was a grip on ourselves.

**RUBY** I have, always till now. We sent out announcements of our wedding. I didn't even do that my first time. My first and me just run off. My sailor, Willy, and me run off and eloped the day before he shipped out. Then he got himself killed at sea.

**EVELYN** He didn't get himself killed at—

**RUBY** Honey, even if you slip off the deck while you're swabbin' it down, it's being killed at sea. I've always thought they shouldn't have those soapsuds on deck. You'd think with all the chemicals they got, they'd invent something less hazardous. And your daddy and me, we didn't let anybody know.

**EVELYN** I'd hope not.

**RUBY** I don't want you to be bitter about your daddy, Evelyn. I've never thought he abandoned us.

**EVELYN** I know you ain't.

**RUBY** He used to drink so bad, and he had such trouble finding the house, I've always thought that one night he just didn't find it.

**EVELYN** I know you have.

**RUBY** Out of all of them, I liked Jose the best.

**EVELYN** Jose Gonzales, Jesus God.

**RUBY** He dreamed.

**EVELYN** Ummm.

**RUBY** And I always had a fondness for Otto.

**EVELYN** I don't remember no—

**RUBY** You know Otto. The gambler. You was just little. I had a fondness for Otto because he had a twinkle in his eye. I mean, it wasn't for me, it was for blackjack, but it was a twinkle. (*Pause.*) I couldn't send you an announcement about the marriage 'cause I didn't know where you was living. And I wanted you there real bad.

**EVELYN** I've just been terrible to you this last two years, ain't I? We ain't had no time together in too long.

**RUBY** Not since you growed up. But you was a nice little girl. That's how I know your heart, because I know how nice you was.

**EVELYN** I know. (*Comes to a decision.*) Can I be perfectly honest, Momma?

**RUBY** Honey, your momma isn't strong. She can't take criticism the way she used to.

**EVELYN** No, this is perfectly honest about me. See, Solly didn't show up and you didn't show up and I said I'd go looking for you. Momma, I got into that air-conditioned taxicab, with the windows rolled up, and pulled away from Ed and Nora's house, and the last thing I'd expect happened to me. It was like a huge weight was being lifted off my body.

RUBY   How big a man is he?

EVELYN   It was like my whole body was just sayin': Oh, thank goodness, I'm not gonna have to go through with it.

RUBY   I don't think that means anything. I think that's just butterflies. I've got 'em every time.

EVELYN   He is big, actually.

RUBY   Oh.

EVELYN   I mean, he ain't tall, but . . .

RUBY   But he's big. But he's nice, though.

EVELYN   Oh, he gets nice sometimes . . . I guess . . .

RUBY   Is it the money? Maybe you ain't used to having money.

EVELYN   Oh, no, Momma, it's never quite the money; it's kinda more like what I gotta do to get it.

RUBY   Solly sounds like a generous person. That's important, honey.

EVELYN   Oh . . . no. I don't think really generous people make millions of dollars. They ain't like us, Momma.

COP   (*Returns, rather bounding onto the platform. He has unbuttoned his shirt to the waist.*) Excuse me, ladies.

RUBY   Oh, my goodness.

EVELYN   Oh, good grief.

COP   Just passing back through. See. I've been feeling pretty bad. I think I projected a misleading impression, and it's been troubling me. See, I think I was kinna soft on the outside and hard on the inside.

RUBY   I don't see anything wrong with that, do you?

EVELYN   Sounds familiar.

COP   But, see, the ticket is to be kinda tough on the outside, and kinna marshmallowy, on the inside, if you follow me. I think that covers a wide range. See, that's good for, say, army personnel. That's good for cowboys—now, I don't want to say that I've actually ridden a horse, but I have a natural athletic ability.

RUBY   I bet you have.

EVELYN   Momma.

RUBY   And I think he'd make a very lovely football player on the television.

COP   Now, see, there it fits again. They're tough outside and kinda puddin'y on the inside.

RUBY   I know, like when their wife has her miscarriage.

COP   I'd just fold up.

RUBY   Or when their best buddy comes down with one of those terminal things they're always havin'.

**COP**  Oh, lord, Miss, see, I'd just crumple. I mean, I wouldn't crack.

**RUBY**  I know, but you'd crumple.

**EVELYN**  Momma.

**RUBY**  Have you had any luck with trying to fulfill your appointed duty?

**EVELYN**  Momma!

**COP**  What? Oh, well, to tell you the truth, I haven't done too well on that. See, nobody in this trailer park seems to know anybody else in this trailer park. And I was trying to concentrate on being kinna—soft, you know—

**RUBY**  On the inside.

**COP**  Yeah. And I'm afraid I didn't get too far. They mostly shut the door in my face.

**EVELYN**  Well, anytime.

**COP**  See, I thought I'd come on all tough, you know. Duty first.

**RUBY**  But that wouldn't fool nobody that could see the real marshmallow that you was hiding.

**COP**  Right.

**EVELYN**  Momma.

**COP**  And they'd say: Yes, this is the Bentley uh—trailer, and then I'd sit down and say: I bring you good tidings of great joy.

**RUBY**  Which shall be to all—

**EVELYN**  Hold it. Hold it. Watta you mean? You got a message?

**RUBY**  Oh, my goodness, why didn't you say that?

**COP**  Yes, ma'am, somebody called the highway patrol with a message for Mrs. Bentley, female, Caucasian, about sixty.

**RUBY**  Sixty?

**EVELYN**  Well, even though this isn't the Bentley uh—residence, and even though we don't know the party of whom you seek—

**RUBY**  But, honey, if it's good, then—

**EVELYN**  Foxy, Momma, I've seen it a hundred times.

**RUBY**  Not this sweet young—

**EVELYN**  Every step of the way.

**RUBY**  Such a nice honest chest.

**EVELYN**  Cool it, Momma.

**RUBY**  Breezed in on a motorcycle.

**EVELYN**  That's what I mean. (*To Cop.*) Even though we're not the party of whom you seek, should we have been such a party, what message of great joy would you have imparted?

**COP**  Oh. Well, ma'am, I'm sorry, but that would come under official, private police department duty and couldn't be divulged.

**RUBY**  You could maybe pretend . . . I'll bet you could do that.

**COP**  No, ma'am, I'm afraid that that—

**EVELYN**  What Momma is sayin' is we wouldn't want you to blow your big scene.

**COP** Oh! Oh, yeah. Oh, boy. Well, it—under the right circumstances—it would go something like . . . ( *Thinks for a very long time. Finally.*) I'll tell you, I'll go home and work on it and come back tomorrow.

**RUBY** Come on, just whatever comes to your mind.

**EVELYN** Just spit it out.

**COP** I'd feel more comfortable if—

**EVELYN** Spit while the iron's hot.

**COP** See, I just wish I had a little more time, 'cause how I do on this is very important to me. I mean, I'm not gettin' any younger.

**EVELYN** I've aged ten years since you come in.

**COP** Well, it would go something like: Mister Solly said that we was to turn over every stone looking for this Mrs. Rose—

**RUBY** Ruby.

**EVELYN** Momma.

**COP** Thank you, Miss Ruby Bentley, 'cause that party was his precious fiancee's mother.

**EVELYN** That's lovely, isn't that lovely. That has great human warmth and hope.

**RUBY** Under every stone?

**COP** And to tell her if she heard from her lovely and talented daughter, that he had lost the address of his best friend in the world and couldn't find the street, and that he would be waiting at Schwab's Drug Store all night, which he is sure he can find.

**RUBY** Oh, honey. It's all come true. It's the answer to an unspoken prayer.

**EVELYN** Did you hear? Is all right with the world? Momma, not once did I doubt. Not in my heart of hearts.

**COP** Excuse me, could I run that through again?

**EVELYN** Honey, it was fine—

**COP** It's important to get it right, I'm not getting any—

**EVELYN** We know, honey—you go home like you planned and you work on it.

**COP** I'd feel much more comfortable doing that. I think the important thing is to relax.

**RUBY** In almost everything you do.

**COP** Is eight o'clock tomorrow morning too early?

**EVELYN** I think you're going to make something really marvelous out of this.

**COP** It's not big; you know, it isn't much—it shouldn't be bigger than the circumstances warrant, if you—

**EVELYN** You work on it, we'll let you know.

**COP** (*Being nudged out.*) Simple, you know, but effective. (*Falls off* *platform.*)

**EVELYN**  That's it: that's the ticket.

**COP**  Warm, you know, but simple and direct.

**EVELYN**  First thing tomorrow.

**COP**  I appreciate it, I do. Thank you. (*Exits.*)

**RUBY**  (*Ruby and Evelyn sit. After a pause. Beaming.* ) My little baby. On her wedding day. I never thought I'd see it.

**EVELYN**  I know. He just couldn't find the house. See, usually he has a chauffeur for that, but we're going on our honeymoon today.

**RUBY**  Sure she is. My little baby on her honeymoon. (*Pause. Evelyn is staring off. She lights a cigarette, sighs, frowning.*) What's wrong honey? (*Pause.*) Are the butterflies back again? (*Pause.*) Did you feel the weight again?

**EVELYN**  Oh . . . Kinda.

**RUBY**  Sometimes good things when they really come are kinda a let-down, I know. But think of your future.

**EVELYN**  Ummm.

**RUBY**  Do you love him? (*Pause.*) You love him, don't you?

**EVELYN**  Oh, it's just . . . I wouldn't want to let you down or anything. I mean the swimming pool and never having to turn your hand. But, Momma, I was beginning to feel so . . . comfortable, here with you. I don't know when the last time it was that I was comfortable. I mean, I can't spread out in here like I'd like and I'm really beginning to feel choked up on that weed, but in spite of that . . .

**RUBY**  I was too. It's nice; we ain't had much time.

**EVELYN**  Not here.

**RUBY**  I know.

**EVELYN**  We ought to get you away from here.

**RUBY**  I know.

**EVELYN**  So maybe the two of us should go somewhere.

**RUBY**  That would have been nice. I was kinda beginning to imagine it.

**EVELYN**  We ain't had no time at all, like we should.

**RUBY**  What do you want to do, honey?

**EVELYN**  Well . . . (*A wondering pause.*) . . . uh . . . (*Off.*) Could I have a spot? I'd like one of your pale amber spots. (*The lights fade to an amber spot on her.*)

**RUBY**  That's just amazing.

**EVELYN**  Momma, I told you, carte blanche. (*This to the audience.*) You see. It's all a question of priorities. Like life is basically a question of priorities. Like that's a big surprise, but that kid said, "I'm not getting any younger," and that changed everything. That just went right through me. I mean, he can say that and mean one thing, but to me it hit something else. It hit like: What are those things that you're gonna wish you'd done, Evelyn? Or like—see marrying Solly is a possible. But where am I? And what are the things that— (*To off.*) Could we get this wide enough for Momma? (*To Ruby.*) Scoot in. You okay? (*To audience.*) Now, see, this is gonna come as no earthshaking revelation, but there are two kinds of people in the world. Everything you read, anyone you talk to knows that. In Sunday school we learned there was the alive and the dead.

**RUBY** Quick and the dead. Amen. (*All these responses, quiet echoes, as in church.*)

**EVELYN** There's the users and the used. Or as Solly says, him being in the produce business, he thinks in food, Solly says there's the eaters and the eatens. And it doesn't take 20-20 vision to see that Momma and me are mainly both eatens.

**RUBY** Eatens, that's right.

**EVELYN** Which is all right—

**RUBY** It's all right.

**EVELYN** I mean, the eaters gotta have something to eat or everybody would be up the creek.

**RUBY** Without a paddle.

**EVELYN** But every once in a while an eaten has gotta get away and store up. 'Cause it takes a lotta fortitude being an eaten.

**RUBY** Once in a while the eatens gotta take a break.

**EVELYN** So what is it that I need and Momma needs? Well, really, not much. There's a little place I know on the ocean, with a breeze and the sun . . . that'd be enough.

**RUBY** That'd be enough.

**EVELYN** A while there, getting to re-know the things we knew. Just the two of us.

**RUBY** Would you like that? I think I'd like that.

**EVELYN** Just to draw a little strength.

**RUBY** Take a little time off.

**EVELYN** We've just both got too tired.

**RUBY** And we're gonna take a little time off.

**EVELYN** That's what I want.

**RUBY** So now we know. That's gonna be nice.

**EVELYN** It is.

**RUBY** What's wrong, honey?

**EVELYN** (*Pause.*) Oh, Jesus. I feel just rotten, 'cause I guess this is the end, and I really can't abide ends. Like they say someone was okay, but he came to a bad end. Well, I'm here to tell you as far as I'm concerned, all ends are bad. And we all come to a bad end. And of course, finding Momma here, I say: Oh, that's terrible, I'll take her out of here. And that damned kid says: I'm not getting any younger, and you know that there ain't no out of here. 'Cause past the two kinds of people, past the eaters and the eaten, it's all just meat, it's all just one kind of people and every man-jack of them comin' to a bad end.

RUBY  Oh, sure.

EVELYN  And every man-jack of 'em living here. With no real getting out of here. (*Blows her nose. To Ruby.*) Did you want to say something?

RUBY  If that place is on the ocean, I hope there's a pool, 'cause I hate gettin' my hair wet.

EVELYN  You can't swim, I thought.

RUBY  Well, no, but it'd be cooling to splash around a bit. That'd be nice.

EVELYN  You ready to go now?

RUBY  I think I'd like that, honey. If you're sure.

EVELYN  I'm sure.

RUBY  But, honey, even though everybody might be livin' here, like you said. And I know when you say "here," you don't mean here, you mean "here," but, honey, even though they might be livin' here . . . it wouldn't hurt them, once in a while—just to kinda restore themselves, like you said—it wouldn't hurt them to get away.

**BLACKOUT**

# BREAKFAST AT THE TRACK  (January 1983)

## AUTHOR'S NOTE

This is one of several very short plays, written for Circle Rep benefit nights. On this occasion the company writers drew times of day out of a hat. I drew 6:30 A.M. Since I'm a night person and have experienced this scene with a succession of lovers and friends, it's the only acquaintance I have of that hour. Actually this should probably be set at 5:30 if the windows are just turning blue in August, but, as I say, I'm a little shaky on specifics at this time of day. I like the 10 minute play form. It makes for a very enjoyable evening. If you don't like the play you're watching you know in a very short time it'll be over and you might like the next one. This was written very quickly, I've never come up with names for the characters. They were played by Conchata Ferrell and Jonathan Hogan, quite ably directed by the author, I thought, till Rod Marriot told me there had been a much funnier production done in Minnesota, with a real director.


BREAKFAST AT THE TRACK was first presented as part of a benefit evening at the Lucille Lortel Theater in January 1983, directed by the author with the following cast:

S: Conchata Ferrell
H: Jonathan Hogan


## CHARACTERS

S  Wife
H  Husband


## SCENE

A hotel room, 6:30 AM.

# BREAKFAST AT THE TRACK

S   Who's there?

H   Just me, love.

S   Whadda you doing?

H   What do you mean?

S   What?

H   Just getting up.

S   You sick?

H   No, I'm getting up. I was lying there, planning the day, it's time to get up.

S   What.

H   What what?

S   Time. Time.

H   It's after six-thirty.

S   Oh, Jesus Christ, what in the yellow hell are you doing up at six fucking thirty in the middle of the night?

H   It's morning, darling, open your eyes.

S   It's pitch fucking black, you do this every morning.

H   It's clear as a bell, the windows have all gone blue, in about eight minutes the sun will be up.

S   You do this every fucking morning.

H   What time did you go to sleep?

S   Shut up.

H   I went to sleep at one thirty, you were reading.

S   I'll kill, I'll kill. You do this every . . . (*Pause.*)

H   I can't just lie there. Wide awake. We have breakfast at the track.

S   Who's there? What's happening?

H   I said we have breakfast at the track.

S   What? Oh, God . . . Oh, God . . . what are you talking about?

H   What time did you go to sleep? How long did you read?

S   Late. Go to sleep. It was morning.

H   It wasn't morning, it's morning now.

S   Late. I don't know, I don't remember.

H   How can you not remember when you went to sleep? You do this every morning. What were you reading?

S   I don't believe you're asking me questions.

H   How long have we been married?

S   You know better than this.

H   You know how long we've been married.

S   I do not. Shut up. At this hour I would not hazard a guess at your first name.

H   It's the fourteenth.

S   What? The fourteenth what?

H   Today is the fourteenth, love, you're not listening.

S   Um. Of what?

H   You're joking.

S   Of what month?

H   August. You know that.

S   How did it get to be August?

H   I don't know how you can do that.

S   Please wake me up when I've slept eight hours.

H   I don't know what time you went to sleep. (*Beat.*) I don't know how you can do that. We came up to Saratoga for a vacation, sunshine, excitement, music, horse racing, and you spend every waking hour asleep. You stay up all night reading and miss the whole day. Why do you do that?

S   (*As before.*) What? Who's there? What's happening?

H   How can you do that on a vacation? We've had no time together. I feel like we're taking separate vacations.

S   Oh, God. I don't believe you're still talking.

H   Very well, we won't talk. We never talk. We never do a damn thing.

S   If you don't shut up I'll kill you, I'm not kidding.

H   . . . You don't have to go to breakfast at the track, I can go by myself.

S   Go where?

H   Breakfast at the track.

S   . . . You can not possibly be talking about food.

H   Steve told us how beautiful it was, going out to the track, watching the jockeys exercise the horses, with the mist rising from the ground; then they serve breakfast—Bloody Marys, eggs, they have kippers—

S   Oh, God.

H   I remember what you said, you were very funny, everyone laughed. You asked when all this took place and he said seven o'clock and you said you weren't as young as you used to be and you very seldom stayed up that late anymore. And everyone thought it was a joke.

S   Do I talk to you? When you're trying to go to sleep? Do I prod you and try to make you feel guilty? Just because you're going to sleep?

H   Are you kidding? Not after I'm asleep, maybe; but if I had my way I'd go to sleep every night by eleven. Eleven-thirty. You're not ready to go out, you're not ready to eat, you're not ready to go home. You keep me up 'till one or two in the morning.

S   And you get up at six-thirty. Water. Water. (*Gets up.*)

H   It's daylight. I get up at the same time every morning. I can't help it. I don't believe in lying in bed all day. And today is very special.

S   Wait a minute. Are we in Saratoga? Isn't this Saratoga?

H   What are you talking about?

S   Are we in Saratoga? Yes or no.

H   Yes.

S   Jesus H. Christ. We're on vacation. (*Flops down.*)

H   That's what I said.

S   We are on a fucking vacation and you get up at six fucking . . . sick. You are sick.

H   Sick is lying in bed all day.

S   Sick is being unable to sleep more than two hours just because you'll miss the sunrise.

H   I like the sunrise. It makes my day. It makes my day. It sets me up. it's Christian.

S   If you try to make a virtue out of neurotic behavior . . .

H   You don't have to go.

S   I'll kill. If you don't shut up.

H   I can go by myself. No one will say anything. They'll think it's funny.

S   After however many years of marriage, you have not yet realized—

H   Two years of marriage. Two. Two. Two.

S   —You have not yet realized that you are a morning person and I am not a morning person. That you require four hours sleep and I require a minimum of eight. I do not wake up. I must carefully re-connect my spine every morning. Vertebrae by vertebrae. My eyes do not open. You wake up ready for the day and I wake up ready for the grave. Please do not do this. Good night. Good morning.

H   I don't know about you but I don't consider this much of a marriage.

S   I will kill. There will be a former husband and a widow. I'll be in prison. I'll get some rest.

H   Well, then, no. I don't understand getting up like that. I don't understand sleeping all day.

S   You do exactly the same thing. Only you do it at the other end of the day. We go to a party. At the stroke of ten forty-five you start to unbutton your spine, bone by fucking bone. I can see it happening. You start at the butt and work up to your neck and then your head begins to nod and you get a martyred expression on your face. Till I agree to be your crutch on the way home. Don't give me you don't understand, you do the same thing. We're home by eleven-fifteen every night, you're asleep by eleven-seventeen.

H   In bed at least.

S   Out.

H   Not always.

S   Out cold. Always.

**H**  Well, what do you expect; I'm up by six-thirty.

**S**  You have been known to be up at four.

**H**  I like it.

**S**  Fine.

**H**  I'm in bed, you sure don't come to bed.

**S**  Are you talking sex? I tried. I got bruised. If I snuggle up to you you elbow me in the ribs. I've gotten bruises.

**H**  If we skip the night, I think maybe in the morning.

**S**  That's obscene.

**H**  I cuddle up to you and I get screamed at.

**S**  I have no memory of you cuddling up to me in the morning.

**H**  Of course not. You're not putting your spine together for another hour. (*Count 10.*) Are you asleep.

**S**  What? What's happening? Who's there?

**H**  It's OK. I have to take a shower. I'll be late. You sleep. (*Exits. Shower sounds.*)

**S**  I'll kill. I truly will kill. Our conversations have been taped for evidence at my trial. (*Beat.*) Breakfast at the fucking track. Mist rising from the fucking ground. Bloody Marys, jockeys, horses, kippers . . . (*Looking at clock.*) Six fuckin' forty. The fuckin' windows are growing blue. I'm a goddamned martyr . . . Jesus.

**H**  (*Off, after a pause.*) Honey? You getting up?

**S**  What? What's happening? Who's there?

### BLACKOUT

# SAY DE KOONING  (August 1983)


## AUTHOR'S NOTE

This was written for the East End Gay Organization.  EEGO has a benefit evening of theater every Labor Day weekend.  (The East End being the far end of Long Island, in the general area of the Hamptons — the watering hole of the brittle upper crust, jet–setters, and general Eurotrash for a hundred years.)  The Hamptons are a hundred miles from Manhattan via the Long Island Expressway which has been called the World's Largest Parking Lot.  I've always thought there was a longer, maybe somewhat different play for these characters and this situation, but it keeps eluding me.


SAY DE KOONING was first presented by EEGO at the auditorium of Southampton College on September 7, 1983.  It was designed and directed by John Hawkins with the following cast:

WILLIE: Joan Copeland
BOB: Kelly Connell
MANDY: Lisa Emery


## CHARACTERS

WILLIE
BOB
MANDY


## SCENE

Friday noon of Labor Day Weekend. The living room of an old house near the beach on the East End of Long Island. Say Bridgehampton. There are a number of cardboard boxes stacked about. One box contains large sketching pads, another is filled with Western gear: chaps, etc. A table holds a decanter of brandy and glasses. There is an exit to the kitchen, another to a front hall, and enough wicker furniture of a quality to indicate a comfortably turned-out summer rental.

# SAY DE KOONING

*Bob is standing in the room. He is twenty-five, slight, soft-spoken, and in no way striking on first notice. Willie enters carrying a plant with a ball of earth in her bare hands. She is 45, striking only in that she is strong, dynamic and controlled. At the moment she is out of control and screaming.*

**WILLIE**  Where the hell is the goddamned box?

**BOB**  I just mopped the floor, Willie.

**WILLIE**  Get your fucking socks out of my fucking King Kullen box. And you're blocking my car.

**BOB**  If you're going to get butch and belligerent, I don't need it today....

**WILLIE**  Get your fucking things out of the goddamned box, if you don't want this dumped in the middle of your goddamned floor. I just want the rosemary and the goddamned African daisy and I'll be out of your way.

**BOB**  OK. (*Dumps the box.*) There. Jesus. And your hand is bleeding.

**WILLIE**  I know I'm bleeding, I couldn't find the goddamned shovel.

**BOB**  It's in the garage. What did you dig that up with?

**WILLIE**  My fucking hands. What in the hell does it look like I—and get your car out of the drive, too.

**BOB**  OK, Jesus.

**WILLIE**  And while you're at it you can tell that bitch friend of yours — (*She dumps the plant in the box. Stops dead. All energy and anger drain away. She takes a breath, begins to wipe her hands with a handkerchief. Sits. Pause. Level.*) I'm a wreck. I'm an idiot. I'm crazy to even be out here. I left the damn city early, which was the popular thing to do as everybody else decided to — you've never seen traffic like that. It looked like Dean and Deluca was giving something away.

**BOB**  They weren't.

**WILLIE**  I loathe Long Island. I loathe the L.I.E. It is flat, boring, badly planned, hot and under repair. With all the goddamned local traffic weaving on and off. I understand what's-his-name drove off the damn thing again last week and hit another tree. Out of sheer boredom probably. If they don't take his license away there won't be a tree left standing on the island. It took me thirty-eight minutes in a driving cloudburst to get from the light to the Monument. And in that mood I had to charm some local, cocky, smirking seventeen-year-old total delinquent into parting with one of the four hundred empty cardboard boxes he was gloating over. Can you imagine me charming and co-quettish?

**BOB**  No.

**WILLIE**  Well I was. Had anyone I work with seen me they would have thrown up.

**BOB**  You drove all the way out here for two plants?

**WILLIE**  (*Glares at him.*) Yes.

**BOB**  Oh.

**WILLIE**  I didn't claim it was rational.

**BOB**  No. (*Beat.*) It didn't rain here. (*Beat.*) Do you think you'd like a drink? I think it's time for a drink.

**WILLIE**  When did you start drinking?

**BOB**  Out here you meet two kinds of people. Those who are alcoholics and go to AA and those who are alcoholics and don't go to AA. This is Mandy's brandy. Are you going to see her, because I'm not if I can avoid it.

**WILLIE**  Skip it then, I don't need it.

**BOB**  What the hell, you probably bought it.

**WILLIE**  I did.

**BOB**  We better drink it before it goes bad.

**WILLIE**  Like everything else.

**BOB**  You didn't get out much this summer, huh?

**WILLIE**  What summer? I didn't see any summer.

**BOB**  (*Re brandy.*) This is good.

**WILLIE**  Forty-eight bucks a bottle, you should only use it for cologne. What a washout. This summer. What a washout.

**BOB**  Ben's party was fun.

**WILLIE**  Ben who?

**BOB**  Forget it, you wouldn't have liked it. Did you get a lot of work done in the city, anyway? A lot of prisoners corrected, or whatever it is you do? (*She stares, looks at him or not, doesn't speak.*) I mean something should come from . . . (*Pause.*) I haven't packed the medicine cabinet so if we have any Band-Aids they should be in there. (*Pause.*) You didn't even get a good tan. For fifteen hundred bucks you should at least get a tan. Unless you paid Mandy's share too, in which case for three . . . (*Pause.*) Are you doing one of those yoga breathing things? (*Pause.*) Well, I've run out of opening gambits. I'll move the car and see you around sometime.

**WILLIE**  (*Looks at her hand.*) It's not that bad. It's just a scratch. As they say in the Westerns.

**BOB**  Just grazed the skull.

**WILLIE**  Tell me about it.

**BOB** You should put something on it anyway. The top seven inches of soil out here are totally the product of the Union Carbide Company. It'll kill anything that moves.

**WILLIE** I didn't pay Mandy's share. Why should I? She makes twice the salary I do. The city is hardly on the same pay scale as *Playboy* magazine.

**BOB** She doesn't exactly work for *Playboy*.

**WILLIE** She works for the photographer who works for *Playboy* and *Hustler* and *Snicker* and *Licker* and *Kicker* and *Fucker* and all the rest of the centerfold come-rags. She *can afford* it. What's his name?

**BOB** Who?

**WILLIE** The damn photographer she works with?

**BOB** Kent. Probably has a sister name True, a brother Winston.

**WILLIE** I didn't much like you at the beginning of the summer. I said when I got to know you better . . . I've been out here twice . . .

**BOB** It's just as well. I don't think I improve . . . I imagined psychiatrists to be more organized. Very firm office hours, lots of leisure time; leave early Friday, come in at noon on Monday.

**WILLIE** Tuesday. Come in at noon on Tuesday. Walk around the office making little practice putts.

**BOB** (*Beat.*) You seem a little steadier now. I mean you're breathing. You weren't breathing when you came in—

**WILLIE** I know, I know.

**BOB** You're better qualified to judge than I am, but you were a little hysterical. That's not the right word, I don't —

**WILLIE** No, that was definitely hysteria. What a washout. This summer. What a washout.

**BOB** You in a hurry? I'll move the car.

**WILLIE** I don't know. I thought I'd get back . . .

**BOB** You have appointments?

**WILLIE** No, I've had this weekend clear since . . . May. I'm clear 'til noon Tuesday. Where's Jack?

**BOB** Who's Jack?

**WILLIE** Wasn't it Jack? Your friend.

**BOB** Joe.

**WILLIE** (*Dismissing it.*) Well, Mandy knew him, I didn't know him. This whole sharing a house with you and Jack was her idea.

**BOB** Yeah. Well, at the time I'd only known Joe about three weeks; Joe doesn't come around anymore.

**WILLIE** Mandy can really pick 'em.

**BOB** Yeah, me too.

**WILLIE** No, maybe you got stung and maybe I work with prisoners six days a week, but Mandy actually has the sensory apparatus to spot a criminal mind from across the room.

**BOB**  Actually Joe came around last week, but he was with some Froot-Loop from the Swamp. He took his stuff. He said the sun had passed its solstice and he was shipping off to either Sarasota or San Francisco, I forget.

**WILLIE**  What's all this rodeo crap, then? That doesn't look like you.

**BOB**  Oh, that's Mandy's. (*Beat.*) I sort of got to like her in spite of herself you know?

**WILLIE**  Mandy's a whore.

**BOB**  No, I don't think Mandy's a whore; she just moves faster than most people. She has this need to be liked, or she likes to stir things up or keep things moving, or she has to be the center of everything that's — no you're right, she's pretty much a whore.

**WILLIE**  God, I'm exhausted, it's not even one o'clock.

**BOB**  Don't you get a month off or something?

**WILLIE**  When you work for the city? You're dreaming.

**BOB**  All these psychiatrists were out during August. I must have met twenty of them. You imagine everyone in Manhattan crawling the walls.

**WILLIE**  They were, but no more than usual. Where did you meet all these shrinks; you been making the rounds of the bars?

**BOB**  No, Ben's party. They're very into free food. It's nicer during the week. I've met a lot of locals; I don't really go out much.

**WILLIE**  You've been painting?

**BOB**  Did Mandy tell you? Yeah, I did about four hundred shelves for one lady, and all the woodwork on another house. It's not much, you know, but it gives me enough to live on so I can stay out.

**WILLIE**  I meant painting. Pictures. Are you still working?

**BOB**  Oh, that, sure. Only I don't paint, I draw. Pen and ink, brush, pencil. Yeah, a lot. Every day. I mean, you know, not a deliberate program, it's just something I've been doing. Kinda compulsively. I mean there's nothing like screwing up your love life to make you interested in work.

**WILLIE**  Tell me about it.

**BOB**  I want to get into etching, but it's too expensive.

**WILLIE**  I've been meaning to tell you, that big drawing Mandy gave me . . . I had it framed for the office. I don't think there's been a person in the room who hasn't asked who did it. It's really very beautiful. Improves my day — for which I certainly want to thank you. I know the flower was supposed to be funny in some way, but I forget what it was. What was it, a Kansas gay feather?

**BOB**  A bull thistle.

**WILLIE**  Oh. I'll remember. Vividly. What are you working on now?

**BOB** Oh — the usual. Plants, shells, any natural thing. I was going to do some of the old buildings but I couldn't get into it. Anything really; some people on the beach, but mostly leaves, shells . . . like that. Plants. Excuse me, but I'm kinda hysterical, too. I mean going back to the city. You know? I don't know if I have an apartment anymore. The phone's been turned off. And I got this note from the super that said I hadn't paid any rent —

**WILLIE** I thought you sent it into town in cash—

**BOB** Yeah, I did — with Joe.

**WILLIE** Oh boy.

**BOB** And he's a little crazy. Well, you wouldn't call him crazy, you'd probably say he had something —

**WILLIE** No, I'd call him crazy. The two of you seemed like a mismatch from the — well, it's none of my business.

**BOB** I think probably it falls into the category of your business.

**WILLIE** I'm not in private practice.

**BOB** You know, I really can't *not* ask. I thought I could, but why did you drive all the way out here for just the African daisy and the rosemary?

**WILLIE** I thought you had an imagination.

**BOB** I've been trying to put them together: take this African flower and this herb . . . but I've strayed into the occult.

**WILLIE** Mandy gave me the African daisy when we came out. She said if we dug it up before a strong frost it would bloom all winter.

**BOB** It will.

**WILLIE** So I've heard.

**BOB** And rosemary is for remembrance. Pray you, love, remember. (*Willie glares at him.*) I was in Hamlet when I was fourteen. Boy's school. Very literary. The school.

**WILLIE** You're not my ideal great Dane, if you'll forgive me.

**BOB** Oh, please. Do I look like a Hamlet?

**WILLIE** What did you play, Ophelia?

**BOB** Thanks. Tragedy of my young life.

**WILLIE** Sorry.

**BOB** Are you kidding? I would have been a fabulous Ophelia. Our Ophelia was a cow. You're supposed to have great insight.

**WILLIE** Usually that just means psyched.

**BOB** Well, then, what do I look like?

**WILLIE** (*After a moment.*) Polonius.

**BOB** You might have lied. I was a very effective Polonius, too. Only I was always being reprimanded for mouthing Ophelia's lines. Actually by the time we opened I stole the damn show. After I got behind the apse or the orris or whatever it was —

**WILLIE** Arras. Apse is part of a church. Orris is a root.

**BOB** After I got behind the arras the play was over. Also the Hamlet was in over his head. Butchy Winkowski. Captain of the gym team — and on stage he moved like a goat. Voice like a tobacco auctioneer.

**WILLIE** How did he get the part?

**BOB** Life in a boy's school is pretty much like like anywhere else.

**WILLIE** The director was fucking him. I didn't know what sex was when I was fourteen.

**BOB** You went to the wrong school.

**WILLIE** Tell me about it. So. What's wrong with you?

**BOB** Huh?

**WILLIE** What's wrong with you?

**BOB** Uh . . . how do you . . . ? Nothing, actually . . . this is just the way I behave. Unless you're noticing something. Am I blinking or limping or listing to the left or something? Nothing's wrong with me . . . I'm fine . . .

**WILLIE** Mandy said you were in trouble.

**BOB** Could I have that again? You couldn't have just said what I thought you just said. You said Mandy said I—

**WILLIE** Mandy said you were—

**BOB** —*Mandy* said *I* was in *trouble*?

**WILLIE** She said you were in trouble.

**BOB** That lesbo, nympho, drugged-over scene-designer for some soft-core porno prick-tease centerfold sleaze-sheet said I was in trouble? That bitch. If I were in trouble it would be because she got me there, but as it happens — (*Under control.*) No. Not me. I'm fine. I'm not in trouble. I don't know what area she had in mind, but . . . Please don't stare at me.

**WILLIE** Sorry.

**BOB** I always think you're seeing some deep-seated neurosis and you're too professional to tell me about it. You always do that.

**WILLIE** Sorry.

**BOB** Every time you leave the room I think you're going to bill me for your time.

**WILLIE** Not at all.

**BOB** Medical people should be very careful about the way they look at people. Especially susceptible people.

**WILLIE** How do you think you're susceptible?

**BOB** Oh . . . kinda like a soft cheese. You know you put a soft cheese in the refrigerator overnight and it comes out tasting like the cucumber and the green onion and the red pepper . . . It doesn't seem to have a definite shape of its own —

**WILLIE** I'm not really much into cheese.

**BOB** Well, I'm susceptible like that. (*Gently scratches his arm.*)

**WILLIE**  So you're not in trouble.

**BOB**  Listen, just tell Mandy to mind her — never mind, I'll tell her my-self, only I won't because I won't see her and if I were to see her I wouldn't talk to her but if I were to talk to her, I'd tell her myself. You're looking at me like that again.

**WILLIE**  Sorry. Do you have a bite or something? You're scratching your arm.

**BOB**  I'm not scratching.

**WILLIE**  My mistake.

**BOB**  It is very important that I'm not scratching.

**WILLIE**  What a washout. This summer. What a washout. When you asked if I was doing a breathing thing, as it happens I was.

**BOB**  What's it for?

**WILLIE**  It's to help you relax. In times of crisis.

**BOB**  You'll have to teach me how to do it.

**WILLIE**  It doesn't work. (*She glances at a stack of notepaper by the phone.*) What are you writing — a book?

**BOB**  No joke. Come on, don't read that.

**WILLIE**  It says it's for Mandy.

**BOB**  They're Mandy's phone messages —

**WILLIE**  That should be interesting.

**BOB**  Come on.

**WILLIE**  They're not yours.

**BOB**  Well, I wrote them. Until I give them to Mandy they're my prop-erty. If and when I decide. Come on, they're all from you anyway.

**WILLIE**  Sure. (*Reads.*) Mandy, Willie called, says please call her. (*Next.*) Mandy, Willie called just to talk, bad week. (*Next.*) Mandy, Willie called, no message except she was belligerent, angry and short and she doesn't know how to talk on the phone. (*Next.*) Mandy, Willie called, she was belligerent, angry and short but I think she said for you to call if you found your tongue. (I said when she found her tongue.) (*Next.*) Mandy, Willie called, said Susan M. is sick and depressed and might lose her job, would like to hear from you. (*Next.*) Mandy, Willie called, says she will come out this weekend, would like not to see you or would not like to see you. She was belligerent, angry and short. (*Next.*) Mandy, Willie —

**BOB**  And so on and so on, you get the picture —

**WILLIE**  I like this — called, said Kent is looking for you; Willie told him she was not your secretary. P.S. Neither am I.

**BOB**  Etcetera, etcetera.

**WILLIE**  (*Next.*) Mandy, Willie called. Your clothes and cat are at your sister's in Yonkers. Her husband says they will only keep them for a week. If they aren't picked up by then he'll take them to the Salvation

Army and the A.S.P.C.A. respectively. (*Tosses notes back on table.*)

**BOB**   Some guy who said he was Lee Bailey's assistant used to call about every twenty minutes but Mandy must have finally given him the brush.

**WILLIE**   Mandy can usually be counted on to give the brush to anyone who'll have it.

**BOB**   I was kinda beginning to like him. Who's Susan M.? That's a new one.

**WILLIE**   Sue's son, Jim. Mandy's stepmother and her kid. Jim's been sick and depressed. He wanted to talk to Mandy. I told him to take a number. He counts on Mandy for support.

**BOB**   Counting on Mandy for support would sicken and depress anyone. Did he lose his job?

**WILLIE**   Yes. He's going back to school.

**BOB**   Is that bad?

**WILLIE**   His mother is happy, Jim doesn't know if he likes it or not.

**BOB**   Oh. You'll have to learn how to talk on the phone if you want me to get the message straight.

**WILLIE**   Thank you.

**BOB**   I don't want to sound like an alarmist, but do you suppose any-thing's happened to Mandy?

**WILLIE**   She can take care of herself, she keeps telling me.

**BOB**   I mean she hasn't slept home in four nights.

**WILLIE**   So I gathered.

**BOB**   Ben said he saw her last Sunday somewhere.

**WILLIE**   Ben who? Oh, the one who had the party I wouldn't have liked. Don't worry about it. I hear from her every night. She leaves messages on the machine. "Hi honey, sorry you're out. Hope you're having fun, I'm not at a place where I can be reached. Good night." So, of course, I tried to reach her anyway.

**BOB**   You don't know anyone out here, do you? They want to meet you.

**WILLIE**   I don't know anyone anywhere. I know forty-nine fucked-up inmates, thirty-five up-tight judges and parole officers and about three-hundred fastidious asshole clerks who slave for the city with indiffer-ent truculence. It tends to make me belligerent, angry and short.

**BOB**   Did you see the piece about you in *The Village Voice*? Well, of course you did.

**WILLIE**   I didn't finish it.

**BOB**   Oh, come on —

**WILLIE**   I couldn't take it. They got everything wrong. I didn't like their "slant."

**BOB**   I got a big kick out of that. Reading something about my house-mate. Mandy gave it to me. Everybody out here wants to meet you.

They called you the "Last Angry Young Man in America."

**WILLIE**   I read that far.

**BOB**   Do you mind that?

**WILLIE**   It doesn't help at work . . . to be in the limelight.

**BOB**   Can't hurt.

**WILLIE**   They're conditioned to think if you grant an interview you're jockeying for a political appointment.

**BOB**   Are you? (*Pause.*) I mean — hello. (*Pause.*) Are you doing your Yoga breathing thing again?

**WILLIE**   Most of my patients need a reference to a doctor who knows something about treating ulcers more than they need me. For starters.

**BOB**   They have ulcers?

**WILLIE**   An alarming percentage, yes.

**BOB**   How come?

**WILLIE**   Because life is tough. (*Rubbing her eyes.*)

**BOB**   Oh. That.

**WILLIE**   That.

**BOB**   Don't rub your —

**WILLIE**   Oh, I know it. What is all this vegetation growing out here, is any of that ragweed?

**BOB**   Ten percent potatoes, ninety percent ragweed. Actually the potatoes are over. The man on the TV news said we're at the height of the irritation season.

**WILLIE**   Tell me about it. I'm allergic to the drive out here. I'm allergic to fresh air, or the ocean or the sand or flowers or the fields full of whatever that is, or weekends or—do you have cats?

**BOB**   No. Are you allergic to cats?

**WILLIE**   Would you know if you visited someone who had a cat?

**BOB**   Right away.

**WILLIE**   Then I'm not. Because I never really thought about it before but every fruit I know has at least two cats.

**BOB**   Not the girls?

**WILLIE**   The women tend to breed pug dogs. Professionally. What are you frowning about?

**BOB**   Was I? Sorry. I mean . . . I think I've been frowning a lot. I uh, met this artist. On the beach.

**WILLIE**   You're in love.

**BOB**   No, not that. Older. Seventyish. Incredibly famous. Abstract Expressionist stalwart. And he looked at my drawings. I don't know . . . and he said . . . Did you hear a door slam?

**WILLIE**   What?

**BOB**   Did you hear a car door?

**WILLIE**   You met an artist on the beach and he asked you if you heard a door slam?

**BOB**  If that's Joe, if he comes back here I don't want to see him. Oh, no. You can't see the front of the house. Listen, I'm going to go to bed, or take a walk —

**WILLIE**  — I thought he left town.

**BOB**  Who ever knows with him . . .

**MANDY**  (*Calling. Off.*) Hey, baby, you made it. Whoopee.

**WILLIE**  Holy Christ. It's Mandy.

**BOB**  Oh, no. I can't take it. (*Starts to leave.*)

**WILLIE**  What the hell is she doing — You. You may not leave this room!

**BOB**  Yeah, well, I'm real sorry, Willie, but this isn't my scene.

**WILLIE**  I'm a brown belt in karate. You touch that doorknob, you better hope it's a donut 'cause you're gonna eat it.

**BOB**  I'm no good to you. Mandy wraps me around her fingers.

**WILLIE**  Try to leave this room, I'll wrap you around that table leg. (*Off.*)

**MANDY**  Hurray, you made it. Hot damn. I should have been here to string up a banner or blow a trumpet.

**WILLIE**  Blow a what did she say? (*Willie enters. She is thin, striking and just under thirty.*)

**MANDY**  (*Kisses Willie.*) Hey, baby. Hi honey.

**WILLIE**  ". . . sorry you're out. Hope you're having fun; I'm not at a place where I can be reached. Good night."

**MANDY**  Must have been a bitch getting away, huh? You've not been home one night this week, or your phone was busy. Drove me crazy. How long you been here? (*Beat. Mandy and Bob remain frozen.*) Traffic on Twenty-seven is brutal. I saw those cars and knew the mood you'd be in. It's going to be like this all weekend. Anxiety is rampant out there. Everyone is desperately trying to fall in love before Tuesday. (*Sees no reaction, goes on a moment.*) They have a deathly fear of going back to the city with nothing to show for the summer except a collection of beach glass. (*Pause.*) Don't tell me; let me guess. Some wicked fairy has turned you to stone. Bob . . .?

**BOB**  Willie is teaching me a yoga breathing thing.

**MANDY**  Get me to show you; it doesn't work for Willie. Willie can't relax; she has a one hundred percent occidental mind.

**WILLIE**  If I relaxed I'd unravel like a sweater.

**BOB**  I thought you were a brown belt in karate.

**WILLIE**  I lied. (*Bob gets up.*) That doesn't mean I can't deck you. (*He sits.*)

**MANDY**  The important thing is you're really here, finally, and we have a four-day weekend to make up for the whole summer. There are two smashing cocktail parties, two obligation parties and at least one fabulous dinner party. Also that movie you wanted to see.

**WILLIE** The important thing is where have you been the last four nights?

**MANDY** You don't know. I'm fuckin' exhausted.

**WILLIE** Well, go easy on yourself.

**MANDY** Also I had to party for ten straight nights.

**WILLIE** I assume you mean ten consecutive nights, yes.

**MANDY** You don't know. At the risk of ruining my good name, I said if I didn't accomplish one thing else all summer I was going to introduce that ass Joe to someone with money who, preferably, lived out of state. Unfortunately times are tight and people with that kind of bread — even the kids — are getting very cagey. What an ordeal. It took me damn near two weeks to find someone who'd buy his particular brand of horseshit — also ended up costing me a fortune, but as far as I'm concerned any price would have been a bargain.

**BOB** You understand this is something she deliberately set out to do. Listen, what's a friend for? And she wonders why I'm angry.

**MANDY** He was really pissed.

**BOB** He still is, Mandy.

**MANDY** Don't give me a hard time. I've worked my butt off this week. Also I've saved your life again. Very important news. I've made an unbelievable deal; I should go into business. Oh, shit! Have you seen my flash attachment? I have to go back to the old Polaroid, I've literally worn the new one out. I spent last Monday and Tuesday — two weeks ago — looking for the perfect beach house interior, put about eight hundred miles on the Mazda, came home ready to drop and realized I'd been living in the perfect beach house all summer. With a little help. So I'm using this. Which is half sentimental clap-trap, but it's still going to work. (*She has been going through the box of rodeo gear.*) Where's the bull whip? There was a big bull whip.

**BOB** On the kitchen table.

**MANDY** I want to dump all this drag out on the porch. Kent is picking it up this afternoon. He's going to hate me so I don't want to talk to him. *Hustler*'s December issue is total leather. Is that sick? For Christmas? What are all these boxes? Are you packing again?

**BOB** Obviously I've been packing, yes. It's the last weekend.

**MANDY** Forget it. (*Looking at the sketch pads.*) Is this new?

**BOB** Don't go through that.

**MANDY** Damn. Mother. Look at that. Who'd think a nerd like Bobby would draw like an angel?

**BOB** You're only saying that because he said that.

**MANDY** But then I understand Leonardo was a total butterfly. Do you think you're going back to the city?

**BOB**  The nerd leaves Tuesday morning . . . or Monday night, or afternoon . . . Nerds have trouble with decisions.

**MANDY**  You're only going to get hives again. He packed up last week and broke out all over. Had to stay inside for two days. **BOB**  I wasn't going to speak to you at all, but I think I do want you to know that I'm fucking angry and I think you're a selfish, lousy person. (*Exits.*)

**WILLIE**  Hey!

**MANDY**  (*Yelling after him.*) Scratching is only going to make it worse.

**BOB**  I'm not scratching.

**MANDY**  You have to give him some resistance or he folds up like a fan. I apologized once and he spent the next two days telling me how it was his fault. He's really in trouble.

**WILLIE**  So I see.

**MANDY**  You're looking great. You got some color.

**WILLIE**  Bob said I didn't get a tan this summer. He's right. I tried, but I didn't.

**MANDY**  Are you kidding? Last week you —

**WILLIE**  I haven't seen you in damn near two weeks — I haven't heard from you in five nights.

**MANDY**  Well, then, two weeks ago, Jesus! You were looking all drawn and washed out.

**WILLIE**  I remember. You said I looked like last year's Madras.

**MANDY**  You did. You look better. You go out to Jones Beach?

**WILLIE**  No.

**MANDY**  Or the pier?

**WILLIE**  No.

**MANDY**  Up on the roof?

**WILLIE**  I got a sun lamp. You look thin.

**MANDY**  I've put on four pounds. I had my hair cut. (*Beat.*) You don't like it.

**WILLIE**  It looks cool.

**MANDY**  I knew you wouldn't.

**WILLIE**  I liked it long. You haven't put on weight; if anything you've lost.

**MANDY**  Basically I'm a loser. It's the weather; nobody eats out here.

**WILLIE**  You've got to be joking — eating is the sole activity of the entire South Fork. If they aren't buying food, cooking food or eating food, they're talking about buying food, cooking food or eating food. The one party I let you drag me to I had to listen to nine former winners of the National Book Award talk about potato salad for forty-five minutes.

**MANDY**  The food was great though.

**WILLIE**   I don't remember — yes, the food was good.

**MANDY**   You've been working late, huh? I haven't been able to reach you on the phone. It was either busy or the machine was on.

**WILLIE**   I got your message. I've not been working any later than you.

**MANDY**   I've not been so late; I've just been working out.

**WILLIE**   I'll bet you've been working out — in the gym or in the john?

**MANDY**   What the hell's wrong with you?

**WILLIE**   You've got to be joking. You haven't slept home in four nights.

**MANDY**   Well, who the hell were you talking to all night every night?

**WILLIE**   None of your damn business.

**MANDY**   I'm sorry. I'm a stylist, I don't have an important job. It's kept me busy fourteen hours a day the past week; I'm ready to drop but it's very humbling being with someone whose work is so valuable to mankind. I get a little flip out of self-defense.

**WILLIE**   My work is not valuable. It's debilitating and useless.

**MANDY**   Oh, come off it. Your work is important. You and Bob are the only people I know who actually do something worthwhile. You think I live with chumps?

**WILLIE**   It might be worthwhile if anything were accomplished. Trying to work within that fucking bureaucracy is beating your head against a wall; it's not getting anything done.

**MANDY**   I thought you were off that kick . . .

**WILLIE**   That is not a kick; that is my life. And my life is not a kick. My life is spent in a system designed exclusively to grind down my energy. The city bureaucracy from clerk to judge is manned by a special sense-less, sexless breed of worker-bee that can not hear, see, feel, smell or taste. They have no eyes, they have no ears, they have no nerve endings. They are untouched by circumstances, argument or pleading. They're drones, gravitated to a job for drones, used by the powers-that-be as a buffer against change. They aren't strong or brave or clever or humane but they have learned right from wrong by the time they're five and the rulebook whole by six and they hew to the by-god line with a chicken-shit tenacity that would defeat the revolution. They have kept the imagination and courage of the species from rising above the repetitious and mundane since the cave. There is no future for us and has never been a future because through some tragic biological accident the species breeds too many of these dedicated automatons with every generation for us ever to rise above them.

**MANDY**   (*Beat.*) I don't agree with you at all.

**WILLIE**   Well, then, you're wrong.

**MANDY**   I think they don't like their jobs; they only work for a two-week vacation, and they love their kids.

**WILLIE**   You're romantic, idealistic, naive and wrong.

**MANDY**   You've had a pretty rotten summer.

**WILLIE**   I. Have. Had. A. Pretty. Rotten. Summer.

**MANDY**   I thought you'd get away more or I wouldn't have taken a job that kept me out here so much.

**WILLIE**   I thought so too. It just wasn't possible.

**MANDY**   The boss or the situation?

**WILLIE**   The boss had a good summer.

**MANDY**   The prisoners and the patients didn't.

**WILLIE**   Generally speaking my summer was better than theirs. Aw, it's been this whole year, but especially during the summer with all the fucking temporary people. They have temporary minds; facing them is like facing the juggernaut.

**MANDY**   You gotta do something about that. I've never really known what a juggernaut was.

**WILLIE**   A mammoth statue of Krishna dragged through the streets while worshippers threw themselves under the wheels to be crushed. And that's what this summer has been.

**MANDY**   That's what a juggernaut is, really?

**WILLIE**   Really. An alternate definition would be the New York City Correctional Facilities.

**MANDY**   I'm sorry I asked. God, I can't believe the summer is over. It's not been what we planned when we rented this house, huh? I was going to cook, you were going to eat —

**WILLIE**   Just as well. How's it been for you?

**MANDY**   Brutal, 'til last week.

**WILLIE**   I heard Ben's party was fun.

**MANDY**   Ben who? Oh, he's Bob's friend. You wouldn't have liked it. Really, everything is going to be good this winter. I promise. I absolutely guarantee this winter. (*Yelling.*) Hey, Bob, this involves you, Get your ass in here. (*Back to Willie.*) Now. For starters I told Kent to go fuck himself.

**WILLIE**   For a change.

**MANDY**   Kent wasn't making it with those models. He wishes. They aren't that desperate. Most of them are working their way through college.

**WILLIE**   I'd rather wash dishes.

**MANDY**   Yeah, me too, but then we don't look like that. So. Do you know Andy Brown?

**WILLIE**   No.

**MANDY**   Think. You're not listening. Andy Brown.

**WILLIE**   Hum a few bars.

**MANDY**   You're impossible. You don't know anyone truly unimportant. Andy Brown is this week's hot photographer. *Architectural Digest,* stuff like that. Three national covers in one month.

**WILLIE**  Not my field.

**MANDY**  Right up my street. And you know Lee Bailey has finally found the courage of his taste and is going practically international.

**WILLIE**  I'm sure we'll all benefit greatly.

**MANDY**  You've got to know Lee Bailey. You've at least been to Bendel's. You've read his book — it's been around the apartment for months; that gorgeous picture-book thing, *Country Weekends.*

**WILLIE**  I've been waiting for the movie.

**MANDY**  You should have heard me bargain. Well, more like spitballing. They're both great — together we're super — what's a threesome? We're a . . . triumvirate.

**WILLIE**  I had a completely different word in mind. (*Calling Mandy.*) Hey, Bob, nerd, damn it.

**MANDY**  Really, I should go into real estate or something.

**WILLIE**  Why not, you've been in everything else.

**MANDY**  (*As Bob enters.*) What the hell's eating you?

**WILLIE**  Me? Damn little lately.

**MANDY**  Stop being snide and listen; this is important.

**WILLIE**  Did you see the way she's chopped off her hair? She looks like every peach on the beach.

**MANDY**  If this is the way you're going to be, we're lucky you haven't been out all summer.

**WILLIE**  What do you want. You waltz in here like a fucking firefly asking has anybody seen your flash attachment; yes, I've seen your flash attachment, it's up your goddamned ass!

**MANDY**  I'm trying to tell you something wonderful, damnit.

**WILLIE**  Why don't you start with where you've slept the last four nights?

**MANDY**  That is part of it.

**WILLIE**  That's it.

**MANDY**  On the North Fork. On the beach. In a bag.

**WILLIE**  In a pig's eye.

**MANDY**  I haven't seen a bed in four nights.

**WILLIE**  They have motel rooms on the North Fork.

**MANDY**  I don't go to motels. I don't stay with someone who's paranoid about me stealing their clothes hangers.

**BOB**  If all you need is a witness, I'm sure the neighbors are listening.

**MANDY**  (*As he would leave.*) Hey, Buster!

**WILLIE**  Leave the room again and you're dead.

**BOB**  The nerd decided if Mandy is going to be here, he would just as soon go this afternoon.

**MANDY**  Go where? You silly fruit, you know you don't have an apartment. You don't have a telephone. You don't have any money; Joe took your last dime. Look at him scratch. No joke, you loathe the city.

**BOB**  Please don't mention the fact that I'm scratching or you'll really bring it on. It isn't funny, Mandy.

**MANDY**  He's incredibly susceptible.

**WILLIE**  We were talking about it.

**BOB**  I had hives, but that isn't going to happen again. It was just a coincidence that that happened when I packed to go back to the city.

**MANDY**  Sure. Look at that spot.

**BOB**  That isn't a spot. Shut up.

**MANDY**  It happens every time he even thinks of New York.

**BOB**  I love it. Stop talking about it. It's going to be OK this time.

**MANDY**  You hate it. New York, New York, New York. (*He screams.*) What does your window look out on? The only window in your apartment. What does it look out on?

**BOB**  It doesn't matter.

**MANDY**  What does your window look out on?

**BOB**  An air shaft.

**MANDY**  What did I tell you?

**BOB**  It happens to be a very interesting air shaft.

**MANDY**  Which is also the ventilation for a Chinese restaurant.

**BOB**  Well, how many people have something like that?

**MANDY**  All his clothes smell like egg foo yung.

**BOB**  It helps me eat less.

**MANDY**  Where's the tub?

**BOB**  Come on, don't.

**MANDY**  Where's the tub in your apartment?

**BOB**  What do you want?

**MANDY**  The tub is in the kitchen sink.

**BOB**  I'm going to look for a different place. It won't be like that anymore.

**MANDY**  The water is cold. He warms it in a sauce pan on the radiator. There is no way to turn off the heat. The room is so hot he's red all over all winter long. He has a cold six months of the year. He's had his stereo ripped off twice. The last time they took everything in the apartment including his underwear.

**BOB**  You are cruel and heartless.

**MANDY**  You know you can't go back there.

**BOB**  You are sadistic . . . and sadistic —

**MANDY**  How can someone live   **BOB**  It won't be that anymore.
in a place gives him hives just       It won't. (*Singing.*)
to think about going back to it? And  I love New York . . .
then he wonders why I call him a nerd.  I love New York . . .

**MANDY**   There's another spot.

**BOB**   That isn't a spot.

**MANDY**   (*Leaving it; moves to the telephone messages idly.*) You are certifiable to think you can go back there.

**BOB**   (*To Willie.*) I'm going to dig up the rosemary before I go because what you have there is the tarragon, and the African daisy if you really want it. There are pots in the garage. You don't have to take them in a box. Also you should put them in a plastic bag or something. And they'll need watering. (*Looking at Mandy who is reading the phone messages.*) Mandy, just leave those alone. Those are mine.

**MANDY**   "While I Was Out" huh?

**WILLIE**   Those don't really apply any more, I was annoyed.

**BOB**   Give them back,

**MANDY**   Buzz off. (*Has read them all, puts them down.*) Where's my cat?

**WILLIE**   He's still at the apartment. Mrs. Basille is looking after him this weekend.

**MANDY**   You took my clothes to Yonkers?

**WILLIE**   I took them one morning and drove back for them the next.

**MANDY**   You should have given them to Goodwill. I don't like anything I own. Who's Susan M.?

**BOB**   Sue's son, Jim.

**MANDY**   Did Jimmy lose his job?

**WILLIE**   Yes.

**MANDY**   Shit.

**WILLIE**   He's going back to school.

**MANDY**   Sue'll love that. What does Jimmy say?

**WILLIE**   He doesn't know how he feels about it. He wants to talk to you.

**MANDY**   If I'd known you didn't want me here, I'd have made some other arrangement.

**WILLIE**   I hadn't heard from you in five days, outside of the machine.

**MANDY**   I called every night but one, either from the trailer camp over there or some bar if there was one around. Your phone was busy.

**WILLIE**   I took it off the hook at midnight. I had to get some rest. It wasn't easy getting away. So what's the new job?

**MANDY**   Listen, I'd just as soon not hang around where I'm not wanted, you know? (*Reads messages.*) "Would like not to see you or would not like to see you." Cute.

**BOB**   Those are all messed up. I put the last one on the first — I was going to change them. It should be: (*Reading.*) Your clothes are at your sister's in Yonkers, I'm not your secretary; Sue's son is sick; I'll be out, don't want to see you; called, no message; had a bad week; Mandy, please call." That was last night.

**MANDY**  Oh.

**WILLIE**  So what's the new job?

**MANDY**  Oh . . . what does it matter? Working for one photographer is like working for another.

**WILLIE**  What were you doing hanging around the trailer camps on the North Fork? (*Shrugs.*) You've joined the migrants. You're picking tomatoes.

**MANDY**  Nothing so useful.

**WILLIE**  Grapes.

**MANDY**  Oh . . . exteriors. We shot about a thousand rolls. We found this very beautiful old house on the beach that we've shot from every conceivable angle from dawn to midnight with a full moon. Plus the beach and water and fishermen and the vineyard and the wharf and gulls and lobsters for days. I've seen so many scallops I'm coming down with hepatitis.

**WILLIE**  This is for a magazine?

**MANDY**  No, the world's most expensive catalog. Over a hundred pages. Like Lee's book only everything's for sale. Lee would have done it himself except he's working on another book; so he was out here and the ad agency people and the printers and we all decided what we wanted to do was one house, June through Labor Day, the perfect summer. Perfect beach house, perfect food, perfect days; very chic, very slick; but that's what I do. It's great fun talking about it with Lee and Andy, and I'm glad he asked for me to do it, but telling you two about it, it all sounds pretty insipid. Just something to keep me out of trouble for four months. The only thing is, Bob, I volunteered you to help us.

**BOB**  Thanks very much, but I don't do that kind of work.

**MANDY**  You don't have to be a damn snob about it.

**BOB**  I'm not. I just don't know how to do it.

**MANDY**  It isn't that, anyway. Judy's leasing us this house for the winter. Most of the time we'll be in the city with a complete duplicate set of the place, but something always comes up where you need the real thing if you expect it to look right. Lighting references and all that. So I volunteered you to house sit. I couldn't get anything more than minimum, which is lousy — about a hundred, hundred thirty a week.

**BOB**  To do what?

**MANDY**  Sit on your can, keep the furnace going, I don't know. To do what you do. Keep it clean, which you'd do anyway, compulsive as you are. I thought it was genius, but if you don't like it they can get someone else.

**WILLIE**  That's what you meant by you should be in real estate?

**MANDY**  I wish you could have heard me convince Lee that his place, which is astonishingly beautiful, was all wrong for this.

**BOB**   And stay here? All winter?

**MANDY**   You never go outside the door in New York. It's not like you'll miss anything.

**BOB**   I work.

**MANDY**   So you can work here. You said you wanted to come out in the winter, work the whole year, see what changes happen.

**BOB**   Yeah, well, I say a lot of things.

**MANDY**   He went outside his door about twice all last winter. The only thing he said is that the people move too fast.

**BOB**   I said they were too loud and they pounce. They jerk.

**MANDY**   He's afraid someone is going to jump on him.

**BOB**   Well, aren't you?

**WILLIE**   You have to realize who you're talking to, there.

**MANDY**   Bob, basically I'm a pouncer. Basically you're a pouncee. Listen, it was just an idea. If you're not interested, fine. I'm kinda out of the mood of selling you on it, you know? (*Looking down at the box of western gear.*) Where's the spurs? There was a pair of spurs . . . The spurs are the entire costume for the Christmas cover. I put them where I'd be sure to see them.

**BOB**   They're on the box of corn flakes. I haven't eaten breakfast in a week.

**WILLIE**   Living with Mandy is a constant joy, isn't it?

**MANDY**   I know, I said. It's very humbling being with two geniuses. I'm a creep. I realize it ten times a day. But I wish you could have been camping out there on the beach with me; you were all that was missing. I mean you've never seen stars before. Sometimes I don't call because I probably tend to take you for granted, which makes me an uncaring slob, but you know that. Maybe Mom used to tell me to call her too much and I resent it; I don't know.

**BOB**   I've never tried to draw in the cold outside. What if my fingers freeze?

**MANDY**   Stick em — in your mouth. I don't know. You're scratching.

**BOB**   I'm not.

**MANDY**   I thought you'd like it. You've been talking about what it must be like in the winter all summer. You said you'd like to do the whole year. Did he tell you about the artist he met on the beach?

**WILLIE**   The one who asked if you heard the door slam?

**BOB**   Yeah, only . . . you know. I keep trying to remember his name. He's really good.

**WILLIE**   Incredibly famous. Abstract expressionist stalwart you said.

**BOB**   Did I? Yeah, he is. Enormous paintings. Hundreds of thousands of dollars each. In every museum. Like de Kooning, only nobody is like de Kooning; de Kooning's the best, but say de Kooning, only de Kooning would never say anything like this, but say de Kooning.

**MANDY**  Bob was drawing these plants and — you know — we're used to the fact he may be a nerd but he's probably the best artist in the history of drawing—

**BOB**  (*Overlapping.*) No, I'm no good, don't say that . . .

**MANDY**  Anyway!

**BOB**  Anyway, I had to stop working because I couldn't do anything with him looking over my shoulder. I mean, just people is OK, but not him. And of course he didn't know I knew who he was.

**MANDY**  Bullshit. You were looking at him like he was Ben Kingsley.

**WILLIE**  Who's Ben Kingsley?

**BOB**  She means I was looking at him like he was Ghandi, and I wasn't at all. I was very cool —

**MANDY**  Fuck you were; I thought you were going to genuflect.

**WILLIE**  Leaving aside the idea of genuflecting to Ghandi.

**BOB**  So he picks up the sketch book and looks at all the drawings —

**MANDY**  — About ten minutes each.

**BOB**  — I mean he turned back to the front and looked at every one. Close.

**MANDY**  Shocked to his soul.

**BOB**  He was not. He didn't show anything but I think he liked them.

**MANDY**  He was pissing nails.

**BOB**  And . . . he was . . . very complimentary.

**MANDY**  Oh yeah, blab, blab, blab, Albrecht Durer; blab, blab, blah, William Holbein.

**WILLIE**  Hans Holbein.

**MANDY**  Blab, blah, blab, Thomas Eakins. Then he said you draw like an angel: I've never seen anything like it.

**WILLIE**  Only . . .?

**BOB**  Only now you must learn to express yourself.

**MANDY**  He said that's the most beautiful work I've ever seen, only now you have to go on and say who you are with the drawing. Go on to express you.

**BOB**  And the trouble is, I do express myself. (*Pause.*) If I don't draw that shell, then maybe no one will, and it'll go . . . un-drawn. And anyway the next day it would be completely different. And plants, anything living. Changes so much overnight, or in different light, just minutes later; if I don't put down the way it is at that moment, no one will ever know. That moment might as well never have happened. I just think that time shouldn't pass, and things shouldn't be let go . . . unknown. And that's all I really want to do. So I really am at least trying to express . . .

**WILLIE**  You're saying what you want to say.

**BOB** Well, as well as I can.

**WILLIE** Like . . . say, de Kooning.

**BOB** Well, if I'm ever able to do it that well. It's like playing the piano. You have to practice all the time. Only musicians have it all over us. Their exercises aren't recorded at least. My fifty years of lame attempts are going to lie around to remind me how inadequate I am. And I know people frame them, and they like them, like you said, in your office — and they think they're OK, but all I see is that it could be better. I mean it's OK that they do, but . . .

**WILLIE** No, maybe you see what you'd have liked it to be, but I wouldn't know the difference.

**BOB** You'll know, if I ever do it right.

**MANDY** God. Tell me it's not humbling living with you two. Willie's trying to save mankind and the nerd is trying to record everything on the planet. Great. And I'm saying, "Piper, honey, you got a touch of mascara on your left tit." Very humbling experience.

**BOB** Why did you introduce Joe to all those people?

**MANDY** You weren't working.

**BOB** Oh. I thought maybe I would.

**MANDY** Also he's the only person I'd ever met who didn't know you were good.

**BOB** Oh. I thought maybe he would.

**MANDY** Forget it. If you weren't both so basically hopeless I wouldn't be able to stand you.

**WILLIE** I've never thought of myself as basically hopeless.

**MANDY** Oh, both of you; you're impossible. That's why I got this job — I mean the pay is brutal. You wouldn't believe it. They spend all the money in the world on sets and lights and props and printing, and pay the photographer and the stylist cab fare. Probably because Lee knows he could do it himself, but I'll learn a lot and he's great, and what I really want is — well, I'll have a chance to do what I'd hoped to do this summer. I mean, I'll be able to make the perfect breakfast for you, and your birthday party that you couldn't come out for, and midnight snacks on the beach, and after-swim refreshers. Rearrange the furniture.

**BOB** What are you going to rearrange?

**MANDY** We won't use this furniture; he has his whole line—you'll love it. It'll only be on the set in New York, not out here . . .

**BOB** Oh.

**MANDY** Also there really wasn't any question of me not taking a job like this, 'cause if you're going to allow yourself to be appointed Health Commissioner — I mean we know from experience that it doesn't matter at all if you're gay, but it really wouldn't look right if your lover was a pornographer, you know?

**WILLIE**  Am I going to be appointed . . .?

**MANDY**  Oh, please, give me a break. All those luncheons with the Mayor you come home crabbing about; all those interviews you hate. The only reason you're always so cross is that you've been realizing that the only way you can accomplish anything is to get to the top and start knocking a few heads together. I mean everyone knows it's going to be you.

**WILLIE**  I've never mentioned once — I've never ever said that I was thinking of accepting, if he decided to appoint me. I've never brought it up.

**MANDY**  I know. We have to talk about that, too. (*Beat.*)

**BOB**  What if the ink in the pen freezes?

**MANDY**  Deal with it.

**BOB**  I can't change my mind like you do, Mandy. I had very definite plans about how terrible this winter was going to be.

**WILLIE**  It's not easy to let go of something like that, is it?

**BOB**  Not at all.

**WILLIE**  (*Ironic.*) Mandy never thinks about the other person's feelings . . .

**BOB**  (*Serious.*) Not at all.

**MANDY**  You try to adjust. Now, honey, I know you really haven't unwound from the drive, but if you relax a little and take a shower, and change, it's going to be time for lunch. Both of you.

**WILLIE**  I'm not hungry.

**MANDY**  I know, but there's all these people who want to meet you, so I thought we'd just get it over with right off the bat. So. Ben's giving you two a lunch.

**BOB**  Ben who? Oh. I don't think I can go.

**MANDY**  Couldn't you just relax and be ordinary people?

**WILLIE**  I don't think so, darling. I love you a lot, but not today. Today's been an ordeal.

**MANDY**  You've got to learn to meet people.

**WILLIE**  Who's going to be there?

**MANDY**  The usual crowd.

**WILLIE**  No way.

**MANDY**  Relax, Willie. Both of you, look at you, you're so wound up.

**BOB**  Well, that's what you do to people.

**MANDY**  Good. Now, unwind. Look at your shoulders; relax. God, you're impossible. Just sit. Look at you. Drop your shoulders. Nobody is going to jump on you here. Let your arms hang loose —

**WILLIE**  Why don't you work on him and I'll go shower and we'll talk.

**MANDY**  Sit down, for god's sake, Willie; you're all wired. Now, I want you to go to this lunch; I want us to go out together.

**WILLIE**   Darling, later, OK?

**MANDY**   Goddamnit, sit. (*Willie does.*) You drive me crazy. Now. What is so difficult? We're going to go to a beautiful house and gently make the acquaintance of about fifty beautiful gentle people.

**WILLIE**   Fifty . . . god.

**MANDY**   Or . . . so. What's the problem?

**WILLIE**   What's expected of me?

**MANDY**   That you be relaxed. It's the end of the summer. We'll come out a couple of weekends this winter and visit Bob. We'll ski and sled. . . You don't have to work or worry this weekend. All you have to do is breathe. I've told you that before.

**WILLIE**   I don't seem to get the knack; I've really tried —

**MANDY**   It's very easy — damnit, Wilhemina, just close your eyes and realize you're breathing, but for hard-core resisters like you, there's a very simple procedure. Simple as counting. You count to eight, then you count to nine, and on up to about twenty. The idea is just to relax.

**WILLIE**   I know the idea. I'm really not into your Zen whatever it is.

**MANDY**   This isn't Zen; it won't hurt you. One of the models taught me this. They can't work if they're tense. You start at eight. You breathe in on the count of eight, hold your breath for the count of eight, and breathe out on the count of eight and then hold that for eight. Then in on the count of nine and so on up to twenty. What could be simpler?

**WILLIE**   Do you really think he's thinking of me for the job? Because I've been thinking he is too.

**MANDY**   If he doesn't appoint you he'll be tarred and feathered in lavender.

**WILLIE**   It'd mean an awful lot of changes, you know.

**MANDY**   I'm the one who welcomes changes. Breathe.

**BOB**   Is that enough money to get my etching stuff? I don't think that's enough.

**MANDY**   You'll talk to Lee, you'll show him your drawings; I think the fee is probably negotiable.

**BOB**   I don't know.

**MANDY**   Breathe. In.

**WILLIE**   How did you know I'd accept?

**MANDY**   Well, I can't say it's telepathetic, can I? You don't believe in that.

**WILLIE**   More and more.

**MANDY**   Breathe in, darling, we've got places to go. Bob, sit down. In on an eight count. (*They do.*) Hold it for eight. Six, seven, eight. Out on a count of eight. Not all at once. Hold it for eight. Leave yourself alone. Six, seven, eight. Now, in on a count of nine. The idea is to feel the air coming onto your body. Hold it for nine. The whole idea is to feel yourself breathing! Close your eyes. (*They do.*) Out on the count of nine. Realize that you're breathing. Hold it. The whole point is to be aware that you're alive. In. Eight, nine, ten. That's good. Hold it. (*They count silently to ten. The lights fade to the count.*)

# A BETROTHAL  (November 1984)
*for Uta Hagen and Herbert Berghof*


## AUTHOR'S NOTE

The John Drew Theater in East Hampton asked four Long Island writers to write a two-character play to star four local married couples. I was given the wonderful task of writing something for Uta Hagen and Herbert Berghof. I talked to Uta on the phone and said I thought the idea sounded like a lark. She informed me she had no intention of performing in a lark. If she and Herbert were going to do a new play by me, they intended to take it seriously. Performing, acting, was not a lark. I think I chose the wrong word. Why didn't I come by for dinner and we'd talk.

I have a number of friends who have studied with one or the other, but I had never met them. God, what wonderful people. God, what a great meal she sat on the table. God, was I intimidated! Herbert, who usually plays very strong, even overbearing men, proved to be one of the gentlest, most elegant hosts it's been my pleasure to meet. Uta is so straightforwardly honest and open it's almost shocking. I said I wanted to write a short comedy for them; they said they loved comedy and would love to do it. I went away and couldn't write a thing. I visited Uta in Montauk. She threw together a brilliant lunch in 10 minutes, showed me her garden, "This is my compost pile. Smell that soil!" I did. It was heaven. I still couldn't write anything.

The evening came and went without the Berghofs or me, and, all things considered, I was very happy not to have been a part of it. But I still felt guilty. I had cadged one of the best meals I'd ever eaten (crown roast of lamb with a stuffing made by some angel) and one of the most charming evenings I'd ever spent, and in no way repaid.

The idea came during the winter when I was planning my garden, pouring over the purple prose of my plant catalogs. I finally got the script to them, but, though they loved it and saw the humor and pain in the characters, with one thing and another (schedules, what to put with it), they never had the opportunity to play it. My loss, certainly, more than theirs. It was first performed in London. Alas, I never got over there to see that production either. Certainly my loss again.

A BETROTHAL was first produced at the Man-In-The-Moon Theatre, a pub–theatre in London, England on September 26, 1986. It was designed and directed by Alison Sutcliffe with the following cast:

MS. J.H. JOSLYN:  Geraldine James
MR. KERMIT WASSERMAN:  Ben Kingsley


**CHARACTERS**

MS. J. H. JOSLYN
MR. KERMIT WASSERMAN


**SCENE**

The corner of a large tent. A flap door nearby. Folding card table, a large coffee urn, paper cups, milk cartons, folding chairs, programs on some chairs. Drizzle outside. An afternoon in mid-May.

# A BETROTHAL

*Ms. J. H. Joslyn enters, miffed. She is perhaps fifty, attractive but doesn't care, maybe a little heavy and doesn't care about that either. She has got herself up in a neat suit and is annoyed that she bothered. She throws off a makeshift plastic bag or some such rain protection.*

**JOSLYN**   But then, what did I expect? What could I possibly have expected? (*Pours coffee from the urn, without skipping a beat she shakes three milk cartons, they are empty, pours the dribble from two into one, pours a bit of coffee in the one, sloshes it about, pours milk into cup.*) I expected nothing. (*Sits, sips.*) I had no expectations. The bastards. It's the way of the world; it's the lay of the land. Well, if they have not eyes in their heads! If they're blind to progress. Pearls before swine. What did I expect? (*Looking off.*) Haven't got sense enough to come in out of the rain. Pouring on them; ruining the whole show. Good. Fogging up their bi-focals. Not that they could see anyway: (*Mincing.*) "Oh, my, isn't that quaint—Oh, how cunning; fetching color, delightful rhythm; amusing play of the various parts. A bit coarse, of course." What faggots. Well, what did I expect? I said there was no hope. I had no hope. The situation was clear from the beginning. It was a hopeless situation. What did I expect? (*Mr. Wasserman enters. Dejected. Sighs. He is perhaps sixty, neat and though he is a large man he is decidedly soft, almost delicate. Looks around, seeing nothing, shakes water from his umbrella, stands it somewhere. Murmurs: "Oh my . . ." Pours coffee. Sits on the other side of the table.*) There's no milk.

**WASSERMAN**   No, fine, thank you, nothing serious . . .

**JOSLYN**   I took the last.

**WASSERMAN**   I'm sorry?

**JOSLYN**   Of the milk.

**WASSERMAN**   Oh. No, no. I . . . just needed to hold something. I'll be fine. (*Pause.*) Oh, dear . . .

**JOSLYN**   They're getting soaked.

**WASSERMAN**   Yes, they'll like that. That's something.

**JOSLYN**   The people. Haven't got the sense to come in out of the rain.

**WASSERMAN**   No, it's stopped. Nearly. Nearly stopped. They're all but finished, anyway. They finished the Tall Beardeds before it started, so no damage done . . . They're on the Arils now.

**JOSLYN**  Damn the Arils. Shouldn't even be in the show.

**WASSERMAN**  No, not my thing. Though interesting. I suppose . . . to those who . . . find them interesting.

**JOSLYN**  Too damn particular.

**WASSERMAN**  Yes, very fussy I'm told.

**JOSLYN**  Ship 'em back to Persia or wherever the hell they came from. Don't belong here,

**WASSERMAN**  I've had no first hand experience with them, I'm sure they're very rewarding . . . to those who . . . find them very rewarding.

**JOSLYN**  Waste of energy.

**WASSERMAN**  Oh, I'm sure.

**JOSLYN**  Look like shit, anyway.

**WASSERMAN**  They are terribly muddy, some of them, for my taste.

**JOSLYN**  Fuck 'em.

**WASSERMAN**  (*Starts.*) Ah, when I was leaving the house, and of course, it was so early, I had this terrible feeling that I was missing something—couldn't for the life of me—that's always so annoying—then, of course, half-way here, in the middle of the Parkway, I realized I'd forgotten my galoshes. I had to pull over, I can't think and drive; it certainly looked like rain. I'd remembered my raincoat, my . . . of course I was so nervous because this is my first time.

**JOSLYN**  (*Beat.*) What are you talking about?

**WASSERMAN**  To show. So I didn't want to be late. So of course it did. Rain. I mean, I didn't go back so of course . . . it. . . .I don't mind ruining my shoes so much, but I hope I don't come down with something. Of course it's probably just nerves. It did rain very hard there for a moment.

**JOSLYN**  I hope it ruins everything.

**WASSERMAN**  I come every year, but this is the first time I've had the nerve to show. Actually the first time I thought I had something really very special. Vanity. Oh, dear, dear . . .

**JOSLYN**  You're a breeder.

**WASSERMAN**  Yes, and you?

**JOSLYN**  Ummm. Pearls before swine, I thought you were a judge. You have that judgy look.

**WASSERMAN**  Oh, no, no, I wouldn't presume.

**JOSLYN**  Your first?

**WASSERMAN**  Uh, yes, and, uh, never again. At least not for years. I haven't the strength. I should have known. Hubris. Ah, well. Oh, dear . . . poor little darling. Such a sweetheart. Never should have exposed her to the harsh . . . light . . . of reality . . . in the world . . . of the real. And me. Oh, dear.

**JOSLYN**  You might as well know I have no use for you or any of your kind.

**WASSERMAN**  I'm sorry?

**JOSLYN**  Vulgar, disgusting, tasteless, showy, and useless in a garden. So expect no sympathy.

**WASSERMAN**  Then, what are you doing here?

**JOSLYN**  (*She keeps her cards very close to her chest.*) I have my own pursuits, thank you, I've been scoffed at before. I'm quite immune. Slings and arrows; roll right off my back.

**WASSERMAN**  I understood you were a breeder, too.

**JOSLYN**  I have my pursuits. Nothing you would understand. For your information I was tickled pink when it started to rain. The spectacle of that huge, vulgar mess of a Tall Bearded that they had just awarded Best of Show, falling right over flat in the mud the moment they turned their backs! Ha! Everyone running to stake it up. In five minutes the whole damn lot of them were leaning and staggering like drunken sailors. No wind, mind you, just a spring shower. And my baby was standing up at attention like a little soldier.

**WASSERMAN**  Which one is your Little Soldier?

**JOSLYN**  I have my pursuits.

**WASSERMAN**  I really must say (*Looking around.*) I have no love for the Tall Beardeds, I'm an Intermediate Breeder. May I take it you're an Intermediate Breeder, too?

**JOSLYN**  I have my pursuits.

**WASSERMAN**  I'm so glad, I never really go to any of the meetings, I couldn't possibly. I get the Quarterly, I pour over the Quarterly . . . uh . . . which one is your Little Soldier?

**JOSLYN**  Never you mind, never you mind. Slings and arrows, l came back to the tent because I thought no one would be here. Everyone was acres away down at the other end, I expected to be alone here.

**WASSERMAN**  Yes, it did look very deserted.

**JOSLYN**  It was. Then you came.

**WASSERMAN**  Yes, yes, I simply couldn't any longer. I was trying to be brave, but I came all over with the feeling I was going to faint. I simply had to sit down. Little Tanya stood up to the rain at first, she just sparkled like dew, but I'm certain she was beginning to feel it. I gave her a little shake, I don't think anyone saw. As soon as I looked around I realized I'd been wrong to enter Big Judy, I told her I was sorry, but for Little Tanya—to be overlooked—I know, of course, she's frail. Part of her charm for me. Oh, such vanity. Never again.

**JOSLYN**  I have no idea whom you're talking about.

**WASSERMAN**  Oh, I'm sorry. I thought–

**JOSLYN**  Who are these women? Why are you telling me about them? I don't know them. I don't know anyone. I wouldn't like them. I want to be alone here.

**WASSERMAN**  Oh, no, they're my babies, of course. They're in the trial garden of the Intermediate Iris Bed. I thought Little Tanya had a very good chance of attracting attention.

**JOSLYN**  You named your iris Big Judy and Little Tanya?

**WASSERMAN**  Maybe you at least noticed Tanya. Many people seemed attracted to her—but, alas . . . not . . . oh, dear. . . .

**JOSLYN**  I noticed nothing. I don't parade about ooing and ahing, thank you. I guarded my entry. I wouldn't put it past some of these—I saw their jealous eyes, their itchy fingers. I stood my ground.

**WASSERMAN**  Over your Little Soldier? I saw everything. I must say I thought some were very inferior. Others, frankly, I know what you mean, made me not jealous at all, but simply burn with envy. I do think the Intermediates are just developing in leaps and . . . such strong branching, what texture.

**JOSLYN**  Branching. You know nothing of branching; nothing of texture.

**WASSERMAN**  It's just that it's something I've neglected horribly. Something I must take the time to work on.

**JOSLYN**  Time, oh, time. Try thirty years.

**WASSERMAN**  I'm sorry?

**JOSLYN**  Of no other thought. Day and night. Try perfection.

**WASSERMAN**  That's remarkable.

**JOSLYN**  Ha. Tell it to the judge.

**WASSERMAN**  Oh, dear. Oh, your Little Soldier wasn't overlooked?

**JOSLYN**  I expected nothing.

**WASSERMAN**  Oh, I must say I was foolish enough to expect Best of Show.

**JOSLYN**, I had no expectations.

**WASSERMAN**  Oh, I so hoped.

**JOSLYN**  I had no hope. What did I expect? Another story of the unsung hero. Slaving in their labs; Marie Curie in that godawful unheated barn, day and night All the nameless laborers of the field. Who knows their plight? Who their hopes and dreams? Who celebrates their tiny joys? The doubling of chromosomes, the increase of bud count. The miracle of texture. Perfectly round falls that stand out utterly horizontally in a hurricane! Triple branching and at ninety degrees not a hundred eighty, who's ever seen it before? Who will ever know who changed the course of history? Who will care? Lost in the shuffle. Taken for granted. The builder of the Trojan Horse, the inventor of the wheel, the discoverer of Pluto, the principle of pi . . . What in the hell are you doing? (*He has been searching through a pocket notebook.*)

**WASSERMAN**  I have it here—"Good blue," no, "Bad yellow," branching, branching, texture . . . somewhere . . . "Lovely white," no . . . AH!

you are (*Reading.*) J. H. Joslyn, Carmel, New York. And your Little Soldier is entry number 3a-I-916.

**JOSLYN**  What have you got there?

**WASSERMAN**  I take copious notes. "Most outstanding falls, utterly round, perfectly horizontal, astonishing branching. holding flowers quite apart, remarkable texture of fall and standard, terribly unfortunate muddiness in —" and so on, and so on. I must say, Ms., er, ah, Joslyn, I'm very pleased to meet the breeder of that Little Soldier. I made special note of Carmel, as I'm from Mahopac, which is a hop skip and a jump down the road.

**JOSLYN**  Were I from Carmel, I'd certainly know the whereabouts of a town so nearby and visibly disagreeable as Mahopac.

**WASSERMAN**  I must say I can't believe your Little Soldier didn't at least receive a citation for extraordinary branching and texture. Why, the branches are at angles to one another instead of directly across from—I must say, what dimension it gives the whole stalk. Like a candelabra; I've never seen it before.

**JOSLYN**  Neither has anyone. Nor do they care, apparently. The builder of the Great Wall of China, the—

**WASSERMAN**  And texture! Like carved ivory. I actually reached to feel the thickness—quite inadvertently, I didn't even realize I'd done it—the way one instinctively smells a rose.

**JOSLYN**  I know nothing of smelling roses. I have no use for them. Or for what you call instinct. Which of course is thoughtlessness.

**WASSERMAN**  I didn't feel it, however. Someone barked at me so fiercely I just moved on, but I certainly took note. You're starred in my book, and there are only four of five entries that are starred.

**JOSLYN**  Humf!

**WASSERMAN**  I'm sorry?

**JOSLYN**  What care I? Slings and arrows. One among four, one among five, right off my back.

**WASSERMAN**  I'm sorry?

**JOSLYN**  (*Looking at him levelly.*) Oh, yes. Hum! Oh, sure . . . I've seen you.

**WASSERMAN**  Oh, well, there you have the advantage, I'm afraid . . . I . . . maybe it's unsocial, but I . . . at a flower show, at least . . . I don't think I see people. I'm taking notes, moving on, admiring, getting so many ideas, that I think perhaps I don't look . . . uh . . . up. And then, of course, I find it so confusing to look at people. What if I should catch their eye? A perfect stranger? What would they think? And maybe it would be a judge, thinking I was trying to influence him . . . or . . . her . . . in some influential way.

**JOSLYN**  At the Grand Union. On Route Six.

**WASSERMAN**  I'm sorry?

**JOSLYN**  Pawing the lettuce and teasing the kiwi fruit. It's only a bad habit, you know, neglectful mother, probably. Father away at sea a good deal, or some such. It could be corrected with a little self-discipline.

**WASSERMAN**  I'm sorry?

**JOSLYN**  Pinching, testing, squeezing, pawing. Some people think they're the only man on God's Earth. Mauling everything, trying to make it their own. How would you feel if you were the iris? How would you feel if you were the fruit?

**WASSERMAN**  I'm sorry?

**JOSLYN**  It can be corrected.

**WASSERMAN**  What's that?

**JOSLYN**  A word to the wise . . .

**WASSERMAN**  (*Reaching out his hands.*) You must admit the texture of your Little Soldier's falls invites the touch. It looks like it would feel of . . . oooo, I don't know of velvet or chamois or ivory or oooo, something extraordinary.

**JOSLYN**  (*Slapping his hand.*) Just never you mind, sir. Never you worry about it. You're not the only one, remember.

**WASSERMAN**  I'm sorry?

**JOSLYN**  Reaching out their grubby paws to cop a feel. There was fifty if there was one. Two judges, if you believe it. With their judgy little thumb and finger. I put them in their places, don't think I didn't. Inadequate guidance at school probably. All this permissive behavior.

**WASSERMAN**  Thirty years . . . my goodness, I've been working that long of course, but I would never presume, l wouldn't know where to begin. I breed for color, so I wouldn't know—

**JOSLYN**  Color, oh, my goodness! Yappidy-yap, yappidy-yap, it's all I hear. Blue this and puce that. Ruby Glow and Pink Reward.

**WASSERMAN**  Oh, when I first saw my first Lillipinkput, I began to work the very next week.

**JOSLYN**  Sing me no first Lillipinkputs, read me no rhymes, thank you. It's all I hear. One has enough to contend with without your Lillipinkputs.

**WASSERMAN**  I was quite inspired by her. I saw a whole clump blooming in Presby Gardens, before she won the Sass Award, and I must say I was bowled over by her.

**JOSLYN**  Sing me no Sass Awards, read me no bowled overs, I've no use for it at all.

**WASSERMAN**  Your world, of course, is of quite a different order.

**JOSLYN**  I have my pursuits.

**WASSERMAN**  You wouldn't see it, I quite realize.

**JOSLYN** I'm not blind. I could be impressed. I can see, and what I see is as far as any of them have gone. There's one today, hardly to be overlooked, tangerine, maybe, orange maybe, I have eyes. Striking color, but then what? I went over to it, one could hardly fail to see it, but on close inspection—the hypocrisy! Flimsy wouldn't begin. Insubstantial, wilting falls lying practically flat against the sheating spathe, crest styles of crepe paper, standards so tissue thin I'm surprised the first drop of rain didn't go straight through them. One branch, mind you, and it hardly held up even this anemic, cobwebby—

**WASSERMAN** (*Hardly audible.*) Madam.

**JOSLYN** —pissant of a—God knows the bud count. Probably not even two. Nothing so wispy could—

**WASSERMAN** Madam.

**JOSLYN**—support more. And a crowd around it ooing and ahing! Over this feeble—

**WASSERMAN** Madam.

**JOSLYN** —debilitated, sapless, pithless, impotent—

**WASSERMAN** (*A little louder.*) Madam.

**JOSLYN** —Lustless, flaccid, feckless, limp—

**WASSERMAN** Madam!

**JOSLYN** Wishy-washy, insipid—!

**WASSERMAN** (*Quite huge.*) MADAM, YOU ARE SPEAKNG OF MY CHILD!

**JOSLYN** (*Beat.*) I beg your pardon?

**WASSERMAN** (*Still outraged.*) You are speaking of Little Tanya! Though she may not be to your liking, many people were very admiring. Several times when I drew close enough to hear their remarks, several people were wondering if the breeder was at the show. Many were struck (*His hand on his throat.*) I think I've injured my voice. I'm terribly sorry. I don't know what I can be thinking, I've never spoken like that before to anyone. Once to a very, *very* truculent raspberry, never to a person. Certainly not a lady. It's the strain of the occasion. I've not been myself all day. I shouldn't be around people, they make me terribly . . . and the agony of competition, it isn't human. Oh, dear. . . .

**JOSLYN** (*After a beat.*) That vapidity is Little Tanya?

**WASSERMAN** (*Eyes closed, a strangled admission.*) Yes . . .

**JOSLYN** That *whisper*?

**WASSERMAN** Please. I know she isn't to your taste.

**JOSLYN** I say nothing of my taste.

**WASSERMAN** I realize you're working in quite a different field.

**JOSLYN** Fields abound, I say nothing of fields.

**WASSERMAN** You have your pursuits.

**JOSLYN**  Just never you mind.

**WASSERMAN**  But you must understand another choosing to endeavor in an endeavor of . . . another choosing.

**JOSLYN**  I say nothing of my understanding.

**WASSERMAN**  That orange has been the achievement of thirty years. And I can't help the vanity of being somewhat . . . vain . . . about . . . achieving it. You understand, failings apart, it is a remarkable orange.

**JOSLYN**  It's a very good color, as colors come and go.

**WASSERMAN**  No rose has an orange like it.

**JOSLYN**  I know nothing of roses.

**WASSERMAN**  Well, I can tell you any orange rose is impossible to use with anything. Little Tanya is the only orange I've seen, and many people remarked on it, that mixes. She's a mixer! She looks charming with other oranges, with lemons, with peaches, with red. Red! With lavender and blue. She blends! People would want her. Many said so. They can use her. She's a blender!

**JOSLYN**  I care nothing about what people can use.

**WASSERMAN**  Well, you should. Many people were remarking about your Little Soldier, you surely heard them . . .

**JOSLYN**  Yammerings of the crowd.

**WASSERMAN**  But it can't be used in a . . . what I mean to say is . . . it's absolutely . . . nothing could . . . well exactly what color would you call it? I mean it isn't a light yellow, it isn't buff. It isn't green, it's muddy, sure, but what? mustard? Bluish maybe, but I was at a loss to make out what . . .

**JOSLYN**  (*She has been collecting her things and rises.*) I see it's quite impossible to hope that you'll ever leave here. Some people are like that. It's a lack of respect for another's privacy. It's a bad habit, of course, it could be worked on, but in your case I doubt any serious improvement. The rain has let up, I'll remove myself and allow you, doubtless, to find another victim.

**WASSERMAN**  (*Looking at her with amazement.*) I know you. How extraordinary. I don't know anyone. I've seen you.

**JOSLYN**  Sing me none of your seens.

**WASSERMAN**  You're a teacher.

**JOSLYN**  I beg your pardon, I am not.

**WASSERMAN**  You most certainly are.

**JOSLYN**  I am not, I know what I am.

**WASSERMAN**  You teach.

**JOSLYN**  I do not.

**WASSERMAN**  You did, you must have.

**JOSLYN**  (*Beat.*) I have my pursuits, thank you. What I do and what I've done are not for the ears of idle strangers.

**WASSERMAN**  Last year you taught!

**JOSLYN**  I did not!

**WASSERMAN**  You came to the gate!

**JOSLYN**  I came to no gate of yours, you can be sure. I peer through no gates, thank you.

**WASSERMAN**  You came just inside, and there you stood. Looking just as you do now.

**JOSLYN**  I did not. I come in gates only when I'm invited in, and I'm invited in only where I ask to be and I did not ask, thank you.

**WASSERMAN**  You came to Castle Crampton. I saw you at the gate. Believe me, I certainly didn't intend to see you, I don't see any of them, they sometimes see me, it can't be helped, they ask their questions, they talk on and on, some of them, it's all very . . . and the children pour in on their field trips, the musicians, you know they have hundreds of them for the chamber orchestras, the quartets, and they're so talky, I'm afraid. You were a chaperon to one of the children's classes.

**JOSLYN**  I beg your pardon, I have no class.

**WASSERMAN**  And in they poured and there you stood. Just inside the gate.

**JOSLYN**  In the line of one's employment one is sometimes called upon, quite against one's will to fulfill the place of those who are irresponsible enough to become ill.

**WASSERMAN**  I would never insist, of course, you know where you did and didn't go. I must say I don't at all feel comfortable around children. They don't seem to watch where they're going, they tend to step on me. But if you're the principal and went along in place of one of the—

**JOSLYN**  I am certainly not a principal.

**WASSERMAN**  Or an assistant principal with the duty of replacing some—

**JOSLYN**  I am certainly no assistant principal.

**WASSERMAN**  Or the librarian and were asked to fill in for—

**JOSLYN**  I am not a librarian for any of your—

**WASSERMAN**  Or the assistant librarian.

**JOSLYN**  I have my pursuits. You, of course, might be interested in the likes of Castle Crampton Gardens, I assure you I would not be.

**WASSERMAN**  Oh, my goodness, no.

**JOSLYN**  I disdained to step one foot into such a place. One look was all I needed to understand the whole of Castle Crampton completely. Tacky little bedded-out beds, looking as though they belonged in front of a gas station.

**WASSERMAN**  (*Loving it.*) Oh, my goodness!

**JOSLYN** Municipal gardening, indeed. Worse here than abroad if you can believe it, and Crampton worst of all.

**WASSERMAN** Oh, yes!

**JOSLYN** I know the philosophy. Rows of wax begonias, never was a plant so aptly named, your cup of tea, well, you can have it. No doubt Little Tanya would blend in well . . .

**WASSERMAN** Oh, dear, no, I'm afraid even Tanya couldn't save the place.

**JOSLYN** All your geometrical beds, squares and circles and triangles. Yellow marigolds, surrounded by a cunning little ring of blue Ageratum houstonianum, surrounded by a nice contrasting lipstick red of, maybe, Salvia Splendens "Harbinger." "Castle Crampton" spelled out in Petunias and Lobelia. They might as well use spray paint. A Spanish castle, A Venetian court, a ballroom lawn, no doubt, with German statuary.

**WASSERMAN** Yes, yes, yes . . . all of it.

**JOSLYN** Tulips by the hundreds, I'm sure, in the spring.

**WASSERMAN** By the thousands! I plant them, they buy them by the truckloads, ripped out the day they're shot and replaced by marigolds, not even stock.

**JOSLYN** You plant them? You? Not just an innocent tourist, but responsible for that mess?

**WASSERMAN** Oh, Lord no, responsible, never, I wouldn't presume. I wouldn't make a decision myself, what if someone saw it? Oh, I'm terribly sorry, I know you and you don't know me, what am I thinking . . . I'm not in the habit of meeting . . . allow me to introduce . . . uh, Ms. J. H. Joslyn, this is Mr. Kermit Wasserman; Mr. Wasserman, Ms. Joslyn. How do you do? It is my misfortune to be one of the assistant gardeners at Crampton.

**JOSLYN** How do you do? I was just going.

**WASSERMAN** Oh, my yes, I'm afraid you'd better, because if you're going to be wicked about Cramptom I couldn't tear myself away and I shouldn't hear it. My own garden, of course, very small is a cottage, Englishy sort of thing, very modest, but enough for me and my iris. And yours?

**JOSLYN** Sing me no yourses, my garden's my garden. Certainly not Englishy cottage. I farm, I don't decorate. I breed. I grow eggplant and squash, kale and kohlrabi. And I breed intermediate iris for strength and substance. I'm none of your watercolorists.

**WASSERMAN** You're not, by any chance, colorblind?

**JOSLYN** I beg your pardon?

**WASSERMAN** I'm terribly sorry, I don't know what came over me. It's just that one who has created such a lovely texture and, as you say, substance, and neglected so completely—

**JOSLYN**  Rolls right off my back. There's no reason for me to stay, what did I expect? I don't know how some people call themselves scientists.

**WASSERMAN**  Ms. Joslyn, I may be vain, I may have expected too much, but you cannot—

**JOSLYN**  How could you have overlooked so basic a thing as stalk?

**WASSERMAN**  I could say the same for you, you know, were I the sort who—

**JOSLYN**  The color may be striking but there's nothing under it!

**WASSERMAN**  You have created a castle without a flag!

**JOSLYN**  I care for more than flashy headgear, thank you!

**WASSERMAN**  And you might as well be breeding galoshes!

**JOSLYN**  I am a great breeder, sir!

**WASSERMAN**  And, madam, so am I!

**JOSLYN**  I've toiled in the fields, sir, for thirty years!

**WASSERMAN**  And so have I!

**JOSLYN**  And you've nothing to show for it.

**WASSERMAN**  No one wants your Little Soldier!

**JOSLYN**  No one needs your Tanya!

**WASSERMAN**  If my Tanya had the texture of your Little Soldier!

**JOSLYN**  If my Soldier had the color of Tanya . . . ! (*There is a dead pause. It extends. Their words hang in the air. They think for a moment. They consider, each with his or her own thoughts. They picture it. She sits.*)

**WASSERMAN**  (*Imagining it.*) Oh, my . . .

**JOSLYN**  Hummm . . .

**WASSERMAN**  Oh, my, that would be something . . .

**JOSLYN**  Hummmmm . . .

**WASSERMAN**  In four years . . . maybe five. Six at the outside . . . Can you see it?

**JOSLYN**  (*Musing.*) Just never mind, I see what I see . . .

**WASSERMAN**  I've never seen anything like it.

**JOSLYN**  There's never been anything like it.

**WASSERMAN**  Not to push, and I don't think it's vanity, but Best of Show would be in the bag.

**JOSLYN**  In a jerkwater show like this? I wouldn't waste our time.

**WASSERMAN**  One might easily interest the nurseries in such a . . . uh . . .

**JOSLYN**  Oh, my good man, beating them away with our umbrellas.

**WASSERMAN**  The Sass Award is not at all out of the question.

**JOSLYN**  Sing me no Sass Awards, we're talking the cover of the Royal Horticultural Society's Garden Magazine.

**WASSERMAN**  Perhaps you had better be listed as breeder. I wouldn't be able to tolerate the limelight. Fame has always . . .

**JOSLYN**  (*Musing.*) Sing me no limelight, read me no fame; we're talking fortune.

**WASSERMAN**  Indeed. Not to be crass, but? . . .

**JOSLYN**  Thousands. Tens of thousands.

**WASSERMAN**  A better income, I would think than assisting at a school library.

**JOSLYN**  Fuck the school library.

**WASSERMAN**  Indeed.

**JOSLYN**  Fuck Castle Crampton.

**WASSERMAN**  Oh, indeed. (*A long pause, they dream. Then delicately turn to particulars. She clears her throat.*)

**JOSLYN**  (*Inquiring lightly.*) Ah . . . how are . . . her . . . uh . . . rhizomes?

**WASSERMAN**  Well actually, now that you ask, very strong indeed, really quite remarkable.

**JOSLYN**  Are they?

**WASSERMAN**  And . . . uh . . . his?

**JOSLYN**  Well, uh . . . adequate certainly . . . uh . . . perhaps not absolutely . . . the . . . uh . . .

**WASSERMAN**  Only that?

**JOSLYN**  I've probably seen better increase.

**WASSERMAN**  Tanya increases like a weed.

**JOSLYN**  *Does* she? The little devil.

**WASSERMAN**  And, uh, his . . . seed pod?

**JOSLYN**  Oh, marvelous, of course with all that upper strength. Unfailing.

**WASSERMAN**  I thought so. I must tell you, Tanya has been known to disappoint me there.

**JOSLYN**  Well she's terribly delicate, it would be uncaring to expect. . . .

**WASSERMAN**  I'm afraid, though, we'd much better have your Little Soldier as the seed parent.

**JOSLYN**  Absolutely. He won't mind playing the girl. Not for Little Tanya. Of the Golden Hair! I assume the bud count, actually . . . ?

**WASSERMAN**  Oh, yes, two. And she's been known to have two branches.

**JOSLYN**  Oh, I'm glad to hear it. That might make it much easier. Though we have to get some starch in her. Strengthen those limbs. Not stout—just strong. He'll do wonders for that.

**WASSERMAN**  And as for color, I'm glad to say, there, Tanya is very dominant.

**JOSLYN**  The little vixen! He's not very sure of himself there, I'm glad to say.

**WASSERMAN** Oh, she'll take care of him nicely.

**JOSLYN** My, my, my . . .

**WASSERMAN** I must say . . .

**JOSLYN** So convenient that you live so close.

**WASSERMAN** Isn't it?

**JOSLYN** Lovely Mahopac. (*Pause.*) You understand, I think this should be exclusive. I don't want to see her red hair pussy-footing around with—

**WASSERMAN** Madam! You overreach yourself. Tanya's fidelity, I assure you is irreproachable. You had much better be concerned about your Little Soldier.

**JOSLYN** You have his word.

**WASSERMAN** Well . . . one hears stories . . .

**JOSLYN** Would you agree to begin with my seed bed? I make all my own soil, pure compost. A good grade of builders sand.

**WASSERMAN** That's quite fine by me . . . You won't mind if I visit the site first, just to . . .

**JOSLYN** Oh, by all means. I think we should begin first thing in the morning. I'll drive over to your place . . .

**WASSERMAN** Oh, excellent, excellent . . . We can collect her lovely pollen at the crack of dawn . . .

**JOSLYN** I have a divine set of sable brushes—never been touched. So exorbitant, but I couldn't help myself.

**WASSERMAN** How impulsive!

**JOSLYN** Oh, I know. I've been waiting for the right occasion . . . I knew it'd come.

**WASSERMAN** Intuition . . . I don't expect to sleep a wink.

**JOSLYN** Nor I.

**WASSERMAN** Well I must say. (*He gets up, walks a few steps, a new dignity.*) They're all drifting back, the judging must be over. Ha! If they only knew.

**JOSLYN** Look at them. Do you watch the presentation of the ribbons? And all their giggling little squeals when they win?

**WASSERMAN** Not usually, I'm afraid. Crowds, you know, with nothing to look at . . . except people, of course . . . but perhaps this year . . . just to see how it's done. Just to get into practice.

**JOSLYN** Might as well get in the habit of being notable. I must say, Mr. Wasserman, you're looking like a championship breeder.

**WASSERMAN** And you, Ms. Joslyn.

**JOSLYN** Ah! The sun's come out. And look who's golden hair is flashing in the light. She must be a hundred yards away.

**WASSERMAN** She has reason to be excited tonight.

**JOSLYN** I'm as nervous as a schoolgirl.

**WASSERMAN**   I think you're blushing.

**JOSLYN**   So are you.

**WASSERMAN**   Well, let us sit here, then, and wait for the onslaught of the unsuspecting crowd. (*They sit.*)

**JOSLYN**   I must say it has been a very good show this year. (*They open their programs and begin to study them.*)

### CURTAIN

# ABSTINENCE   (1986)


## AUTHOR'S NOTE

Another play written for a Circle Rep benefit. This one is based on
the experience of being the friend of about fifty people in A.A. The people
in that group are so tight I've always thought we could benefit from an organization called Friends of A.A.


ABSTINENCE was first presented on October 24, 1988 by Circle Repertory Company as part of their Twentieth Anniversary Celebration gala benefit honoring Lanford Wilson. It was directed by Marshall W. Mason with
the following cast:

MARTHA: Bobo Lewis
DANNA: Debra Mooney
WINNIE: Mary McDonnell
LON: Mark Blum
JOE: Steve Bassett

> ". . . Abstinence engenders maladies."
> *Love's Labour's Lost*


## CHARACTERS

MARTHA  The maid.
DANNA  Thirty, sharp and a little hysterical just tonight.
WINNIE  Thirty, sweet and charming. Always.
LON  Winnie's husband, thirty-five and mild.
JOE  Thirty, The All American Sweetheart of a man. Unfortunately mad.


## SCENE

The very dark front hall of a New York apartment. Maybe track lighting.
Chic.

# ABSTINENCE

*Martha, the Maid, stands at the front door. Lon enters, lighting a cigarette.*

**LON**  I think all the guests are here, Martha.

**MARTHA**  Is this the shoplifters or the smokers or the sex offenders or the drunks?

**LON**  I think it's the weight-watchers, but just in case it's the smokers I stepped out here to have a cigarette.

**WINNIE**  (*Enters from another way.*) Happy anniversary, darling. I'm so thankful you're here.

**LON**  Happy anniversary, Winnie. My helpful little helpless wife. I thought you were in with your guests.

**WINNIE**  I just popped up for a moment to tuck in the children.

**LON**  Why is it that every anniversary we have to give a party for one of your charity groups?

**WINNIE**  I just feel our life is so perfect we should help those less fortunate. (*They exit arm-in-arm.*)

**MARTHA**  (*To the audience.*) Already you know we're in trouble, right? (*The doorbell rings. Martha reaches to open it, turns to look at audience.*) One tip. Always bet on somebody named Winnie. (*She opens the door. Danna staggers in a step.*)

**DANNA**  Thank God someone's here! You're not Winnie. You're . . . she talks about you all the time . . . you're Abigail or Eleanor or Lady Bird . . .

**MARTHA**  Martha.

**DANNA**  Martha!

**MARTHA**  And whom should I say . . . ?

**DANNA**  Oh. I'm a friend. I've just come from a meeting—this is the closest place I could think of. Tell her—My name is—God, I knew it a minute ago. Danna! I'm Danna Walsh.

**MARTHA**  Danna Walsh. (*In one move Martha takes a book from nowhere, pages quickly to the back, checks, raises her eyebrows.*)

**DANNA**  Now, Jackie, darling . . .

**MARTHA**  Martha.

**DANNA**  Martha, darling, you've got to get me a drink.

**MARTHA**  No way.

**DANNA**  I'll give you money. I'll give you my jewels. I'll give you my husband—no, I dumped him, I'll give you my mother.

**MARTHA**  I was weakening but you blew it.

**WINNIE**  (*Entering.*) Martha, who was at—Danna, darling! I so wanted to be there for you tonight but we have this dinner party every year.

**DANNA**  I hate to burst in on you like this but you've always been so helpful. I have to talk to you alone.

**WINNIE**  Oh, Martha knows everything.

**DANNA**  You do? (*Beat. Goes to Martha.*) What is a . . . (*Whispers. Martha raises her eyebrows, whispers back into Danna's ear.*) Well, of course it is. It's absurdly simple if you think about it. (*To Winnie.*) Winnie, you've got to help me.

**WINNIE**  You don't look well at all. How did it go?

**DANNA**  How did what go?

**WINNIE**  The meeting. A.A. The first anniversary of your sobriety.

**DANNA**  Who remembers, it must have been twenty minutes ago. I was a wreck. I qualified. Everyone applauded. I could have ripped their hearts out. I was congratulated. The rich bitch who runs things called me a brick. I've never wanted a drink so badly in my life.

**WINNIE**  Don't be silly. We're all so proud of you! You've gone an entire year today without a drink.

**DANNA**  A year? Are you mad? What would be so unusual about that? This is leap year you idiot. Three hundred sixty-six long tedious days. And three hundred sixty long hopeless nights. I've read over five hundred books. I've written four. I've knitted some things: a bed cover, wallpaper for the living room. Johnnie Walker Red! Now there's a man with spine. Aren't you going to ask me in?

**WINNIE**  You're in, darling.

**DANNA**  This is your apartment? This well? It's pitch in here!

**WINNIE**  Would you like a cup of tea?

**DANNA**  (*All hope gone. Musing.*) Oh . . . no . . . I've been haunted all day by a scene in one of the Thin Man movies. Nick is at the table when Nora comes in late, and she asks him how much he's had to drink; Nick says he's had five martinis. And when the waiter comes over Nora says, "Would you please bring me five martinis?" (*Beat.*) I want to live like that. I want charm in my life. I want my alcohol back. I used to have a wonderful life. I mean, I didn't have friends, but I didn't notice.

**WINNIE**  Why don't you come join us? Just twenty or so, they're sitting down to eat. They're Liars, I'm afraid, Liars Anonymous, but you know how charming they can be.

**DANNA**  Food? How shallow. People I don't know? Without a drink? I'll just steady myself against the wall here—where is it?—and I'll be fine. If Dolly could just bring me a . . .

**MARTHA**  Forget it.

**WINNIE**   I know, love. I'm a drunk too. I've had some—

**DANNA**   Ha! You call yourself a drunk? You haven't had a drink in three years. Put me in front of a bottle of Cuervo Gold and I'll show you a drunk.

**WINNIE**   You know what we say: One day at a time.

**DANNA**   I've experienced one day at a time for three hundred sixty-six days —end to end. Twenty-four hours in every day, eighty-six thousand four hundred seconds. I know, I counted them once. A year ago I could celebrate the Fourth of July, come home; go to bed; wake up, it would be November.

**LON**   (*Enters. Sees Danna, maybe hesitates one step, smiles.*) Winnie, are you coming back to the . . .

**WINNIE**   Lon, I want you to meet a dear friend of mine. This is Danna. We've been friends for, oh, my, how long is it?

**DANNA**   Three hundred sixty-six . . . endless . . .

**WINNIE**   Is it a year already? Danna, this is my husband, Lon.

**DANNA**   You don't happen to be carrying, do you?

**WINNIE**   Danna was just admiring the foyer.

**LON**   Yes, my wife did the entire apartment herself.

**DANNA**   I haven't seen it.

**LON**   I was just talking to the most remarkable man in there. He says he climbed Mount Everest completely by himself.

**WINNIE**   Let me just—oh, you know what a terrible organizer I am—I'll just get the next course started and then I'm all yours. (*She goes out, smiling. Just before she leaves she stops. Thinks. Looks at Martha, then goes out thinking. A calm beat. You can't tell, but they are listening to Winnie's retreat.*)

**DANNA**   (*They stare at each other an intense moment. Then:*) Alonzo! (*They kiss passionately, fall to to ground in a 69 position, Lon's head up Danna's dress, both growling and barking like dogs. They sit up. Danna's hair is a mess. They stare at each other a frozen beat.*)

**MARTHA**   (*To audience.*) I turned down a paying job to do this play.

**LON**   (*To Danna.*) Every moment without you has been hell!

**DANNA**   You can't possibly be Winnie's husband. You're that pompous miser she talks about? She said you were eighty! She said you had no teeth.

**LON**   Where did you meet Winnie?

**DANNA**   Ha! You think she really goes to ballet class five times a week? Have you once asked to see her plie? You told me your wife was Catholic, blind, and confined to a wheelchair.

**LON**   I didn't want to worry you.

**DANNA**   I mean she's a kind-hearted helpless thing, but you might have told me you were married to Miss Ripple of 1985.

**LON**  Don't be jealous, Danna. Winnie never drinks.

**DANNA**  Ha! I could tell you stories about that Sweet-pea that would turn your piss green. Ever wonder why she carried a sewing basket for twelve years without ever so much as darning a sock?

**LON**  Winnie is the most charitable woman in the city.

**DANNA**  If you mean she's known for giving it away.

**LON**  This is not becoming, Danna.

**DANNA**  She can't help it, poor dear. While you're down on Wall Street that poor helpless thing is down on half of Spanish Harlem.

**LON**  You could hardly know her.

**DANNA**  I know you have two olive-skinned sons with flashing black eyes.

**LON**  (*Moving closer, becoming aroused.*) If anything, Winnie is almost too gentle and kind. She has none of the shocking terms of endearment that you have. Or the voracious appetite. None of the inventive positions ... certainly none of the improvisationally creative—before I met you I had no idea of the things that could be done with raw vegetables. If I were to think one of you had a broad experience ...

**DANNA**  I wasn't myself, Lon. I was sober. And as for the potato trick, I learned that one at ... (*Remembering herself.*) I mean to say ... "Winnie" you said her name was? No, we've only met a couple of times. Meetings or something, a few friends. I had no idea she was your wife. I doubt that I could allow myself to see you again now that I know— (*Losing it.*) —unless you either take me right here in this dungeon of a foyer or bring me a Manhattan. Oh, god! With a Manhattan who needs a man? A Manhattan asks nothing from you. It doesn't deceive or sulk or play games. And it has, God knows, more interesting conversation. A Manhattan ... listens!

**LON**  (*Love talk.*) You said to pick—

**WINNIE**  (*He shuts up as she enters, she notices but doesn't show it.*) Now, I'm all yours.

**DANNA**  Winnie! You poor deceived darling. You weak and caring ...

**WINNIE**  Could you wait just a little moment? (*She exits.*)

**LON**  (*Adjusting back.*) You said to pick up a zucchini ... I got three. And a cucumber. And a baby eggplant. And a crooked necked squash. The mind boggles.

**DANNA**  (*Torn, but.*) Woah ... no, no Lon. It's not enough. The night with the pumpkin was fun, but it's not enough.

**LON**  Martha might ask the cook if she has any sherry.

**MARTHA**  This woman is loaded for bear, she'd blow a glass of sherry to hell.

**LON**  Really, I don't believe there's any alcohol in the house.

**DANNA**  You're goddamned right there isn't. You'll find there's no nail polish remover either. That tit-mouse wouldn't trust herself in the same room with vanilla extract. Why do you think the radiator kept freezing on your car? It's the trusting ones who need our help, Alonzo. She needs you. A charming intelligent dynamo of a man who inherited thirty-seven million and has parleyed that, now, into . . . how much?

**LON** (*Proud.*) Well . . . a little over twelve. But I could never leave you. You're special. Who else has a living room with cable-knit walls?

**DANNA** (*Pleased.*) For one, my mother. I did hers too.

**LON** But, you're right—Winnie does need me.

**DANNA** If it were anyone but that lovely, uncomplicated . . .

**LON** But she doesn't have to know.

**DANNA** The woman has gimlet eyes. She's been sober for three years, she can see through six feet of concrete. (*Winnie enters with Joe, a very handsome young man indeed.*)

**WINNIE** Danna, darling. I wanted you to meet Joe. Joe is a friend of Bill Wilson's too.

**JOE** Sorry, Winnie, I'd love to meet the fellow but I don't know Bill Wilson at all. Sounds like a lovely guy. Do you?

**DANNA** Know him? I've practically had his child. If he were here I'd saute the sanctimonious son-of-a-bitch in Marsala. Whoever— (*She notices Joe for the first time and does not take her eyes off him again.*) Oh. Hi, Joe.

**JOE** Hi.

**DANNA** You're leaving soon?

**JOE** I don't know. My pilot had the jet warmed up to go to Buenos Aires, but I saw you in the hall here and called him to cancel the trip.

**DANNA** And then, Buenos Aires is so . . . hot this time of year.

**JOE** And I don't like to fly without a drink and my doctor says my liver's shot. All those years in the P.O.W. camps.

**DANNA** You poor dear. What was your drink? Bourbon?

**JOE** Well, since we have our own vineyards, I mostly just stick to Dom Perignon. Family loyalty and all that.

**DANNA** With me it's a cold vodka martini. Or two.

**JOE** Twist or an olive?

**DANNA** Hold the garbage.

**JOE** So this is your anniversary.

**DANNA** My first. It's been little nervous-making.

**WINNIE** Remember, you don't have to worry about tomorrow. You just have to get through tonight.

**DANNA** Oh, suddenly, I don't think that's going to be such a problem—I don't know though. You sound like a playboy.

**JOE** Actually, I'm a physicist.

**DANNA** My. (*Winnie is helping Joe on with his coat.*)

**JOE**   And you live close-by.

**DANNA**   Twenty or thirty blocks.

**LON**   Danna? Aren't you going to say goodnight? Danna? The crisper?

**WINNIE**   Oh. And Joe.

**JOE**   Yes, Winnie?

**WINNIE**   Happy anniversary.

**JOE**   Thanks.

**DANNA**   It's your anniversary too?

**JOE**   Well, I don't talk about it. My wife, the Dutchess, had a passion for collecting Iranian pewter. Nothing would do but she had to go there just one more time.

**DANNA**   Oh no.

**JOE**   Caught in a terrorist crossfire.

**DANNA**   You don't have to talk about it.

**JOE**   Should we walk?

**DANNA**   Let's take a cab. (*They leave.*)

**WINNIE**   (*After a beat.*) I do hope she'll be all right.

**LON**   You worry too much about other people. She can look after herself. Not like my helpless darling. It's his anniversary, too?

**WINNIE**   Yes. Such a pity. But they let him out this one night every year. We must go in and join our guests . . . take my arm. Now, remember, this is my Liars Anonymous group; don't believe a word anyone says . . . Darling. I was looking in the refrigerator. You must show me what you plan to do with all those vegetables. (*Martha is left alone as at the beginning. A pause.*)

**MARTHA**   . . . "The night with the pumpkin . . . was fun? . . ." (*Beat.*) Liars Anonymous. Wouldn't you know. I had two marriage proposals and a tip on the market from that group. (*Going.*) What a nasty little play. I don't know about you but I'll never touch a crudité again. (*Gone.*)

**END**

# A POSTER OF THE COSMOS  (August 1987)
*for Tom Noonan*

## AUTHOR'S NOTE

I received a letter from two writer friends, saying they thought artists had not responded fully to the AIDS crisis. This, as you can imagine, was some time ago, 1987.  Since I was in rehearsal for BURN THIS, a play about the loss of a dear, important and talented gay dancer, a play I'd been agonizing over for 2 years in response to the almost weekly loss of some of the most beautiful people I'd known, I thought I had covered the subject pretty well. Still, I wanted to do something for the evening.

I met John Ford Noonan, a friend and very talented playwright, who reminded me that three years earlier I had promised to write a play for his brother Tom. That's a promise, believe me, I rarely make. With Tom as a physical model for the character, and the desire to participate in the AIDS evening, late one night I woke up at 5 A.M. with POSTER completely intact.  I wrote the first half of the play, in pencil, that morning and was late for rehearsal. The next night the same thing happened and I got up and finished it.  I realized the play was much too long for what my friends wanted, but I thanked them for the kick that got it started.  Their evening never came off, but by that winter it was clear that artists all over the world, gay and straight, were certainly responding to the AIDS crisis.  We had no alternative.

A POSTER OF THE COSMOS was first presented on June 8, 1988 by Curt Dempster in the Ensemble Studio Theatre's Marathon '88 in New York City. It was directed by Jonathan Hogan with the following cast:

TOM:  Tom Noonan

## CHARACTER

TOM   a large, brooding, and most of this time, quite angry man of thirty-six.

## SCENE

A police station in Manhattan, 1987.

# A POSTER OF THE COSMOS

*Tom, most of the time, sits at an institutional table in an institutional chair. There is a tape recorder on the table. He is in a white pool of light in a black void. He wears a white T-shirt, white work pants and sneakers. He is addressing a cop who would be at the other end of the table, and another off left or right who would be slouching against a door. When he gets up, something in the cops' posture tells him he'd better sit back down. When he smokes, the smoke rises up in the white downspot like a nebula.*

**TOM** (*He is standing and quite pissed off.*) All right, I'm *sitting* down and I'm staying down. Okay? (*He sits.*) Now, are you happy? (*Glares at the cops in disgust.*) Jesus, you guys slay me with that crap. "You don't look like the kinna guy'd do somethin' like dat." You're a joke. Cops. Jesus. I mean you're some total cliché. I don't have to be here lookin' at you guys, I could turn on the TV. "What's that white stuff on your shirt?" Jesus. I'm a baker, it's flour. You want a sample, take to your lab? (*Shaking his head in wonder.*) "You don't look like the kinna guy'd do somethin' like dat." What does dat kinna guy who'd do somethin' like dat look like to a cop, huh? And what kinna thing? You don't know nothin'; you know what you think you know. You seen every kinna dirty business there is every night, lookin' under the covers, spend your workin' day in the fuckin' armpits of the city and still ain't learned shit about people. You're totally fuckin' blind and deaf like fish I heard about, spend their life back in some fuckin' cave. (*He looks around, taps the tape recorder, looks at it.*) Is this on? You got your video camera goin'? 'Cause I told you I'd tell you but this is the only time I'm tellin' this. So, you know, get out your proper equipment, I'm not doin' this twice. (*He looks around, still disgusted.*) "You don't look like the kinna guy'd do somethin' like dat." Johnny said I didn't look like no kinna guy at all. Just a big ugly guy. Said I was like Kurt Vonnegut or somebody. Somebody had the good sense not to look like nobody else. He said that, I read every word Vonnegut wrote. He's good. He's got a perverted point of view, I like that. There was a time I wouldn't of understood that, but we change, which is what I'm sayin' here. (*Beat.*) "You don't look like the kinna guy'd do dat." What kinna guy is *that*? *What* kinna guy? Oh, well, you're talkin' dat kinna guy. The kinna guy'd *do* that. *Dat* kinna guy. . . . Well, I *ain't* dat kinna guy. I'm a kinna guy like you kinna guys. That's why you make me want to puke sittin' here lookin' at you. "Hey, guys, dis guy is our kinna guy. I can't believe he's dat kinna guy." Well, I *ain't* that kinna guy. (*He is almost saddened by the cops.*) You guys move in the dark, inna doorways, if you didn't look right through people 'steada at 'em, you'd maybe know there ain't no "*kinna guys.*" You'd maybe know you can't sort guys out like vegetables. This is a potato, it goes wid the potatoes; this is a carrot, this here's celery—we got us an eggplant, goes wid the eggplant. That's vegetables, that ain't people. There's no kinna guys, 'cause *guys,* if you used your *eyes,* you'd know, are V-8 juice, man. You don't know *what* kinna thing's in there. (*Tom pauses, takes cigarettes from his pants pocket, puts them on the table with a Zippo lighter, takes one from the pack and lights it. He has a new thought that annoys him lightly.*) For all you know Johnny was a junkie. Didn't see you lookin' for tracks, and you'da found 'em by the way, so what kinna guys are we talkin' about here? It depresses people to sit here and talk to this kinna massive stupidity. (*Beat.*) Johnny'd love it. He'd laugh his ass, man. No shit, he'd wet himself over you guys. And I don't wanna make him sound simple. He was like this anything-but-easy sort of person. He used to, you know, when he was a kid, had this prescription for hypertension medication, but he said he didn't take it 'cause it messed up his bowels so bad. *Thinking* was Johnny's problem. Like 'cause his mind was goin' like on all these tracks, like it had all these connections and he was always repluggin' everything and crossin' over these wires, till you could almost like *see* this complicated mess of lines in his head. Like he'd wait till he was like fuckin' droppin', like his eyes had been closed for an hour before he'd even get in bed at night. And then he'd lay there and in a minute he'd be up again. And like, you know, you'd think, aw, shit, 'cause he's smokin' all these cigarettes and this shit and half the time he don't know if he's sittin' up or layin' down. The whole apartment could go up and he'd never know it. He'd just have to go on repluggin' those wires till finally, sorta totally unannounced, somethin' would short out in his head. You could almost hear like his whole system shut down, and he'd be out cold somewhere. Maybe ona floor, ina chair. (*Maybe a beat, but he continues the same.*) Then, you know, he was a twitcher. Like a dog. Even in his sleep, which was something I never saw on a human being while they was sleepin'. Like a dog is chasing maybe a rabbit, or gettin' run after by a wolf, but you'd watch Johnny and say, Johnny what the hell are you dreamin' you're chasin'? Then he'd wake up and keep right on twitchin'. You know, the foot is goin' or the fingers are goin'. He'd be biting at his lip or digging at his cheek like a fuckin' junkie, which I don't think he ever was, 'cause he worked for a hospital, procuring, and coulda brought anythin' home but never did, except stories about the fuckin' nurses and orderlies tryin' to steal him blind, falsifying records on him, but he never said he was, and he'd lie, but his lies was always telling things on himself like he was worse than he was. Like he said he'd left his wife and kid, back in Arkansas when he was seventeen, and really missed the little daughter, but like he fuckin' never had no kids. The wife, yeah, but—and a lot of shit like he'd been in jail, which he hadn't and all. But he, you know, used to shoot up but he never worked up a habit, 'cause probably he never, at that time, had the bread for it and you can't imagine a worse thief than Johnny, so he'd never make it as a junkie, 'less he had some john supportin' him in it. But he never said he was even an out-and-out user, so you can be pretty sure he wasn't. Which also he wasn't the type 'cause junkies are zombies even before they get hooked. They're basically lazy people don't want the responsibility of livin'. Anyway, you're not gonna catch no twitcher on the shit, 'cause it'd be like, you know, a waste of good shit. And Johnny was this, you know, he'd get his fingers goin' in his hair, I'd look over and say, "Aww, Jesus, Johnny," 'cause there'd be this like patch of red hair in the middle of all his like dirty blond and he'd say, " What, have I got myself bleedin' again?' And you couldn't figger what a basically nice-lookin' guy was always fuckin' himself over like that, but that was just all those wires he was repluggin' all the time. Like the only reason he had a good body was he had these weights, but he'd use 'em like to work off energy not to build himself up. That's what I say, his mom said he was born with it. But he like burned calories like nothin' I ever saw. Ate more than me and he's what? Five-six, which he thought was short but it isn't like freakish or nothin' to worry about and weighed maybe a buck thirty but he used to say like basically his body was a very inefficient machine. He was like a real gas burner. (*Beat. He thinks a minute.*) He was gonna open a delivery service. This from a guy who had a money job—and he'd be the only deliverer. On his bike. He used to sit and map out routes one place to another. He called himself the Manhattan Transit. Used to make practice runs; you know, during rush hour. But this was just a way to blow off that nervous stuff he had but it didn't work out 'cause he had no business sense. He could organize anything, but he couldn't start something. He went so far he made up this ad and put it in the *Village Voice* two weeks running with our phone number on it. This was during a two-week vacation he had. We was goin' to go down to St. Pete, then he got this idea. Only the damnedest thing, the phone never rung once. No, that's not true. Once about six months later I picked up the phone, said, hello, this guy says, "Is this the Manhattan Transit?" I said it used to be but they sold their bicycle. (*Beat.*) He would of been good at it. I said he should work at some place where they use messengers but he wasn't interested in workin' for somebody else. He was already doin' that, he had a regular job you'd think kept him so crazy he wouldn't have time to dream up some schemes, but you got to remember all those wires in his head—and he wasn't meant to work in a office. Twitchers are hell in a office. He was at St. Vincent's first, then up to Doctors Hospital and back to St. Vincent's, runnin' procurements for like the whole hospital. Ordering truckloads of rubbing alcohol and all the prescription stuff, the bedpans and walkers, so you know it wasn't no snap, but one wire in his head was always out in the rain on his bike using this like photographic map of the city: the one-way streets, and places blocked off for school kids at recess time. You probably seen him. He's the guy goin' about five times faster than the traffic. And fightin' everythin'. Nothin' was easy. Went at everythin' crazy. He'd get off work, his face all red, you'd know he'd been diggin' at himself again. That he'd be up all night workin' on the bike. So I don't want to make him sound easy. He was anything butta easy sort of person. I was the easy one. (*Pause. He stretches, or even gets up, then sits back down. He looks off, thinking.*) I was the easy one. He was always wantin' to change things, I didn't care how things was. Then he was always changin' jobs, or tryin' to. He'd blow up at somebody and walk out, they'd always ask him to come back and I been workin' at the same bakery twenty years. Since I was sixteen. And I like it 'cause they're old fashioned and do it the same way they always did. You'd think bakin' bread is nothin' with the machines they use. Doin' all the measuring and mixin' and kneadin', what's to do but carry the trays to the ovens and back, but yeast is a livin' thing; it can't be taken for granted. One batch ain't like the next, and the humidity and temperature in the room makes a difference. Johnny liked it. I couldn't smell it on me but he liked the smell. He said people take on the character of their work and I figured I was gradually becoming this nice crusty loaf of Italian bread. But the way I think of it it's good, 'cause, like I said, it's nourishing and it's a live thing. Bread. But I wasn't foolin' myself that it was a job that calls for a lot of thinkin'. Like Johnny's. Instinct, maybe. Also the money ain't bad and you always got fresh bread. Only thing I didn't like was I worked nights and he worked days. (*Pause. He looks at the cops.*) Hell, that got a reaction, didn't it? Now you're thinkin', "He ain't our kinna guy after all. Good, we ain't gotta worry about it." But I was, I used to be, I know all that. But circumstances are crazy things; the things that can happen all of a sudden change everything. Like I'd never thought much of myself as a part of anything. I was, you know, I thought I was above everything. I just watched it. But really, I didn't know how to get involved in it. (*Beat.*) So, I get off work at seven, I'm eatin' at this place I always did, Johnny's havin' breakfast. He's depressed 'cause the Cosmos folded. Soccer team. I think they'd folded about five years back but he'd got to thinkin' about it again. And we're talkin' about atmospheric pressure, which is something it happens I've read a lot about, and we're both readers that only read factual stuff. Only I read slow and forget it and he reads like tearin' through things and remembers. And we'd both been married when we was kids, and had a kid of our own, only, you know, it turned out he didn't. And he said he was gay now and he'd been like fuckin' everythin' in sight for five years only he'd got frustrated with it and hadn't been laid in a month, and we're bitchin' our jobs and he got up and goes off for a minute and comes back and says why don't we go around the corner to his apartment 'cause we're takin' up two seats at the counter and this is a business based on volume and I said, no, you got to go to work and he said . . . "I just called in sick." (*He smiles, then thinks about it. A frown, a troubled pause.*) That's funny. He really did, first time I met him, called in sick. I never thought about that—till right now. (*Beat.*) Jesus, all that talkin' about food makes me realize I ain't eaten in two days. (*A beat. He looks at the cops expectantly. Apparently there is no reaction.*) Fuck it, skip it. So anyway, if you'da said I'd be livin' wid a guy I'da said, you know, go fuck yourself. And it stayed like that. It was somethin' that always surprised me, you know? Well, of course you don't. Assholes. But I'd wake up, go in the livin' room, he'd be in a chair or somethin', you know, twitchin' like he was deliverin' somethin' somewhere. Or actually sometimes he'd be in bed there. And it always like surprised me. I'd think, what the hell do you know about this? If he'd been like a big old hairy guy or something probably nothing would have happened, but Johnny didn't have hair on his body, he had like this peach fuzz all over him that made him feel like . . . skip it. I'm your kinna guy, right? I don't think. I don't analyze. So you know . . . we had like . . . three years. We did go down to St. Pete. He'd heard about it, he'd always wanted to go. We didn't like it. We went on down to Key West, he'd heard about that, too. That was worse. We come back, rented a car, went up' to Vermont. And that was good. Except for Johnny drivin', I couldn't let him drive 'cause he'd go crazy. We'd get behind a tractor or somethin', he'd go ape. Also I'd get dizzy on the roads all up and down and curvin' and Johnny being this like aerobic driver. (*Pause.*) So after three years, when he started gettin' sick—they was very good about it at the hospital. They let him come to work for a while. Then, you know, like I said, he'd dig at himself and bleed, so that wasn't possible. That'd be real bad. So then *I* started being the one that was crazy all the time and I'd get off and come home in the morning, he'd be starin' out the window or somethin'.

He'd say, "I slept fourteen hours." It was like this blessing for him; like this miracle, he couldn't believe it. I guess everything that was goin' on in him, I guess was interesting to him. He was like studying it. I'd say, "What?" And he'd hold up his hand for me to be quiet for a long time and then he'd say, "I'd never have believed pain could be that bad. This is amazing." You know, he had like his intestines all eaten out and that and he had insurance and the hospital was good to him. They all visited him, but he didn't take the painkillers. He was curious about it. (*He looks around, then goes on rather flatly.*) Then he got worse and started takin' 'em. (*Beat.*) You could see by his expression that he hadn't thought he was gonna do that. The staff, the nurses and you know, the volunteers, the ghouls that get off on that, they were okay. They didn't get in our way much. (*Searching, becoming frustrated.*) What I couldn't believe was that I didn't have it. I got the fuckin' test, it was negative. I couldn't believe that. Twice. I couldn't figger that, 'cause like the first time I was with him, I just fucked him and he like laid up against me and jerked off. And that was sorta what we did for a while. That was our pattern; you know, you fall into routines. But after a while, you get familiar with someone, I was all over him. No way I wasn't exposed to that like three times a week for three years. What the hell was goin' on? I got to thinkin' maybe he didn't have it, maybe it was somethin' else, but . . . (*He settles down, pauses, thinks of something else.*) He had these friends at the hospital, offered him somethin', I don't know what, take him out of his misery, he didn't take it, he wanted to see it through to the end like. (*A little frustration creeps back.*) See, my problem was I didn't really know what he was goin' through. You help and you watch and it tears you up, sure, but you don't know *what*, you know, whatta you know? (*Beat.*) He wanted to come home, but . . . uh . . . (*Pause. He regards the cops.*) This is the only part you fucks care about, so listen up. We wanted him to be home for the end, but it slipped up on us. We thought he'd come home another time but he went into this like semicoma and just went right outta sight, he just sank. I didn't know if he recognized me or not. I got this old poster of the Cosmos and put it up on the wall across from the bed. They had him propped up in bed, but he just looked scared. He saw it and he said, "What's that?" You know, you know you know everythin' in the room and it's all familiar, and he hadn't seen that before. Probably it was just this big dark thing in front of him that he couldn't tell what it was and it scared him. He didn't understand it. (*Looking around.*) This gets bloody, so if you're faint of heart or anything. (*Looking up.*) All you fuckers out in TV land, recordin' this shit for fuckin' posterity; check your focus, this is hot shit, they're gonna wanna know this. (*Pause.*) So the nurse comes by, I said he's restin'. She was glad to skip him. And I took off my clothes and held him. He was sayin', it sounded like, "This is curious." And there was just like nothin' to him. (*Pause.*) See the problem is, like I said, I was the one who was crazy now. And, uh, well, to hell with it. I'm your kinna guy, fellas, I won't think about it. We do what we do, we do what's gotta be done. (*And rather coldly, or that is what he tries for.*) So he died in my arms and I held him a long time and then I cut a place on his cheek where he used to dig and on his chest where he used to gouge out these red marks and in his hair. And when the blood came I licked it off him. Cleaned him up. So then the nurse come, you know, and shit a brick and called you guys. But they let me hold him till you came. I guess they was afraid of me. Or maybe of all the blood. Then they knew I had to be crazy, 'cause like we agreed, I'm not the kinna guy'd do somethin' like dat. What they thought, I think, was that I'd killed him, but that wasn't what he wanted and what I had to consider now was myself. And what I wanted. (*Pause.*) So if it don't take again, then I'm like fucked, which wouldn't be the first time. I guess there's gonna be maybe some compensation in knowin' I did what I could. (*A long wandering pause, then he looks at them.*) So. Are you happy now? (*A pause. Eight counts.*)

**BLACKOUT**

# THE MOONSHOT TAPE (1990)

*for Michael Warren Powell*


## AUTHOR'S NOTE

This was written a while after Poster as a companion piece. The one act play-in-monologue form is one of the best and most difficult exercises I know. Both for the writer and actor. I was going to write a short comic piece to go with the other two, but some inner voice said it was inappropriate and the play wouldn't come. When the two were done at Humboldt State, the evening seemed quite complete without a third piece.

THE MOONSHOT TAPE was first presented at Humboldt State University, the California State University, in Arcata, California, as part of CSU Summer Arts '90 on August 11, 1990 with the following cast:

DIANE: Roxanne Biggs

It was presented with A POSTER OF THE COSMOS, acted by Richard Thomas. Marshall W. Mason designed and directed both plays.


## CHARACTER

DIANE


## SCENE

A room at the Ozark Cabins Motel in Mountain Grove, Missouri. It is late on a drizzling spring afternoon. The set is a motel bed and nothing else. A pair of motel pillows and a motel bedspread. Diane has an ashtray, a notebook, a pen, a Bic lighter and a package of cigarettes. There is a motel glass on the floor and a bottle of no-name vodka beside it. The light is from motel lamps that we can't see, and toward the end perhaps the hint of a light from a sign outside blinking: Red, Blue, Lavender, Off. Red, Blue, Lavender, Off.

# THE MOONSHOT TAPE

*Diane is thirty-five. She has short hair, jeans and a T-shirt, socks, no shoes. When she reads, she uses dime-store reading glasses. She speaks to an interviewer who would be sitting against the fourth wall. She is trying to be cordial, but she has a "to hell with it, let the chips fall where they may" directness that hides a natural warmth, and also masks a pain and grievance of which she is only partially aware. Diane is sitting cross-legged in the middle of the bed, reading a typed list that runs to two pages. After a moment she takes off the reading glasses and folds them.*

**DIANE**   Well, that covers all the usual bases, I think. I'm sorry, I was reading, what did—oh, sure, smoke, use a tape recorder by all means, I usually won't be interviewed without, do whatever it takes—(*She puts her glasses back on and looks at the list again. Reading.*) "How did living in a small town, essentially a rural area, prepare you for a career and living in a metropolitan area. Or not?" "When did you leave Missouri?" "Where do you get your ideas for your stories?" "How much of an influence has Mountain Grove been on your writing, your life?" "What is your favorite of your own work? Why?" "What do you think is the current state of short story writing?" "What do you see as the future of S.S. Writing?" That sounds like a steamship. Stories are a little skiff. "Why are your stories so downbeat?" "Do you plan to write a novel?" Now, that's a steamship. S.S. Madam Bovary; S.S. The Sun Also Rises. That male chauvinist, anti-Semitic closet case. He says the same about me. (*Pause. She is probably thinking of the questions unasked. She comes out of it slowly and looks at her interviewer.*) I like the way you do your hair. When I was in school here we were all hippies and wore our hair down to our ass. We just washed it and brushed it—in public—as nature intended. Consequentially I never learned how to do anything with it and am insecure about my hair. Anyone over thirty was untrustworthy. You wore a suit, you were the enemy. Everything was visible, you knew immediately where you stood; black and white. No grey areas like now, everywhere is a grey area now, isn't it? I was mightily ashamed of the excitement I felt watching Neil Armstrong walk on the moon. He was there, but he was still an American Establishment Pig. "One small step for Man, one giant leap for Mankind." Which means nothing. He had obviously rehearsed it to say "One small step for *a* man," but he fucked it up. And then lied about it which was perfect. I was a, I guess, sophomore. The Surgeon General had just issued his warning that cigarette smoking was hazardous to our health so I'd started to smoke. (*Beat.*) It was over, of course. We didn't know. The writing was on the ol' wall if we'd taken the trouble to learn to read. I went to my cousin's eighth grade graduation, the 13-year-olds were Yuppies already, rebelling against either our parents who were still stuck reliving Dunkirk and Saipan and buying new refrigerators, or against their hippy, sloppy, be-glittered, older siblings, god knows we must have looked like we definitely didn't have the answer. All the little 13-year-old girls were done up like Donnie or Marie, whichever one is the girl. I was class of '71, that'd make them class of '75, that's about right. You don't have any idea what I'm talking . . . doesn't matter, you would have been about a year old. All those names that were burned into our skin back then are . . . William Calley, My Lai, Alan Shepard, the Native Americans who took over Alcatraz to be a what? Cultural Center I think, god help us. Rest in peace. (*She looks over the list a second, then takes off her glasses again, breaking off, preoccupied.*) I'm expecting a call from Mother, so—she's going to call me when Edith leaves. That's one of my stepfather's kids. I said I was—well, I was meeting you—I said I had to work, that's always my excuse. We—Edith and I, my stepsister and I—how to say this in the briefest possible—hated each other. So Mom's going to call me when she clears out. She's just dropping through from wherever she lives now, wherever it is that her husband has been sent to assistant manage the new Pizza Hut or Burger King. Someplace, Kansas. She's busy packing up photo albums and pots and pans and sweaters and sheets and quilts and refrigerator jars. I don't know where she'll put—add them to what is already one of the world's largest private collections of Tupperware. (*Looking around.*) This isn't bad, this joint. I used to wonder about it. I passed it every day on the way to school. We lived down on Church Street. I mean there couldn't be more than what? Ten rooms? Who's going to stop at a moldy little Masonite motel just an hour from Springfield where there's an actual Great Western? You wouldn't even come here for a rendezvous, it's too crummy. How to end a liaison. I mean, you know, as it turns out the rooms are perfectly adequate, they're clean, the heat's a little eccentric but there's a bathroom with at least a shower. Luckily it's only—you know, it's just a mile up the hill to the Nursing Home, so it couldn't be more convenient. I've triangulated that trip: here, to the house, to the Nursing Home, back to here, about forty times in the last two days. I'd imagined I'd stay at home but Mom, ever ahead of schedule, had my bed taken apart, tied together and stacked out in the yard with most of the other contents. The Home lets you keep a dresser and bed table from your belongings, so—But all those years I passed this place I couldn't imagine who stayed here. Now I know. (*Looking toward the window.*) If this damn weather wasn't so typically foul we could walk. That wouldn't make your job any easier, but I only have five days and I want to spend as much time with Mother as possible. I won't even get a chance to see the town. I haven't been here in . . . God! Well, Mom likes to travel and I hate it, I get enough of it, so I try to bring her to New York once a year. I'm not going to have time to look up—you know how many kids from my graduating class still live here? Exactly two. Out of thirty-six, which we thought was an enormous class back then. Well . . . (*She puts her glasses back on and looks at the list.*) "How did living in a small town, essentially a rural area, prepare you for a career and living in a metropolitan area. Or not?" (*Pause. She starts at the paper.*) "How did living in a small town, essentially a rural area, prepare you for a career and living in a metropolitan area. Or not?" (*Beat. She continues to stare at the list. Finally.*) "When did you leave Missouri?" We graduated on June 11th the day the Federal Marshals took over Alcatraz—so much for the Native Americans' Cultural Center—and I left for Boston the next day. Early. I'd been staying most of the year at a girlfriend's place; I'd had my bags packed for a month. I got to Boston, saw what they were wearing, or not wearing, and threw everything away. I'd been accepted at B.U., I flew from Springfield to St. Louis to Boston, found the room I'd arranged for, found the campus, took this huge sketch pad and an assortment of pencils to the Lobster Claw, ordered a beer and hung out for three months. Till the fall semester started. I was going to be a painter, you understand. My drawings, and the few paintings I'd done, about ten, swung wildly from doe-eyed but determined young women with flowers in their hair to what I imagined the apocalypse would look like. (*She breaks off and looks around her bed for a moment.*) I've managed to build a nest here without the foresight to get another bottle of vodka. With things as they are, half a bottle is definitely not going to do it. Long as I pick up one before they close—at five-thirty if you believe it. The evening sessions, getting Mom to sleep, take it out of you. It was her idea to go there, insisted on it, looked forward to it almost, but . . . (*Beat.*) Half the inmates are insane or senile or something. Some ex-telephone operator rolls up and down the halls looking helplessly lost, yelling, I swear to God— "Operator? Operator? Help me. Operator, help me." The lady in Mom's room—she asked for a roommate and she drew this gal who can't remember from one minute to the next anything that's happened before in her life. She doesn't know if she has to go to the bathroom, if she's eaten, if she's slept. So she says, "Lady? Lady? Lady? Whatta I do now? Lady? Whatta I do now?"

(*Beat.*) That's going to wear thin, I can tell. Even for Mom who has the patience of the angels. (*She looks at the list.*) "Where do you get your ideas for stories?" (*She sighs, then thinks seriously.*) Well, why not? To begin with most of my critics would have you believe I've never had an idea for a story. And, you know, for all I know or care they're right "Where do I get" . . . I'm gonna try to answer this truthfully. I've lied to dozens of interviewers about it. A lot of the time they're flat-out portraits of people I know; things in their lives they've been foolish enough to tell me or I've witnessed or surmised. Then I swear it isn't them, how could they think I'd do that? Or, you know, sometimes it's just raw speculation. You see someone, you start making up a story about them. There's a little old woman, probably lives with fifty cats. That guy is a wife beater. Someone on the subway, it's a game, you know, I've always done it. Like the song: (*Singing conversationally.*) "Laughing on the bus, playing games with the strangers. You said the man in the gabardine suit was a spy. I said 'Be careful, his bow tie is really a camera . . .'" It makes them less of a stranger. Or at least it's easier than the trouble it would take to meet them. It's a good exercise to get the imagination going. And sometimes it ends with a story. Or, you know, sometimes—well, it's always, unfortunately, just yourself you're writing about, but sometimes they're blatantly autobiographical. My side of the story, that's always fun. Never underestimate the power and excitement of revenge. (*Without a beat she breaks off.*) What in the hell is Edith taking so much—probably dishing me to filth. In that superior Christian tone. She's what? Holy Roller, whatever it is, there's a name for it. No lipstick, no movies. Probably married him just so she'd have a legitimate excuse not to read my work. Fiction, good God forbid, the devil's door; and salacious fiction at that. They don't know the half of it. I could curl her toes good but what's the point? Mom married Edith's dad when Edith was about two, I was eleven. Tom, Edith's dad, was a case. Well, actually he was only about three six-packs. And half a fifth of J. W. Dant. The smell still turns my gut. It didn't keep me from drinking, but it kept me from drinking J. W. Dant. "Where do I get my ideas?" Sometimes I start writing something, it turns into a piece that's been kicking me around forever; and I think, oh, good, I'm finally doing that. Then I'll go months with nothing. One thing I haven't done, at least in years, is sit in front of a blank sheet of paper—or now a blank P.C. screen—and force myself to write. "Now is the time for all good women to come to the aid of their party." If they had one. I always wait till I'm—well, I started to say inspired, that's a little sweeping—at least until I have some*one* or some incident or some place or some event in mind. Like if you weren't here now I might be writing a story about a woman coming home to help her mother move into a Nursing Home. Or just coming back for a visit and seeing the town or someone from school, or any of the things coming back home does to you. Being invaded by those memories, those times, those voices, the pictures. The moonshot, watching it on TV, imagining that silence, that airlessness, weightlessness, kicking up that dust that hadn't been kicked up before and doesn't settle immediately because of the weak gravity. That barren place. Or graduation; *that* barren place. Or being interviewed by a terminally shy young high school reporter and filling her tape with maundering stories of the first moonshot. . . . And the various lies you tell of your history to protect the guilty. But probably coming back to this particular town I'd just be getting drunk so don't feel you're usurping my time; no other interviewer has. I'd more likely be watching TV. We get channels two, seven and almost ten. So. (*She looks at the paper again, tired of this, exasperated, almost pissed.*) "How much of an influence has Mountain Grove been on your writing comma your life?" Buckets. Whole bucketsful. (*Pause.*) I'm sorry. You've caught me at low ebb, or a bad time. I have all these feelings, guilt-trips, ghosts, bombarding me here. How much of an influence has Mountain Grove been? Never underestimate that either, and in little ways. The first boyfriend I had at B.U.—for all our free love talk in high school, I'd managed to remain a virgin, squirming out from under basketball players in the back seats of Camaros. I can't imagine *why*. What kind of morality is that? It's all right to be felt up till you're literally raw, french-kiss all night, jerk 'em off even, if that's what it takes, but preserve the integrity of your hymen at all costs. Oh, lord. For all the flaws in our design, and with Mother lately I'm beginning to realize the human body is not nearly the miracle it seems when you're eighteen, but as for the hymen: *Think* of the sweeping changes it would make in the history of Man if Woman had never been designed with that particular membrane. Anyway, I had this boyfriend for about a month. We went on a picnic, walking through the woods. The poor guy had never been in the country before in his life. I'm stomping through the underbrush, I look back and this bastard is getting slapped in the face with every sapling in the forest. He had no idea how to walk in the woods. So I lost some respect for him in that hidden place where we judge men, and didn't see him much after that. I'd say over by the oak tree and he'd say, which one is that? No. I couldn't seriously consider someone who can't tell a birch from a beech. I was thankful that he took my virginity with him, but that was about it. And introducing me to Swinburne which was important to me then. And tells you quite a bit about both of us. (*Suddenly remembering.*) Oh! The sketch pad that I took to the Claw to draw in. It was too dark, just the light on my table, so I started writing in it. Started out a diary and ended up my first story, that first day in Boston. And by the time the fall semester rolled around I matriculated as an English major, minor in art history. All my life I'd said I was going to be a painter. Made all the protest signs: "The Draft Sucks!" charming things like that. After that afternoon, if anyone had asked I would have said I write stories; I'm a story writer. And saying makes it so. Sympathetic magic. If you want it to rain, make the sound of rain. (*Beat.*) I'm going to have to go up there if Edith doesn't leave, and I have no desire to see her. She's had three kids, in four years, and lords them over anyone who hasn't. Her dad died, my stepfather, Tom, about four years ago. I thought I'd seen the last of her at his funeral. Well, she's taking Mom's giving up of the house—she's studying to be a nurse, she didn't go to college so she had to take all this other crap, aside from equivalency tests, math courses, civics for godsake. And actually she does care about people. One of the few Christians I know who takes her religion seriously, which doesn't make her any easier to be around but will surely get her into heaven. And of course after I left Edith was still at home, she was only about nine, so Mom's her mother too. Mother says the vilest things behind her back but that's behind her back, and she shouldn't but—well, fuck it, never mind. (*She picks up the list, puts on her glasses and reads without looking up, quite pissed now at this imposition.*) "What is your favorite of your own work?" The one I'm working on at the time. "Why?" Because it might actually be good. "What do you think is the current state of short story writing?" I don't read other people's work, not fiction. I read mysteries to keep my mind off writing and life and non-fiction. "What do you see as the future of steamship writing?" I couldn't tell you where it's going, I don't know where it's been. "Do you plan to write a novel?" Why not? Plans are easy. (*She stares off. Pause.*) Oh, brother. There are good days and bad days and then there are days when some nice girl from your high school comes to interview you for the Mountain Grove Sentinel! I wrote for the Sentinel, you know. I started a continuing saga about— God knows. No, even God wouldn't remember this one. Anyway, I didn't finish it. It ended with "to be continued." And I suppose was. (*Pause. She looks back at the list.*) "How did living in a small town, essentially a rural area, prepare you for a career and living in a metropolitan area? Or not?" (*Beat.*) Living in one place is very much like living in another. You see, the environment tries to work its way with you—the verdant hills, the necessity to plow the land, the perk of stealing honey, or making sugar from sugar cane. The closeness of the cows—I mean the emotional closeness, but what the environment has to work with is human nature and the human being. And human beings have not evolved much in the last several thousand years, so we are

what we are, which is a pretty hard-sell and all environmental con-
straints do is make us more or less wiley, and though I could pick a
mess of greens in Central Park and quote chapter and verse from the
Bible, unless we are reared in an area of particularly hazardous waste,
and maybe I was, we are not going to be nearly as deftly molded by the
environment as we are by the People. Who. Inhabit It. (*Beat*.) As for
instance, my father left Mom and me when I was five. Mom didn't remarry until I was eleven: Tom and Edith and little Sam, who was three
and a half and never spoke and if he did Tom told him to shut up. Or as
for instance Tom. (*Beat*.) Mom was frail and quite a bit older than Tom
and always the peacemaker, nothing was to upset the order of the
household, the sanctity of the home we hear so much about. Just put a
lid on it and let it boil. And Tom was the quietly expansive, friendly
type that everyone loved. Good job at the cheese factory, nothing
flashy or threatening, just a good Ol' Joe who started coming into my
room sometime during that first year. Edith and Sam had a room on
one side of the bathroom and I had a room on the other. The house
hadn't been built that way, my room was added. Tom built it—with in-
tent, I'm sure now. After all I was eleven, nearly twelve, I had to have
my space. (*Beat*.) He'd stand by the side of my bed in the dark, pull the
covers back and feel my breasts, rub his enormous dick against my
cheek, turn my head over and fuck my face. Or stick his dick in my
mouth and come. Then he'd cover me up and go to the door. Stand
there, very quiet, forever . . . I never knew why . . . then go back to
bed. (*Pause*.) That was only when he drank. Maybe once every three
weeks. The room would reek from him. Cigarette sweat and boiler-
makers. I thought, of course, that it was some sort of punishment. You
can't imagine how good I was. I'd help in the kitchen, set the table, do
the dishes, wipe the counter, clean the refrigerator, do my homework
for the next month, read all the elective outside reading assignments,
fall asleep, and in a few hours I'd wake up with his hand brushing my
forehead, and lay very still. The two or three times I tried to turn my
head he yanked it back with such violence I thought he'd break my
neck. So. Eleven, twelve, thirteen, fourteen, fifteen, sixteen. If you believe it. I put a lock on my door when I was fourteen, he took it off. I
went to Mom, said, "Mom, at night, after you're asleep, Tom comes
into my room"—and she slapped me half way across the house. Told
me never to lie again. All I thought was, my God, you really do see
stars, just like in Looney Tunes. So most of my last year in school I
lived at a friend's house. Moved in with her. Used Edith as an excuse.
Said I'd kill her if I had to live with her. But really I was gonna kill
Tom. Which I didn't, by the bye, he died of emphysema about four
years ago. So. "How did living in a small town, essentially a rural area,

prepare you for a career and living in a metropolitan area? Or not?" and "How much of an influence has Mountain Grove been on your writing comma your life?" Coping with Tom was my adolescence. Anything else was peripheral. He was a good looking man. Tall, thin, blond, younger, nearly ten years, than Mom. All the girls were crazy about him. I never told them. Well, even after I was in high school, I still thought it was some discipline. Had to be some reason. I was looking at it from my point of view, of course, not Tom's. But from his the act is still degrading. I didn't realize that it made me feel dirty—well, fuck it, who am I kidding, it didn't. Or the amount that it did I could cope with, with those endless resources we have at your age. (*Beat.*) At B.U. having been a virgin for eighteen years, I tried very hard to make up for lost time. After the lousy Boy Scout candidate I slept around most of the Big East. Actually most of the Eastern Seaboard. The current cry was, "Make Love, Not War," and of course I leapt at the opportunity, ripped my clothes off with the least provocation, desperately angry that I had missed Woodstock by four years, making it up as I went along. The usual trip: acid, mushrooms, vodka. Then, as you may know, I was published by the time I was a sophomore, so I was writing a lot and milling with my gang, trying hard to be one of the crowd, not stand out, don't be above anything. And god knows I wasn't. I spent my college years either at my typewriter, marching, or on my back. First position, second position, third position. Didn't go home once in those four years. Talked to Mom on the phone; always when Sam and Edith would be in school and Tom would be at work, making cheese and whey. (*Beat.*) All that fucking, of course, was a search, but I didn't know it. Tangled in the blankets, beating the bushes. This goes back to feeling a little dirty, or only a little dirty, I rationalized that I was striving to cleanse myself, put my adolescence behind me. (*Pause.*) So, I didn't come back here till our class reunion. Our fifth. I'd moved to New York by then, got a job as a copy editor, left it, started writing advertising copy, quit that. Finally realizing that I didn't want a job where I had to write someone else's bidding, so I worked—office temp, legal, medical—until the first collection came out and I was like: Oh, wow, discovered! By which I mean two stories were sold as movies and I bought a brownstone and began to move in the literary circles, still moving in circles. So I didn't really know I hadn't been trying to cleanse myself with semen, or douche—I'd been trying to get myself dirty again. And very unsuccessfully. So I came back here, for our fifth high school reunion, contrived to get everyone but Tom out of the house one Sunday afternoon. Tom was very respectful. I was important, of course, and an adult now. And Tom had found God. So I showed him how the police tied us up to take us off to jail—they hadn't actually, and as a matter of fact, I was never in jail, but it comes in handy from time to time to be able to tell a story. Which he told me later was just lying and getting away with it. So there he was, with his feet belted together and his hands tied behind his back, lying on the living room floor. I wish you could have seen it gradually . . . dawn on him that he was helpless . . . (*Pause. She lights a cigarette. Maybe she pours a couple of fingers of vodka and has a belt as well.*) Never underestimate the power and excitement of revenge. (*Beat.*) I wandered into the kitchen, got myself a soda from the fridge. Tom started calling, "Diane? Where'd you go, honey? Diane, this ain't funny, sweetheart." I looked around the kitchen, some of the drawers. I hadn't realized, lord above, Mom had a regular slaughterhouse in her knife drawer. Mallets and cleavers and a collection of butcher knives that was absolutely *sobering*. But I selected the weapon of my trade—an indelible, permanent ink felt tip pen that mom used to mark packages of meat for the locker plant or deep freeze and I went back into the room with Tom. He was thinking very fast, but he didn't say anything. So I sat down beside him on the floor and very slowly started unbuttoning his shirt and pants, with him starting to say now, "Oh, don't do that, Diane, Honey, I'm gonna tell your mother," if you can believe it. I went back into the kitchen, got the scissors, scared him to death, but only to cut his clothes off him, around the rope and my belt and his belt that I had hog-tied him with. Which *really* pissed him off—his Sunday suit pants and good new Arrow shirt. I just said, "Tom, don't tell me you've forgot all our nights together." I was stroking his stomach and his dick. You've never seen anyone struggle so hard not to get an erection. I just said, "You're coming into my room, it's dark and quiet and smells like Evening in Paris body powder. You pull the covers down off my perky little breasts." He's yelling, "I don't know what you're talking about, you just dreamed that." I said, "Why, Daddy, that's every little girl's dream—in the minds of men." And "Oh, there, finally, is that big ol' fat stubby hard dick with the pointy head I been lookin' for." He's trying to roll over so I straddled him. He's saying, "Don't do nothin', whatta you doin'?" I told him, "Now, Tom, Peepin' Tom, you taught me about love in the village, I'm gonna show you how we do it downtown." And I got him up in me—he's going, "Oh, God, no, oh, God forgive her." Maybe if he'd said, Oh, God, forgive *me*—and I told him, "And I'm gonna write you a little story, Tom— that I want you to treasure, 'cause I get about three thousand dollars for something like this." And I took that nice indelible pen and took his shirt and wiped the sweat off his pretty blank white hairless chest and wrote: "Once there was a little girl whose guardian came to see her in the night." Keeping my hips going and writing was like trying to rub your stomach and pat your head. He's bucking around, yelling, "You're not really writin' that, don't mark me up." I said, "Oh, honey, you marked me up." My story went something like—I'm saying it aloud, writing: "He liked to put his hands on her adolescent breasts to excite himself and he liked to rub his hot dick on her red cheeks—her cheeks must have felt like flames. And when he got so hot and hard he couldn't stand it any longer he'd put it in her mouth to cool himself off and pump till he came. And that's how he took care of his little ward. And that's how his little ward took care of him." (*Beat*.) Probably a little more Dickensian than most of my work. Of course he was screaming and bucking. I wasn't proud of my penmanship, but under the circumstances—and I went slow enough to make sure it was legible. Then he was trying not to come. Saying, "Stop it, don't do that I don't do that anymore. I was drunk. It was the devil, darlin'," wailing like a revivalist and I said, "When you come Daddy, let's both yell 'Oh, yes,' but I yelled, "Oh, yes," and he yelled, "Oh, God!" I lay down, stretched out, against his chest. I told him, "All those other times were for you, Daddy, but this one was for me." (*Beat*.) So I got my overnight bag and got the car keys that had fallen out of his pocket onto the rug. And left him there, hog-tied and inscribed in the middle of the floor. Naked as the day he was born —looking like the pot-gutted tattooed man. I said, "Thank you, Tom." Then I stood in the doorway for a long while like he used to do. Only he wasn't pretending to be asleep, he was twisting around on the rug, yelling, "Untie me, dammit Diane, where do you think you're agoin'? Don't leave me here all marked up." I went out to the car, drove it to the airport and left it there. (*Pause*.) Mother was livid. He told her it was a game but she didn't see the fun in it. She liked everything to be peaceful. So she came to visit me, I didn't come back here. Not until Tom got so bad that she was nursing him and couldn't leave. Right toward the end I came here to see her. I was only in the room with Tom for a few minutes. Edith was there. Tom said he'd tried to read my stories but they were filthy and depressing and he told me that writing was just lying and getting away with it. And I said, "No, Tom, writing is the only place I know of where you can tell the truth and get away with it." (*Beat*.) He died about two weeks later, I had to come back for the funeral. Only to be with Mom, who really gets along better with Edith but won't admit it. Edith is less complicated. She's more fun to be with. Edith isn't on some quest for the Holy Grail, she's found it. And more power to her. (*Glancing at the list*.) "How much of an influence has Mountain Grove been on your writing, your life?" Check. "How did living in a small town, essentially a rural area, prepare you for a career and living in a metropolitan area? Or not?" Check. "When did you leave Missouri?" *No. One. Ever. Leaves. Any. Place. Or. Any. One!* Jesus Christ. (*She rubs the back of her hand across her eyes and continues, pushing it out.*) "Where do you get your ideas for stories?" Experience is the better teacher. "Why are your stories so downbeat?" Well, that's all point of view. I think they're funny. Maybe Mom's everlasting positive lid; even now, putting her best face on. Always trying to change me into something acceptable. Admonishing me against dirty talk and negative thoughts. Every sentence begins with "don't." How you feeling, Mom? "Don't ask questions all the time. I'm fine." Why do I write short stories instead of novels? Obviously I like ending things, that's all I've done. You can end eight or ten stories in a space that you could only end one novel. I like tying things up. Or I wouldn't be here now; where it's so much fun with all those memories of childhood; walking back over Mountain Grove where everything is sweet and fine and nobody has any secrets, everything is—what did I say, I want to remember that, where everything is "visible." (*Pause. Ironic.*) Jesus, dear God. "Operator? Operator? Help me. Lady? What do I do now?" (*She looks around.*) You know, with all the interviews, I've never asked to see any of them, but I might be interested in this one. I didn't realize it had got dark outside. Why not? I think I've covered . . . (*She turns off the tape and looks at her interviewer.*) Honey, you want to go in the john and get one of those glasses before you leave, you look like you could use a drink. (*Beat. Beat.*)

**BLACKOUT**

# EUKIAH  (April 1991)

*for William Leavengood*

## AUTHOR'S NOTE

This short piece was a response to the 10 minute play festival that Jon Jory presents in Louisville. Another one of those rare times when an entire play comes to you from nowhere and complete. It even seemed appropriate for Louisville – horses you know – but it wouldn't come. I couldn't get it down on paper. Probably because half the fun of writing is finding out how it ends, and I already knew.

When Bill Leavengood and I were driving around the country ( I have this arrangement with a number of my friends – I pay, they drive) we stopped at the Actors Theater of Louisville. As we left town, talking about their 10 minute play festival, I said that I had once thought of an idea for the festival, but it hadn't panned out. Bill asked what it was and I told him. Bill has a morbid little (actually big) imagination and loved the idea. He said I had to give it another try.

EUKIAH split the first prize at the 10 minute play festival that year with a wonderfully fanciful play, LYNETTE AT 3 A.M., by Jane Anderson.

The workshop premiere of EUKIAH took place on June 17, 1991 at the Actor's Theater of Louisville, directed by Marcia Dixcy with the following cast:

BUTCH: Arthur Aulisi
EUKIAH: Jim Dubensky

EUKIAH subsequently premiered at the Humana Festival of New American Plays on March 21, 1992. directed by Jon Jory with the following cast:

BUTCH: Mark Shannon
EUKIAH: Shaun Powell

# CHARACTERS

BUTCH
EUKIAH


# SCENE

A dark empty stage represents a long abandoned private airplane hangar. The space is vast and almost entirely dark. A streak of light from a crack in the roof stripes the floor.

# EUKIAH

*Butch walks into the light. He is a young, powerful, charming man; everybody's best friend. He is also menacing. Nothing he says is introspective. Everything is for a purpose. During the indicated beats of silence he listens; for Eukiah to answer, for the sound of breathing, for the least indication of where Eukiah is. The play is a seduction. Voices have a slight echo in here.*

**BUTCH**  Eukiah? (*Beat.*) Eukiah? (*Beat.*) Barry saw you run in here, so I know you're here. You're doin' it again, Eukiah, you're jumping to these weird conclusions you jump to just like some half-wit. You don't wanna be called a half-wit, you gotta stop actin' like a half-wit, don't ya? You're gettin' to where nobody can joke around you, ya know that? What kind of fun is a person like that to be around, huh? One you can't joke around? We talked about that before, remember? (*Beat.*) Eukiah? What are you thinkin'? You thinkin' you heard Harry say something, you thought he meant it, didn't you? What did you think you heard? Huh? What'd you thing he meant? Eukiah? (*Beat.*) You're gonna have to talk to me, I can't talk to myself here. (*Beat.*) Have you ever known me to lie to you? Eukiah? Have you ever known that? (*Pause. He might walk around some.*) Okay. Boy, this old hangar sure seen better days, hasn't it? Just like everything else on this place, huh? Been pretty much a losing proposition since I've known it, though. Probably you too, hasn't it? Hell, I don't think they have the wherewithall anymore, give even one of those ol' barns a swab a paint. You think? Might paint 'em pink, whattaya think? Or candy stripes. Red and white. Peppermint. You'd like that. (*Beat.*) This'll remind you of old Mac's heyday, though, won't it? Private airplane hangar. Talk about echoes, this is an echo of the past, huh? Ol' Mac had some winners, I guess, about twenty years ago. That must have been the life, huh? Private planes, keep 'em in your private hangar. You got your luncheons with the dukes and duchesses. Winner's Circle damn near every race. If they wasn't raised by Ol' Mac or their sire or dam one wasn't raised by Ol' Mac, I don't imagine anybody'd bother to bet on em, do you? Boy that's all gone, huh? Planes and limos and all, dukes and duchesses—good lookin' horses, though. Damn shame we can't enter 'em in a beauty contest somewhere. I know, you're attached to 'em, but I'll tell you they make damn expensive pets. What was you? Out by the paddock when Barry was talkin' to me? You think you overheard something, is that it? What do you think you heard? You want to talk about it? I know you'd rather talk to me than talk to Barry, huh? Eukiah? (*Pause.*) Is this where you come? When you run off all tempermental and sulking? Pretty nasty old place to play in. Echoes good though. Gotta keep awful quiet if you're trying to be secret like you always do in a place like this. Why do you do that? You got any idea? I'm serious, now. Run off like that. They're waitin' supper on you, I guess you know. You know how happy they're gonna be about it, too. (*Beat.*) Eukiah? What was it you think you heard, honey? What? Was it about the horses? Cause I thought I told you never trust anything anybody says if it's about horses.

EUKIAH  (*Still unseen.*) I heard what Barry said. You said you *would,* too.

BUTCH  (*Butch relaxes some, smiles.*) Where the dickens have you got to? There's so much echo in here I can't tell where you are. You back in those oil drums? You haven't crawled up in the rafters have you? Watch yourself. We don't want you getting' hurt. I don't think those horses would eat their oats at all, anybody gave 'em to 'em 'cept you. I think they'd flat out go on strike. Don't you figure?

EUKIAH  They wouldn't drink, you couldn't get 'em to.

BUTCH  Don't I know it. Pot-A-Gold, for sure. You're the only one to get him to do anything. I think he'd just dehydrate. He'd blow away, you wasn't leadin' him. We could lead him to water but we couldn't make him to drink, isn't that right? (*Beat.*) What are you hiding about? Nobody's gonna hurt you. Don't I always take up for you? You get the weirdest ideas. What do you think you heard Barry say?

EUKIAH  He's gonna burn the horses.

BUTCH  What? Oh, man. You are just crazy sometimes, these things you dream up. Who is? Barry? What would he wanna do something crazy like that for?

EUKIAH  I heard you talkin.'

BUTCH  Can you answer me that? Why would he even dream of doin' something like that?

EUKIAH  For the insurance.

BUTCH  No, Eukiah. Just come on to supper, now, I got a date tonight, I can't mess around with you anymore. You really are a half-wit. I'm sorry, but if you think Barry'd do something like that, I'm sorry, that's just flat out half-witted thinkin'. It's not even funny. The way you talk, you yak all day to anybody around, no idea what you're saying half the time; anybody heard something like that there wouldn't be no work for me or you or anybody else around here, 'cause they'd just lock us all up.

EUKIAH  You said you would.

**BUTCH**  *I* would? I would what?

**EUKIAH**  You said it was about time somebody did somethin'.

**BUTCH**  Eukiah, come out here. I can see you over by that old buggy, my eyes got used to the dark. There ain't no sense in hiding anymore. (*Beat.*) Come on out, damn it, so we can go to supper. I'm not going to play with you anymore. Come on. Well, just answer me one thing. How's burnin' 'em up gonna be any better than splittin' a hoof or somethin' like that? Come on, crazy. The least little thing happens to make a horse not run, it's the same as if he had to be destroyed, you ought to know that. (*Eukiah is just visible now. He is maybe 16 years old. He is slow and soft; he has the mentality of an 8 year old.*)

**EUKIAH**  Yeah, but they already took Pot-A-Gold and Flashy and that gray one, the speckled one, off. They already sold 'em.

**BUTCH**  Which one do you call Flashy, you mean Go Carmen? The filly? And Old Ironside? Why would they do that?

**EUKIAH**  Cause they're the best ones. Then they put three no good horses in their stalls, so nobody would know. And they're gonna burn 'em and nobody would know. And they're gonna burn 'em and nobody can tell they ain't the horses they're supposed to be, Butchy.

**BUTCH**  Nobody could run Pot-A-Gold somewhere else, Euky. You know those numbers they tattoo in his mouth? That's gonna identify him no matter where he goes, anybody'll know that's Pot-A-Gold.

**EUKIAH**  Some other country. They wouldn't care.

**BUTCH**  Anywhere on earth.

**EUKIAH**  They got some plan where it'll work, 'cause I heard 'em.

**BUTCH**  I don't know what you think you heard, but you're really acting half-witted here.

**EUKIAH**  Don't call me—

**BUTCH**  Well, I'm sorry, but what would you call it? A person can't burn down a barn full of horses, Euky. What a horrible thing to think. No wonder you get scared, you scare yourself thinking things like that. Those horses are valued, hell I don't even know, millions of dollars probably. Insurance inspectors come around, they take a place apart. You tell me, how would somebody get away with a trick like that?

**EUKIAH**  What was you talkin' about then?

**BUTCH**  I don't even know. Where it was you heard what you thought you heard. You're too fast for me. You'll just have to go in to supper and ask Mac what Harry was talking about, won't you? Would that make you feel better? Instead of jumpin' to your weird conclusions. Now, can you get that out of your head? Huh? So we can go eat and I can take a bath and go on my date? Is that all right with you? Then I'll come back and tell you all about it. Got a date with Mary, you'd like to hear about that, wouldn't you? (*Eukiah begins to grin.*) Yes? That's okay with you, is it?

**EUKIAH**  I guess. (*He moves into the light, closer to Butch.*)

**BUTCH**  You guess. You're just going to have to trust me, Eukiah, nobody needs money that bad. Not even on this place. I don't even think nobody could get away tryin' to pull something like that. (*He puts his arm around Eukiah's neck and they start to move off, but Butch has Eukiah in a head lock. He speaks with the strain of exertion.*) Not unless there was some half-wit on the place that got his neck broke being kicked in the head and got burned up in the fire. (*Eukiah goes to his knees. Butch bears down on his neck; it breaks with a dull snap. He lets Eukiah slump to the floor. Butch is breathing hard, standing over Eukiah's body.*) I thought I told you. Never trust anything anybody says if it's about horses.

**END**

**Smith and Kraus** *Books For Actors*

## THE MONOLOGUE SERIES
> The Best Men's Stage Monologues of 1992
> The Best Men's Stage Monologues of 1991
> The Best Men's Stage Monologues of 1990
> The Best Women's Stage Monologues of 1992
> The Best Women's Stage Monologues of 1991
> The Best Women's Stage Monologues of 1990
> One Hundred Men's Stage Monologues from the 1980's
> One Hundred Women's Stage Monologues from the 1980's
> Street Talk: Character Monologues for Actors
> Uptown: Character Monologues for Actors
> Monologues from Contemporary Literature: Volume I
> Monologues from Classic Plays
> Kiss and Tell: The Art of the Restoration Monologue

## FESTIVAL MONOLOGUE SERIES
> The Great Monologues from the Humana Festival
> The Great Monologues from the EST Marathon
> The Great Monologues from the Women's Project
> The Great Monologues from the Mark Taper Forum

## YOUNG ACTORS SERIES
> Great Scenes and Monologues for Children
> New Plays from A.C.T.'s Young Conservatory
> Great Scenes for Young Actors from the Stage
> Great Monologues for Young Actors

## SCENE STUDY SERIES
> The Best Stage Scenes for Women from the 1980's
> The Best Stage Scenes for Men from the 1980's
> The Best Stage Scenes of 1992

## CONTEMPORARY AMERICAN PLAYWRIGHTS SERIES
> Seventeen Short Plays by Romulus Linney
> William Mastrosimone: Collected Plays
> Eric Overmyer: Collected Plays
> Terrence McNally: Collected Plays

## GREAT TRANSLATION FOR ACTORS SERIES
> The Wood Demon by Anton Chekhov

## OTHER BOOKS IN OUR COLLECTION
> The Actor's Chekhov
> Women Playwrights: The Best Plays of 1992
> Humana Festival '93: The Collected Plays
> Break A Leg! Daily Inspiration for the Actor

If you require pre-publication information about upcoming Smith and Kraus mono-
logues collections, scene collections, play anthologies, advanced acting books, and
books for young actors, you may receive our semi-annual catalogue, free of charge,
by sending your name and address to **Smith and Kraus Catalogue,
P.O. Box 10, Newbury, VT 05051.**